EXPLORING French

THIRD EDITION

Joan G. Sheeran

EMC Publishing

ST. PAUL • LOS ANGELES

Developmental Editor
Diana Moen

Production Editor
Amy McGuire

Text Designer
Lisa Beller

Cover Designer
Leslie Anderson

Production Specialist
Jack Ross

Copy Editor & Proofreader
Jamie Bryant, B-books, Ltd.

Illustrations
Lachina Publishing, Rolin Graphics

Photo Credits

Arnold, Bernd: iii (bottom), 85 (bottom)
Bettmann/Corbis: 178 (bottom)
Chapel House Photography: ix (top left), x (middle right), xiii (bottom left), 224 (all)
Corbis: 178 (top); *Bianchetti, Stefano:* 220 (top); *Bognar, Tibor:* 123; *Cardinale, Stephanie/People Avenue:* 180 (left); *Fougere, Eric:* 179 (bottom); *Fulz, Tina/Zuma:* 180 (right); *Hash, Mary R./Sygma:* 179 (top); *Karnow, Catherine:* 109 (bottom); *Mayer, Francis G./Corbis:* 124 (top); *Mascolo, Jean/Sygma:* 221 (bottom); *Sayer, Kim:* 29 (top right);
Corbis Royalty-Free: iv (bottom), 1, 85 (top left & right), 97 (top right & bottom), 109 (top), 149, 177 (top & middle), 189 (all), 203 (bottom), 233 (top left & right, bottom right), 259 (top right)
da Veiga, Hannah: 76 (left)
Digital Stock: 29 (left & bottom right), 71 (bottom), 103 (left), 163, 219
Digital Vision: 103 (right)
Englebert, Victor: viii (bottom right)
Fotosearch: 13
French Government Tourist Office: viii (top left), 41, 47
Fried, Robert: xii (bottom left & middle right)
Getty Images: 71 (middle)
Gibson, Keith: xiii (middle right), 123, 265
iStockphoto.com/Barskaya, Galina: 135 (bottom left); *Croizer, Jacques:* 209; *Lazare, Benjamin:* 173; *Pollack ,Chris:* 128 (left); *Pomares, Alberto:* 135 (top left); *Sachs, Francois:* 128 (right); *Trenchard, Jennifer:* v (bottom), 135 (right)
Kraft, Wolf: 167
Larson, June: x (top left), xi (top & middle left, bottom right), 247
Louvre, Paris/Bridgeman Art Library: 125 (top left)
Maison de la France: xi (top right), viii (bottom left), 42 (bottom), 43 (bottom), 45
Messerschmidt, J./Leo de Wys Inc.: 59
Musée Fabre, Montpellier/Bridgeman Art Library: 124 (bottom)
Ollivain, P./SNCF/CAV/La Documentation française: 259 (bottom)
Peccoux, Daniel/Carel Gallery: 125 (bottom)
PhotoPaq: 42 (top), 177 (bottom)
Reuters/Corbis: 233 (bottom left)
Saint Martin Tourist Office: ix (bottom right), xii (bottom right)
Simson, David: 97 (top left), x (bottom left), 264
Stadelsches Kunstinstitut, Frankfurt-am-Main/Bridgeman Art Library: 125 (top right)
Stapleton Collection/Corbis: 220 (bottom), 221 (top)
Sternberg, Will: 71 (top), 203 (top), 222
Stockbyte: iv (top)
Strumhoefel, Horst: 76 (right), 207
Switzerland Tourism: ix (middle left), xii (top left), 50
Tremblay, Jon: ix (top right)
Tunisia Tourist Office: viii (top right), xii (top right)

Softcover Edition: ISBN 978-0-82193-479-1
Hardcover Edition: ISBN 978-0-82194-040-2

875 Montreal Way
St. Paul, MN 55102
E-mail: educate@emcp.com
Web site: www.emcp.com

Printed in the United States of America

17 16 15 14 13 12 5 6 7 8 9 10

Introduction

Congratulations on starting your exploration of French! It is a good language choice because more than 200 million people in the world speak French. One of our geographical neighbors, the province of Quebec in Canada, speaks French. There is also a history of French in New England and Louisiana. French is one of the official languages of many African countries that used to be French colonies. Besides France, Canada, and Africa, it is also spoken in Haiti and other Caribbean islands, Switzerland, Belgium, and Luxembourg.

French is derived from Indo-European, an ancient language that influenced many modern European and Middle Eastern languages. The Roman soldiers who invaded the area known as Gaul (now France) spoke Latin, which evolved over time to become modern French. Cousins of the French language are Spanish, Italian, Portuguese, and Romanian.

French explorers helped chart the New World. Jacques Cartier explored the St. Lawrence River in Canada. Samuel de Champlain explored the eastern coast of North America and got as far west as Lake Huron. Father Marquette and Louis Joliet explored the northern Mississippi River. They were followed by Robert LaSalle, who

20

traveled south to the mouth of the Mississippi and claimed it for France. In fact, the name Louisiana comes from the name of the French king, Louis XIV. Other place names in the United States come from French, for example, the St. Croix River in Minnesota, Trempeauleau County in Wisconsin, and the city of Dubuque in Iowa.

Do you know what a cognate is? It is a word from another language that looks and/or sounds like an English word. Many examples abound in French, for example, *le shampooing, le rap, le weekend, le fast-food, le basketball, le stress, le walkman,* and *le parking*. Besides nouns such as these, there are cognates for adjectives, for example, *intelligent/intelligente, sérieux/sérieuse, petit/petite, excellent/excellente,* and *rapide*. Recognizing cognates means that you begin your study of French already knowing a lot of vocabulary. English also has cognates from French, for example, croissant, restaurant, tennis, café, chauffeur, and à la mode. How many more can you think of?

There is a section toward the end of each unit with symbols. Each symbol represents a word or expression in French. This learning method is called "Symtalk" (symbols + talking). You will be asked to "read" the sentences and then to engage in a directed dialogue with a partner or describe a scene. When you write sentences in this section, you will be talking about the characters shown below. You can refer back to this page as often as you like until you learn the names of all the characters.

Symtalk Characters

Gérard
Sylvie
Hiko
Antoine
Brigitte
Alain

As you start your study of French, remember to be curious and ask questions and to not be afraid to practice new sounds and sentence patterns. Someday you may use French in your job or when traveling, so it will have useful applications. Have fun with French!

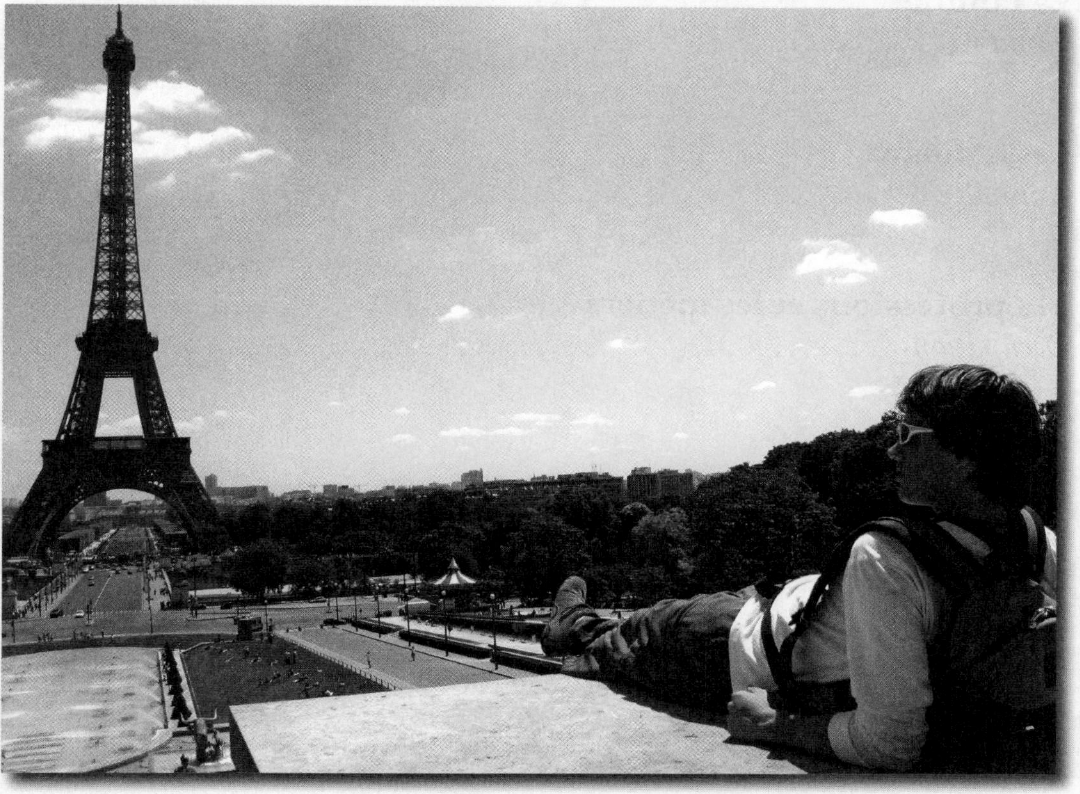

Table of Contents

Exploring

. . . countries and cities

Eiffel Tower—Paris, France

Market, or souk, *in Tunis—the capital of Tunisia*

Picturesque town along the French Riviera, or Côte d'Azur

The Grand-Place in Brussels, Belgium

Palace of Versailles, where French kings and queens lived

The Canadian flag and a statue of Jacques Cartier in Quebec City, Canada

Skiing in the Swiss Alps

Horseback riding in Saint Martin, an island in the Caribbean

. . . language

SEPTEMBRE
1 V Gilles
2 S Ingrid
3 D Grégoire
4 L Rosalie 36
5 M Raïssa
6 M Bertrand
7 J Reine
8 V Nativité N.D.
9 S Alain
10 D Inès
11 L Adelphe 37
12 M Apollinaire
13 M Aimé
14 J La Ste Croix
15 V Roland
16 S Edith
17 D Renaud
18 L Nadège 38
19 M Emilie
20 M Davy Q.T.
21 J Matthieu
22 V Maurice
23 S AUTOMNE
24 D Thècle
25 L Hermann 39
26 M Côme, Dam.
27 M Vinc. de Paul
28 J Venceslas
29 V Michel
30 S Jérôme

Saints' names calendar

FRITES BOISSONS SALADES CRÊPES

Angers, France

La Galerie du Chat

Shop sign in Paris

Restaurant
La Martinique
Spécialités Créoles Fruits de Mer
Cocktails exotiques Coupes glacées
75, rue du Mail
49000 ANGERS
02.41.87.22.25
Ouvert du lundi soir au dimanche midi.

A taste of the Caribbean in Angers

Ring
Liège-Luik D
Namur-Namen L
Antwerpen-Anvers NL
Bruxelles National
Brussel Nationaal
Institutions Européennes
Europese Instellingen
Botanique
Kruidtuin

Directional signs in Brussels, Belgium

L'ÉVÉNEMENT MUSICAL DE LA RENTRÉE
NRJ
PARIS
100.3
LE MÉGA MUSIC DANCE
MD
A BERCY
solidarité sida
SAMEDI 24 SEPTEMBRE
A BERCY à 20h30
Plus de 30 artistes pour chanter et danser avec vous

A concert coming to Bercy, a concert hall in Paris

. . . daily life

ISABELLE HUPPERT
SAINT-CYR
Madame de Maintenon
leur avait promis tous les
bonheurs du monde...
UN FILM DE PATRICIA MAZUY
JEAN-PIERRE KALFON - SIMON REGGIANI - ANNE MAREV
NINA MEURISSE - MORGANE MORÉ

Movie posters at the cinéma

AU PERE TRANQUILLE
AU PERE
TRANQUILLE
SALLE AU PREMIER
VUE SUR FORUM
AU PERE
TRANQUILLE
CAFE

Busy Parisian café

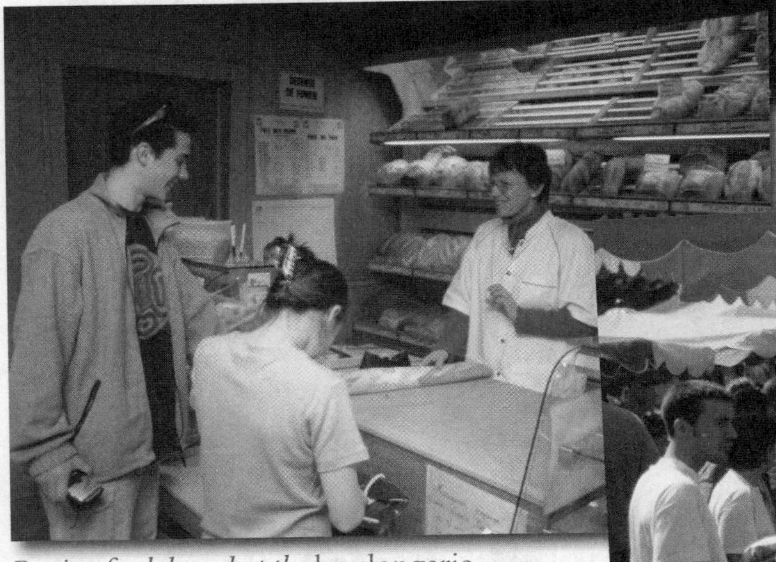

Buying fresh bread at the boulangerie

Shoppers at an open-air market, or marché

. . . people

Traveling by camel through the Sahara in Tunisia

Historic re-enactors in Geneva, Switzerland

Friends, or les copains, get together downtown

Restaurant worker about to serve mussels and frites

Wearing traditional costumes at a festival on the island of Saint Martin

. . . and culture.

Tahitian Women (On the Beach) *by Gauguin—Musée d'Orsay, Paris*

The Centre Pompidou, *or* Beaubourg, *and its distinctive architecture*

Salmon with hollandaise sauce

Mousse au chocolat

Paris's Opéra Garnier, *known for its ballets*

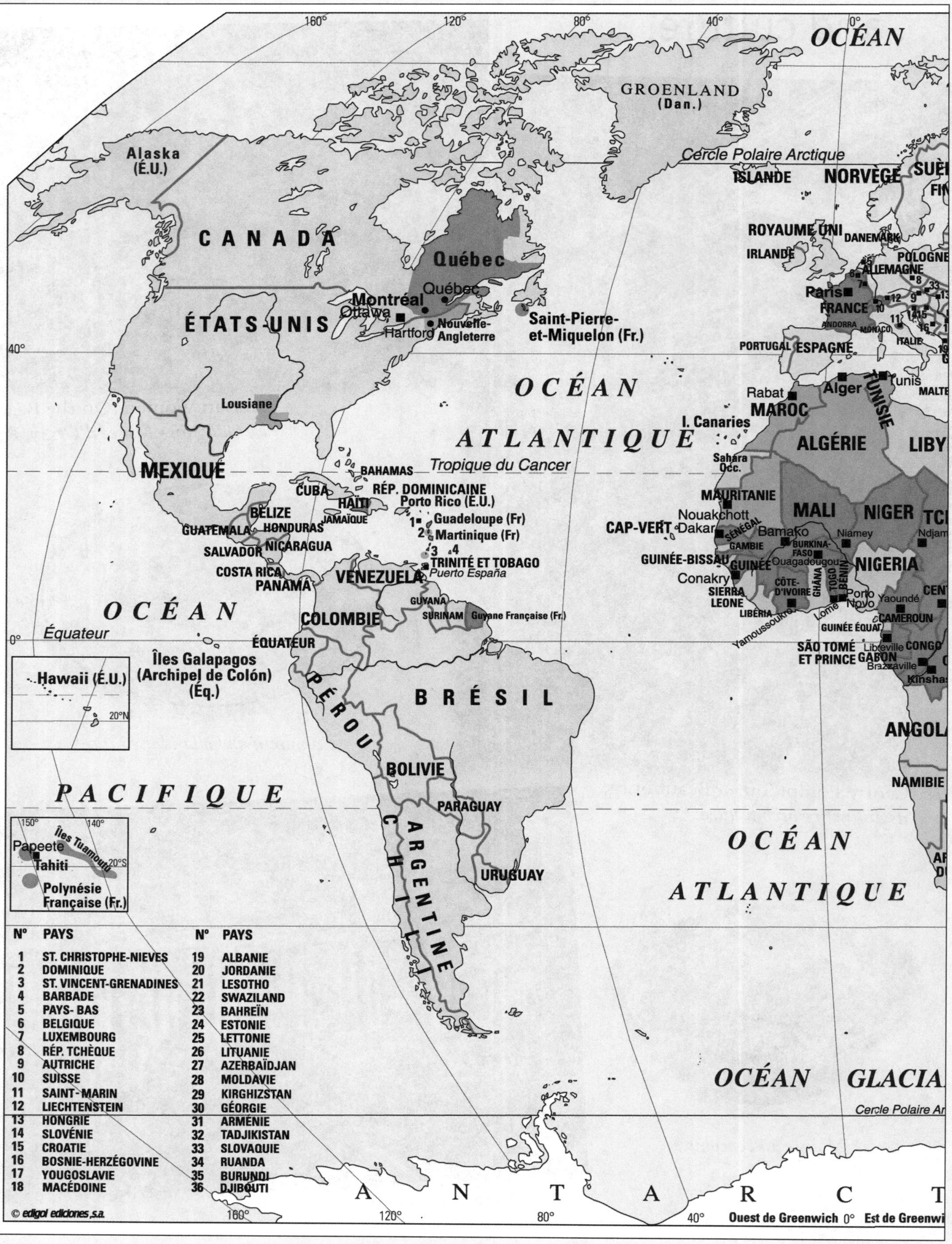
160°
120°
80°
40°
0°
OCÉAN
GROENLAND
(Dan.)
Cercle Polaire Arctique
Alaska
(É.U.)
ISLANDE
NORVÈGE
CANADA
Québec
ROYAUME UNI
DANEMARK
IRLANDE
POLOGNE
ALLEMAGNE
Paris
FRANCE
ANDORRA
MONACO
ITALIE
PORTUGAL
ESPAGNE
Montréal
Québec
Ottawa
Hartford
Nouvelle-Angleterre
Saint-Pierre-et-Miquelon (Fr.)
ÉTATS-UNIS
40°
OCÉAN
ATLANTIQUE
Lousiane
Rabat
Alger
Tunis
TUNISIE
MALTE
MAROC
I. Canaries
ALGÉRIE
Sahara Occ.
MEXIQUE
Tropique du Cancer
BAHAMAS
CUBA
HAITI
RÉP. DOMINICAINE
Porto Rico (É.U.)
JAMAÏQUE
BELIZE
GUATEMALA
HONDURAS
SALVADOR
NICARAGUA
COSTA RICA
PANAMÁ
Guadeloupe (Fr)
Martinique (Fr)
TRINITÉ ET TOBAGO
Puerto España
VENEZUELA
GUYANA
SURINAM
Guyane Française (Fr.)
COLOMBIE
ÉQUATEUR
MAURITANIE
Nouakchott
Dakar
CAP-VERT
SÉNÉGAL
GAMBIE
GUINÉE-BISSAU
GUINÉE
Conakry
SIERRA LEONE
LIBÉRIA
Yamoussoukro
CÔTE-D'IVOIRE
GHANA
TOGO
BÉNIN
Lomé
Porto Novo
MALI
Bamako
BURKINA-FASO
Ouagadougou
NIGER
Niamey
NIGERIA
Ndjamena
Yaoundé
CAMEROUN
GUINÉE ÉQUAT.
SÃO TOMÉ ET PRINCE
Libreville
GABON
CONGO
Brazzaville
Kinshasa
OCÉAN
Équateur
0°
Îles Galapagos
(Archipel de Colón)
(Éq.)
Hawaii (É.U.)
20°N
PÉROU
BRÉSIL
BOLIVIE
ANGOLA
NAMIBIE
PACIFIQUE
PARAGUAY
CHILI
ARGENTINE
URUGUAY
150°
140°
Îles Tuamotu
Papeete
Tahiti
20°S
Polynésie Française (Fr.)
OCÉAN
ATLANTIQUE
OCÉAN GLACIAL
Cercle Polaire Arctique
ANTARCTI
Ouest de Greenwich 0° Est de Greenwich
© edigol ediciones, s.a.

Nº	PAYS	Nº	PAYS
1	ST. CHRISTOPHE-NIEVES	19	ALBANIE
2	DOMINIQUE	20	JORDANIE
3	ST. VINCENT-GRENADINES	21	LESOTHO
4	BARBADE	22	SWAZILAND
5	PAYS- BAS	23	BAHREÏN
6	BELGIQUE	24	ESTONIE
7	LUXEMBOURG	25	LETTONIE
8	RÉP. TCHÈQUE	26	LITUANIE
9	AUTRICHE	27	AZERBAÏDJAN
10	SUISSE	28	MOLDAVIE
11	SAINT-MARIN	29	KIRGHIZSTAN
12	LIECHTENSTEIN	30	GÉORGIE
13	HONGRIE	31	ARMÉNIE
14	SLOVÉNIE	32	TADJIKISTAN
15	CROATIE	33	SLOVAQUIE
16	BOSNIE-HERZÉGOVINE	34	RUANDA
17	YOUGOSLAVIE	35	BURUNDI
18	MACÉDOINE	36	DJIBOUTI

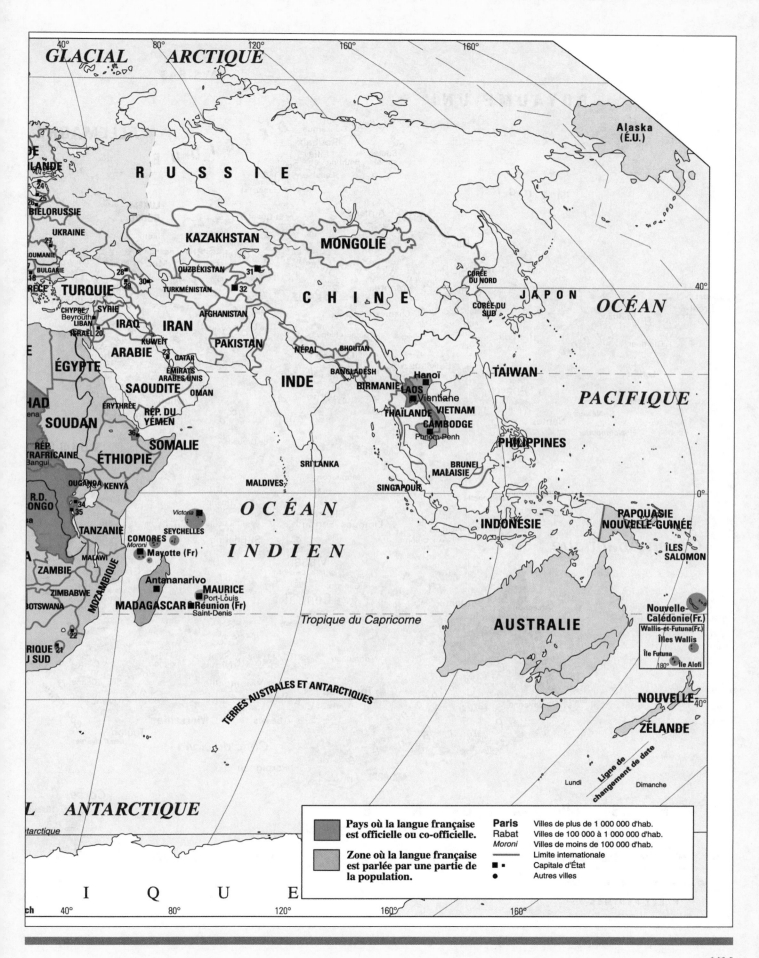

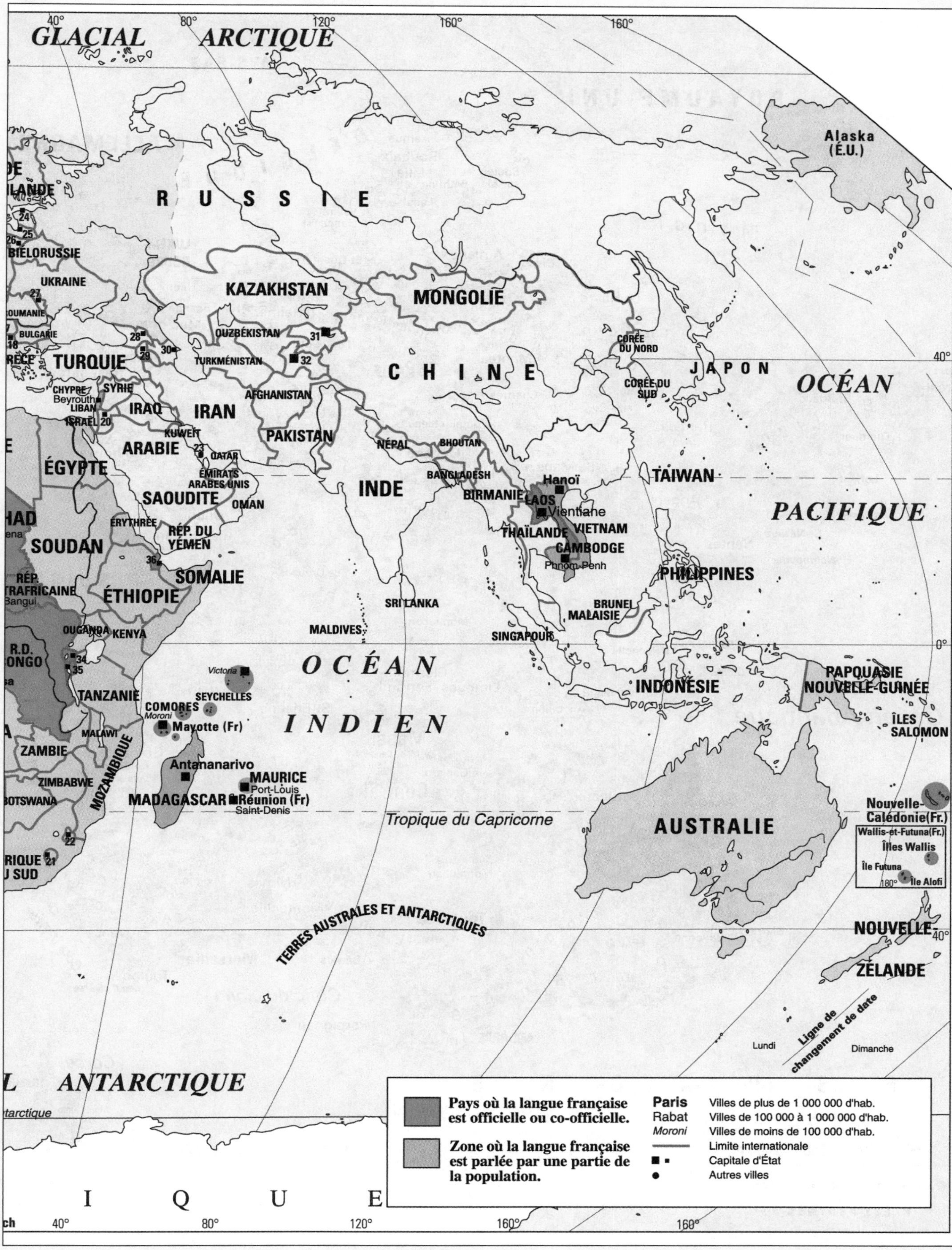
GLACIAL ARCTIQUE
Alaska (É.U.)
RUSSIE
BIELORUSSIE
UKRAINE
ROUMANIE
BULGARIE
TURQUIE
CHYPRE
Beyrouth
LIBAN
ISRAËL
SYRIE
IRAQ
IRAN
KOWEÏT
ARABIE SAOUDITE
QATAR
ÉMIRATS ARABES UNIS
OMAN
KAZAKHSTAN
OUZBÉKISTAN
TURKMÉNISTAN
AFGHANISTAN
PAKISTAN
MONGOLIE
CHINE
CORÉE DU NORD
CORÉE DU SUD
JAPON
OCÉAN PACIFIQUE
NÉPAL
BHOUTAN
BANGLADESH
INDE
BIRMANIE
Hanoï
LAOS
Vientiane
THAÏLANDE
VIETNAM
CAMBODGE
Phnom-Penh
TAIWAN
PHILIPPINES
SRI LANKA
MALDIVES
BRUNEI
MALAISIE
SINGAPOUR
INDONÉSIE
PAPOUASIE NOUVELLE-GUINÉE
ÎLES SALOMON
ÉGYPTE
TCHAD
SOUDAN
ÉRYTHRÉE
RÉP. DU YÉMEN
RÉP. CENTRAFRICAINE
Bangui
ÉTHIOPIE
SOMALIE
OUGANDA
KENYA
R.D. CONGO
TANZANIE
COMORES
Moroni
Mayotte (Fr)
SEYCHELLES
Victoria
MALAWI
ZAMBIE
ZIMBABWE
BOTSWANA
MOZAMBIQUE
MADAGASCAR
Antananarivo
MAURICE
Port-Louis
Réunion (Fr)
Saint-Denis
AFRIQUE DU SUD
OCÉAN INDIEN
Tropique du Capricorne
AUSTRALIE
Nouvelle-Calédonie (Fr.)
Wallis-et-Futuna (Fr.)
Îles Wallis
Île Futuna
Île Alofi
NOUVELLE-ZÉLANDE
TERRES AUSTRALES ET ANTARCTIQUES
Ligne de changement de date
Lundi
Dimanche
ANTARCTIQUE
Pays où la langue française est officielle ou co-officielle.
Zone où la langue française est parlée par une partie de la population.
Paris Villes de plus de 1 000 000 d'hab.
Rabat Villes de 100 000 à 1 000 000 d'hab.
Moroni Villes de moins de 100 000 d'hab.
Limite internationale
Capitale d'État
Autres villes

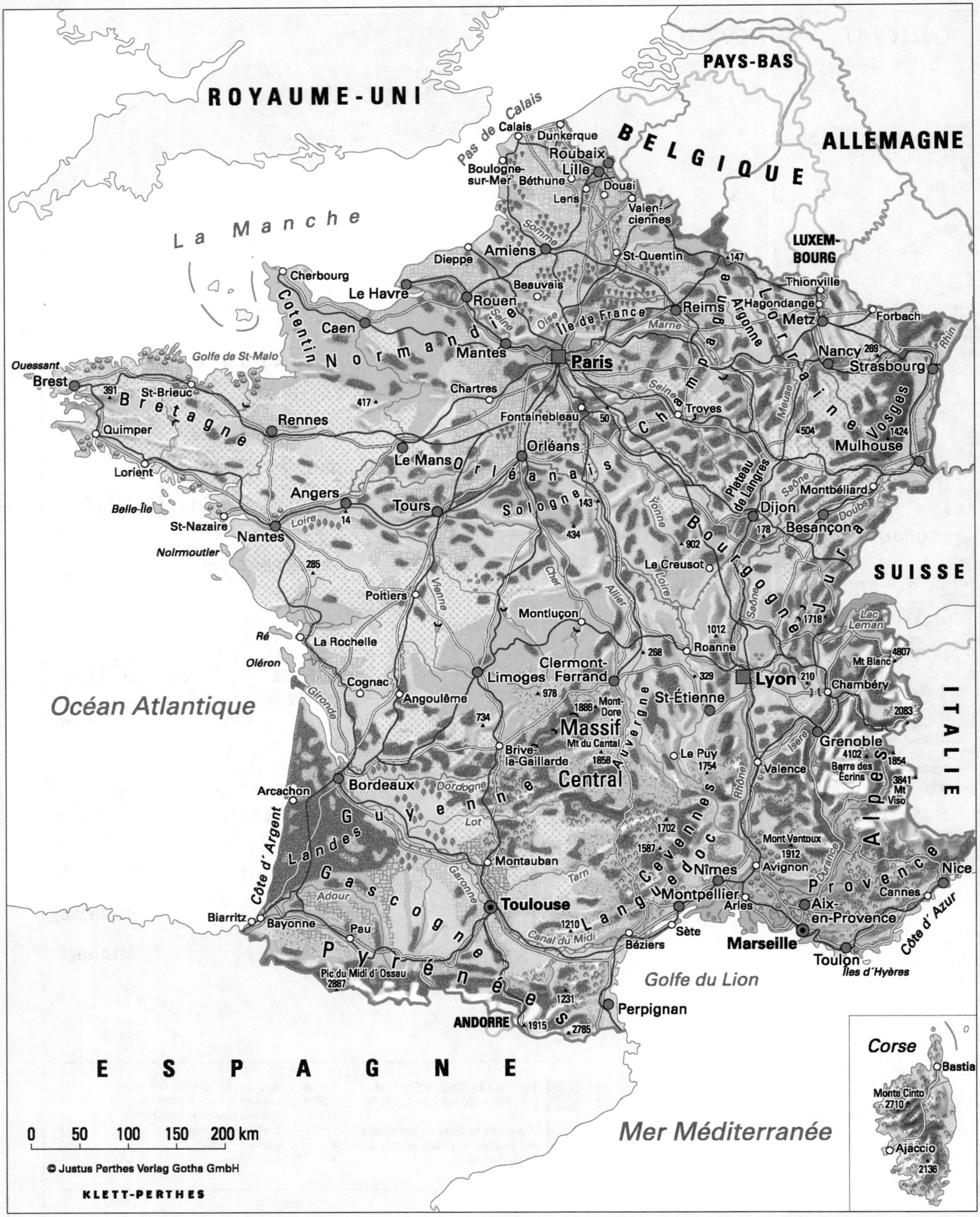
ROYAUME-UNI
PAYS-BAS
BELGIQUE
ALLEMAGNE
LUXEM-BOURG
SUISSE
ITALIE
ESPAGNE
ANDORRE
La Manche
Pas de Calais
Océan Atlantique
Golfe du Lion
Mer Méditerranée
Golfe de St-Malo
Calais
Dunkerque
Roubaix
Lille
Boulogne-sur-Mer
Béthune
Douai
Lens
Valenciennes
Amiens
Dieppe
St-Quentin
Cherbourg
Le Havre
Rouen
Beauvais
Reims
Thionville
Hagondange
Metz
Forbach
Caen
Mantes
Paris
Nancy
Strasbourg
Ouessant
Brest
St-Brieuc
Chartres
Rennes
Quimper
Fontainebleau
Troyes
Le Mans
Orléans
Mulhouse
Lorient
Montbéliard
Angers
Tours
Dijon
Belle-Île
St-Nazaire
Nantes
Besançon
Noirmoutier
Le Creusot
Poitiers
Montluçon
Ré
La Rochelle
Roanne
Oléron
Clermont-Ferrand
Lyon
Cognac
Limoges
Chambéry
Angoulême
St-Étienne
Mont-Dore
Grenoble
Brive-la-Gaillarde
Le Puy
Mt du Cantal
Valence
Barre des Écrins
Mt Viso
Arcachon
Bordeaux
Mont Ventoux
Montauban
Nîmes
Avignon
Nice
Cannes
Montpellier
Arles
Aix-en-Provence
Biarritz
Bayonne
Toulouse
Pau
Sète
Béziers
Marseille
Toulon
Îles d'Hyères
Pic du Midi d'Ossau
Perpignan
Mt Blanc
Lac Leman
Cotentin
Normandie
Bretagne
Île de France
Champagne
Lorraine
Argonne
Vosges
Orléanais
Sologne
Plateau de Langres
Bourgogne
Jura
Massif Central
Auvergne
Alpes
Cévennes
Languedoc
Provence
Côte d'Azur
Guyenne
Landes
Côte d'Argent
Gascogne
Pyrénées
Somme
Seine
Oise
Marne
Meuse
Rhin
Saône
Doubs
Loire
Yonne
Cher
Allier
Vienne
Gironde
Dordogne
Lot
Tarn
Garonne
Adour
Rhône
Isère
Durance
Canal du Midi
Corse
Bastia
Monte Cinto
Ajaccio
0 50 100 150 200 km
© Justus Perthes Verlag Gotha GmbH
KLETT-PERTHES

Unit 1

Les salutations et les courtoisies
Greetings and Expressions of Courtesy

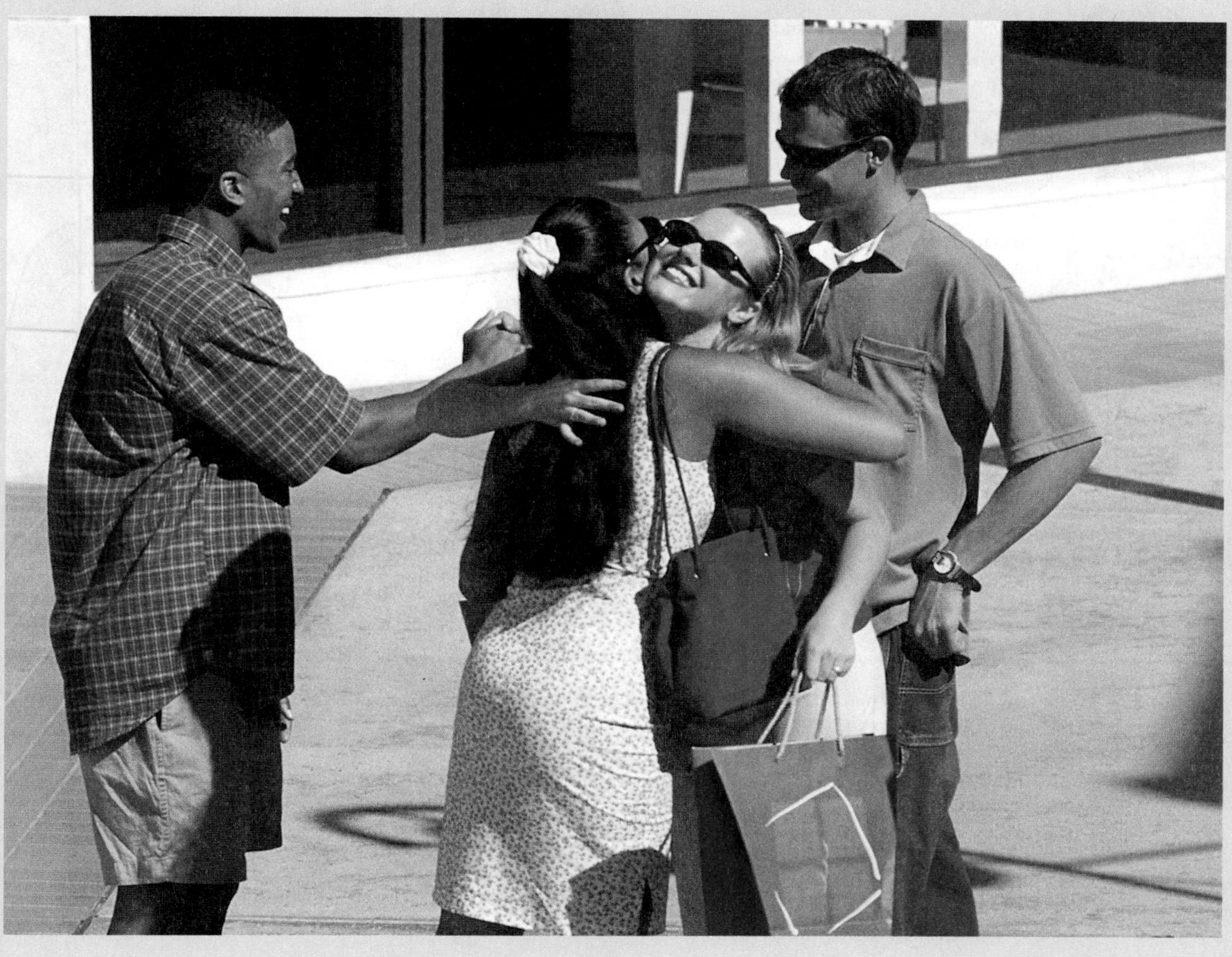

Vocabulaire

Bonjour.	Bonsoir.	Bonne nuit.
Good day. Good morning.	Good evening.	Good night.

La courtoisie

S'il te plaît.	Please.
Merci.	Thank you.
De rien.	You're welcome.
Pardon.	Excuse me.
Desolé.	Sorry.

Bonne chance.
Good luck.

Je m'appelle Jacques. Et toi? Tu t'appelles comment?
My name is Jacques. And you? What's your name?
Je m'appelle André.
My name is André.
Enchanté, André.
I'm delighted to meet you, André.
Oui.
Yes.
Non.
No.
Tu parles français, n'est-ce pas?
You speak French, don't you?
Oui, je parle français.
Yes, I speak French.
Comment vas-tu?
How are you?
Bien, merci. Et toi, comment ça va?
Fine, thanks. And you, how's everything going?
Pas mal. Ça va.
Not bad. All right.

A traditional warm French greeting is to give up to four kisses, alternating between the right and left cheek.

When you say hello to an adult, use the formal greeting: *Bonjour, Madame!* or *Bonjour, Monsieur!* Add the person's last name if you know it: *Bonjour, Madame Pilorget! Salut,* an informal and casual greeting, is usually said to a friend: *Salut, Pierre!*

When meeting someone, a girl says *Enchantée* (spelled with an extra "e"), which means "I'm delighted to meet you."

Another expression, *Avec plaisir,* means "I'm pleased to meet you."

The term *Mademoiselle* (Miss) refers generally to a young girl, while *Madame* is used to address any woman, regardless of marital status.

Parles-tu italien?
Do you speak Italian?
Non. Je ne parle pas italien.
No. I don't speak Italian.

Les langues	Languages
l'allemand	German
l'anglais	English
l'arabe	Arabic
le chinois	Chinese
l'espagnol	Spanish
l'italien	Italian
le japonais	Japanese
le portugais	Portuguese
le russe	Russian

Salut.
Hello. Hi.
À bientôt.
See you later.
Au revoir.
Good-bye.
À demain.
See you tomorrow.

Vocabulaire Extra!

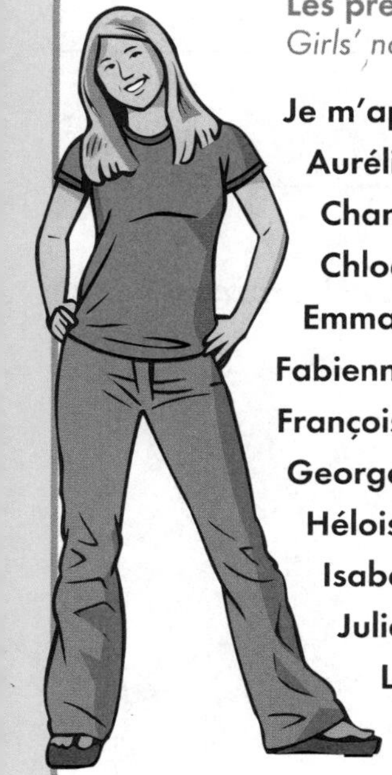

Les prénoms de filles
Girls' names

Je m'appelle. . .

Aurélie
Chantal
Chloé
Emmanuelle
Fabienne
Françoise
Georgette
Héloise
Isabelle
Julie
Laure
Léa
Lucie
Marie-Alix
Manon
Noëlle
Renée
Sophie
Thérèse
Yvette

La fille s'appelle Georgette.
The girl's name is Georgette.

Les prénoms de garçons
Boys' names

Je m'appelle. . .

Alexandre
Bernard
Charles
Didier
Étienne
Fabien
Gilles
Guillaume
Henri
Jacques
Jean-François
Louis
Maxime
Michel
Olivier
Philippe
Robert
Samuel
Théo
Thierry

Le garçon s'appelle Jacques.
The boy's name is Jacques.

Activités

A **Choisis l'expression inapplicable.** ***(Choose the word or expression that doesn't fit with the rest.)***

1. Oui.	Enchanté.	Avec plaisir.	Bonjour.
2. À demain.	Au revoir.	Pardon.	À bientôt.
3. Bonne nuit.	Bonne chance.	Bonjour.	Bonsoir.
4. S'il te plaît.	Merci.	Bonjour.	De rien.
5. allemand	anglais	japonais	Non.

B **Encercle les prénoms de filles.** ***(Circle the girls' names.)***

1. Fabienne fille
2. Guillaume garçon
3. Thierry g
4. Sophie f
5. Didier g
6. Laure f
7. René g
8. Jean-François g
9. Noëlle f
10. Chantal f

C **Écris des réponses aux questions.** ***(Write answers to the questions.)***

1. Parles-tu français?

   Oui. Je parle français

2. Comment t'appelles-tu?

   Je m'appelle Brigitte

3. Comment ça va?

   Ça va bien et toi

D **Écris une expression en français pour chaque illustration.** ***(Write the French expression that corresponds to each picture.)***

1. Bonne chance

2. Salut, Allô, Bonjour, Bonsoir, Au Revoir, Bonne Nuit, A bientot

Comment vas-tu?
Bonjour.
Je m'appelle...
Merci.
S'il te plait.

3. Je parle francais,

4. Enchanté, Avec plaisir

Hello!
Please.
Excuse me.
Yes.
Thank you.

5. Je parle anglais

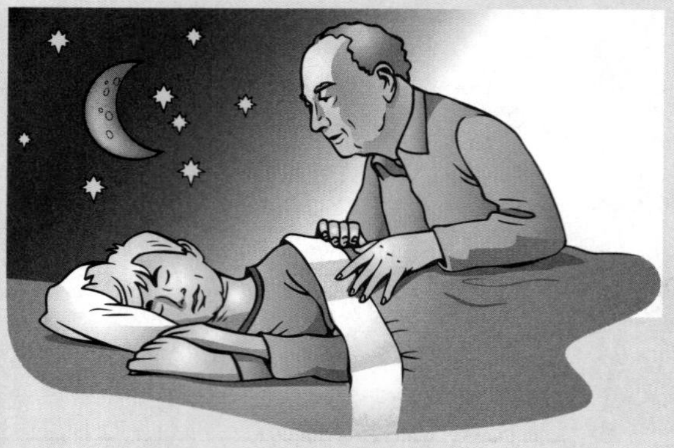

6. Bonne Nuit

7. Bonne Voyage

E

Écris des réponses brèves en français, s'il te plaît. ***(Write out short answers in French, please.)***

1. How do you greet someone in the morning?

   Bonjour

2. How do you greet someone in the evening?

   Bonsoir

3. What is customary to say after meeting someone?

   Enchanté

4. How do you wish someone luck?

   Bonne chance

5. Finish the following sentence:

   Je parle français et anglais.

6. *Salut* would generally be used to greet: A

   A. a friend, *Robert* or B. a gentleman, *M.* (Mr.) *Dubois.*

7. Is Fabienne a name for *un garçon*?

   Non.

8. Answer this question: *Comment t'appelles-tu?*

   Je m'appelle Brigitte

9. One expression of leave-taking is: Bonne voyage

10. *Oui* is the opposite of Non.

F **Complète les dialogues en français par écrit.** ***(Complete the dialogues in French in writing.)***

1. JULIETTE: Salut! Je m'appelle Juliette. Et toi?
   BERNARD: Salut! Je m'appele Bernard. Enchanté
2. OLIVIER: Comment vas-tu, Thérèse?
   THÉRÈSE Bien, merci. Et toi?
3. GUILLAUME: Parles-tu français?
   THIERRY: Oui, je parle français. Et toi?.

G **Parlons!** ***(Let's Talk!)*** **Pretend you are meeting a classmate for the first time. Role-play a simple introduction.** Bonjour. Je m'appelle Brigitte. Comment t'appelle tu? Enchanté. Comment ça va? Oui? Ça va bien

H **C'est à toi! Que sais-tu en français?** ***(It's your turn! What do you know in French?)***

1. Shake hands as you say hello to a friend. Salut
2. Wave and say good-bye to the friend. A plus tard
3. Say what your name is. Je m'appelle Brigitte
4. Say that you speak English. Je parle anglais

Proverbe

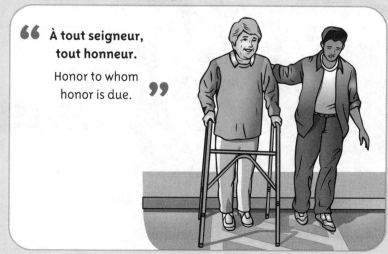

“ **À tout seigneur, tout honneur.**

Honor to whom honor is due. ”

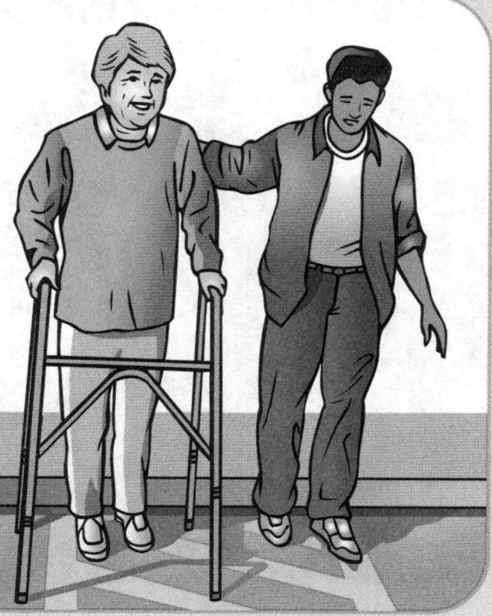

Langue vivante!

bienvenue
à paris
à votre service
MEILLEURS VOEUX
Pour La Nouvelle Année
bonjour!
www.franceguide.com
Bienvenue
dans le vallon
de Tamié
Je note mes coordonnées
❒ M. ❒ Mme ❒ Mlle Nom
Prénom
N° Rue
Code postal Ville
E-mail
❒ Je souhaite être informé(e) des offres commerciales du groupe Prisma Presse et de celles de ses partenaires.
MERCI
Bonne Chance
Bonnes Vacances
Et
Bonne Chance
Que chaque instant
de ce voyage
soit un enchantement
pour les yeux
comme pour le coeur
et apporte de nombreuses
satisfactions.
BON VOYAGE

I Find the French words for:

1. Hello

   Bonjour

2. Good luck

   Bonne chance

3. Have a nice vacation

   Bonnes vacances

4. Welcome

   bienvenue

5. Thank you

   merci

6. Best Wishes for the New Year

   meilleurs voeux pour la Nouvelle Année

J The word *coordonnées* means information about your name and address. What do these abbreviations and words mean?

1. *M.*

   Monsier/messiurs (plural)

2. *Mme*

   madame/mesdame (plural)

3. *Mlle*

   mademoiselle

4. *Nom*

   name

5. *Prénom*

   First name

6. *N^o Rue*

   House number/ Street

7. *Code postal*

   zip Code

8. *Ville*

   City

Symtalk

K **Écris le mot ou l'expression en français dans l'espace blanc.** ***(In the space, write the correct word or expression in French.)***

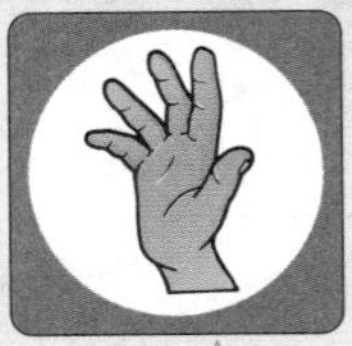

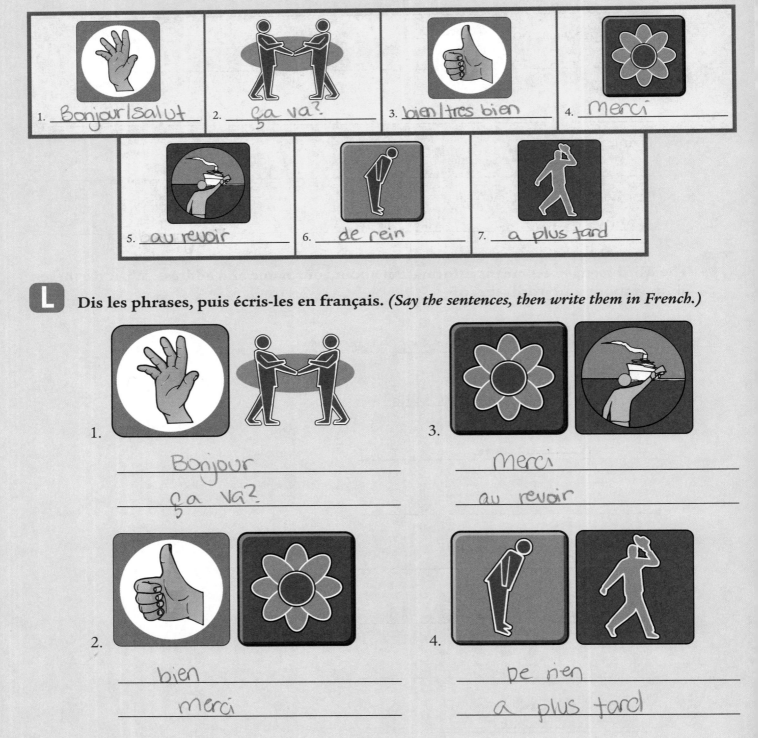

1. Bonjour/salut

2. ça va?

3. bien/tres bien

4. merci

5. au revoir

6. de rein

7. a plus tard

L **Dis les phrases, puis écris-les en français.** ***(Say the sentences, then write them in French.)***

1. 

Bonjour
ça va?

2. 

bien
merci

3. 

merci
au revoir

4. 

De rien
a plus tard

M **Regarde les scènes, puis écris les dialogues.** ***(Look at the scenes, then write the dialogues.)***

1. 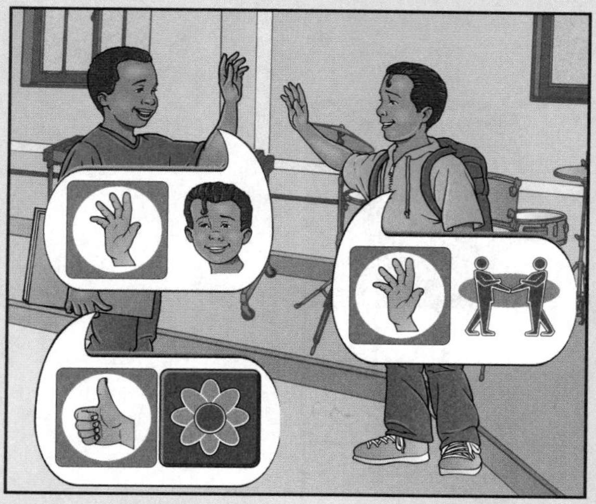

Bonjour Alain

Bonjour, ça va?

Bien, merci

2. 

merci, a plus tard

De rien, au revoir

3. 

Au revoir Brigitte

A plus tard Sylvie

Mots croisés

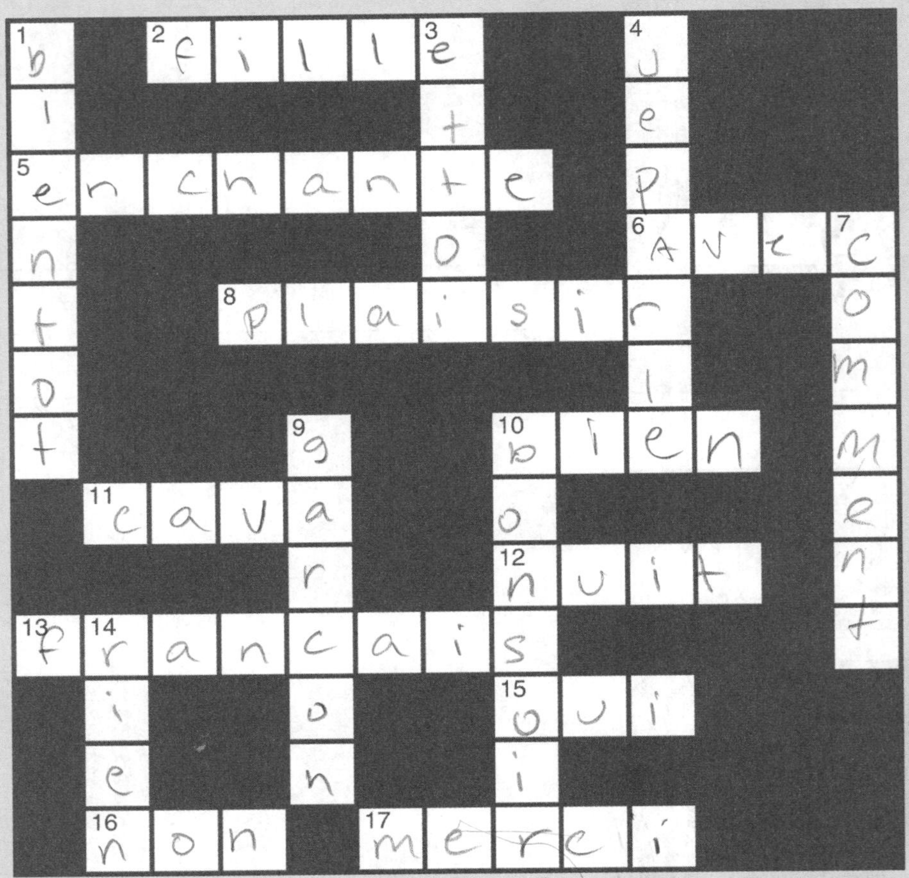

Horizontalement

2. girl
5. Pleased to meet you.
6. ____ *plaisir*
8. *Avec* ____
10. Fine
11. All right
12. Night
13. French
15. Yes
16. Opposite of *oui*
17. Thank you

Verticalement

1. *À* ____*!* (See you soon!)
3. And you?
4. I speak.
7. ____ *t'appelles-tu?*
9. boy
10. Good evening
14. *De* ____

Unit 2

Les objets et les ordres de la salle de classe
Classroom Objects and Commands

Vocabulaire

Qu'est-ce que c'est?	C'est un...
What is this?	C'est une...
	It's a...

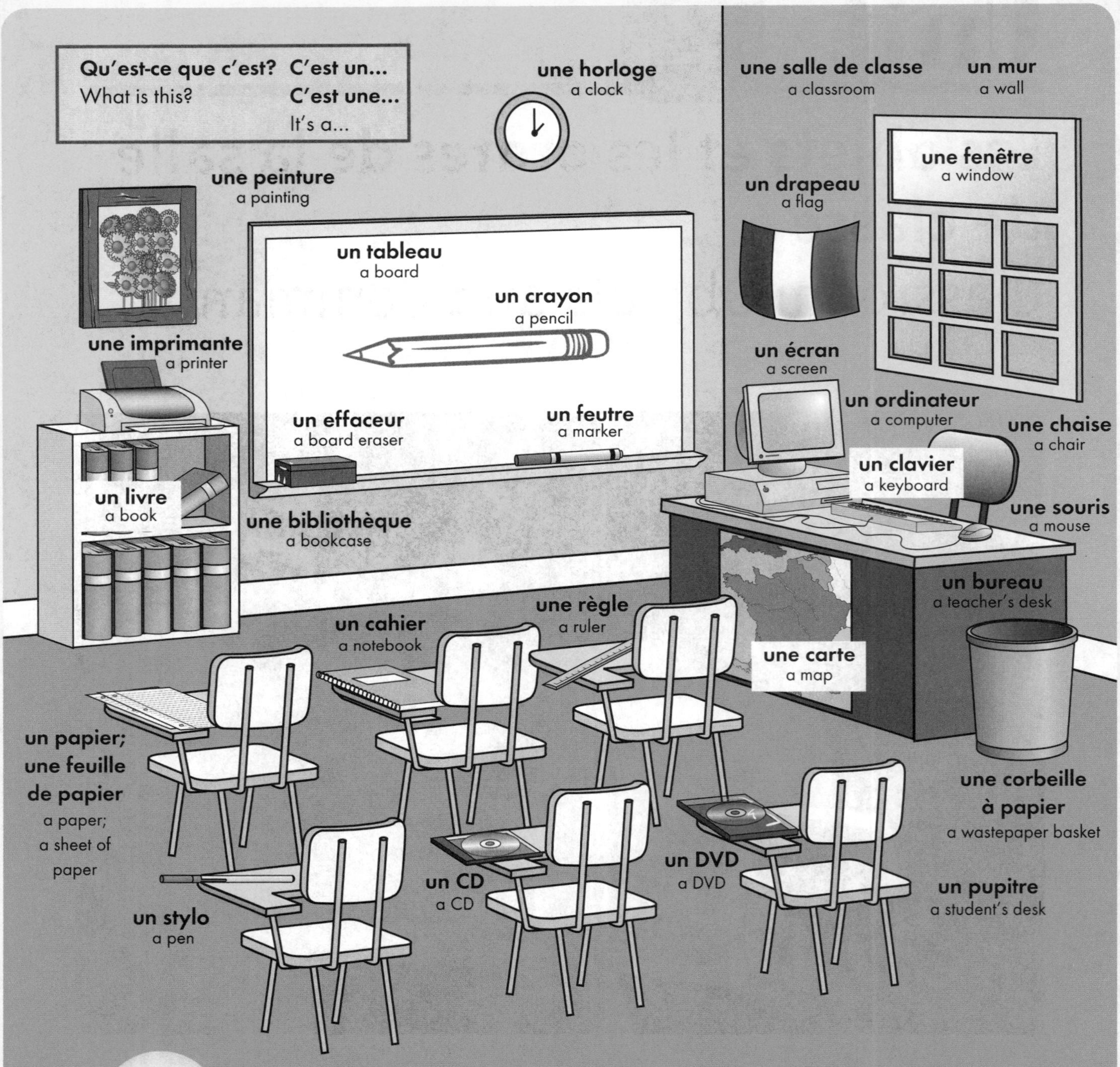

une horloge
a clock
une salle de classe
a classroom
un mur
a wall
une peinture
a painting
une fenêtre
a window
un drapeau
a flag
un tableau
a board
un crayon
a pencil
une imprimante
a printer
un écran
a screen
un ordinateur
a computer
une chaise
a chair
un effaceur
a board eraser
un feutre
a marker
un clavier
a keyboard
un livre
a book
une souris
a mouse
une bibliothèque
a bookcase
un bureau
a teacher's desk
une règle
a ruler
un cahier
a notebook
une carte
a map
un papier;
une feuille
de papier
a paper;
a sheet of
paper
une corbeille
à papier
a wastepaper basket
un DVD
a DVD
un CD
a CD
un pupitre
a student's desk
un stylo
a pen

Une classe refers to a class of students. It is also a short reference to **la salle de classe,** or classroom.

table / table
ciseaux / scissors
gomme / eraser
colle / glue
marqueurs / markers
piano / piano

Va faire un tour!
Walk it off!

Les ordres donnés en classe

Classroom commands

Dis-le en français!
Say it in French!

Parle!
Speak!

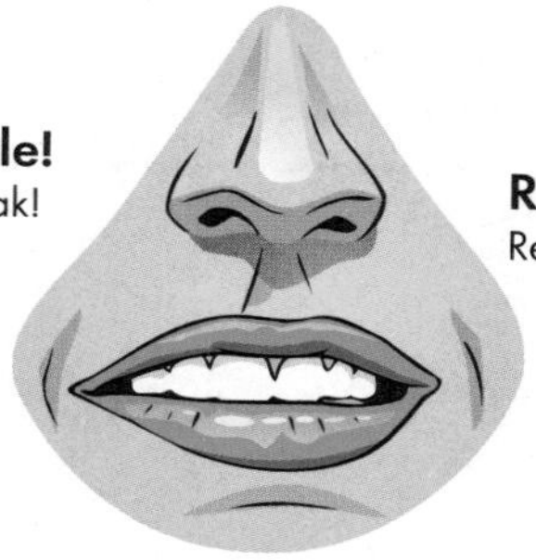

Répète!
Repeat!

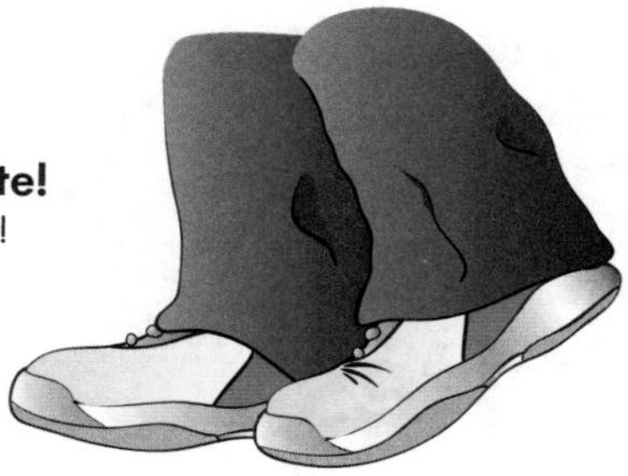

Écris!
Write!

Réponds à la question!
Answer the question!

Va au tableau!
Go to the board!

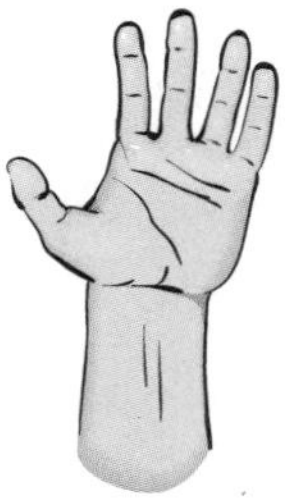

Lève la main!
Raise your hand!

Prends une feuille de papier!
Take out a sheet of paper!

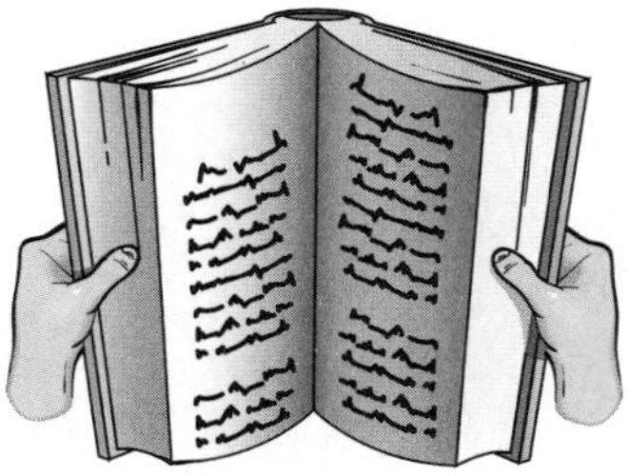

Ouvre le livre!
Open the book!

Ferme le livre!
Close the book!

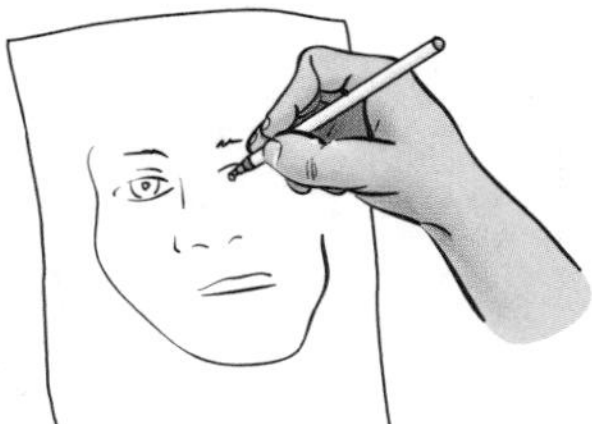

Dessine une image!
Make a sketch (drawing, illustration)!

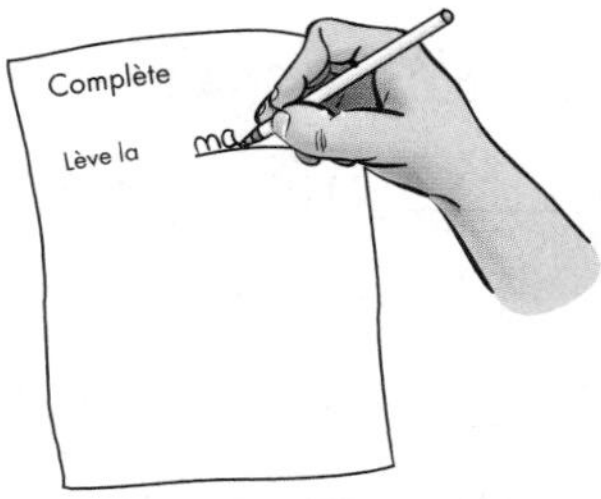
Complète
Lève la

Complète les phrases!
Complete the sentences!

Lis!
Read!

Écoute!
Listen!

ON

Allume l'ordinateur!
Turn the computer on!

OFF

Éteins l'ordinateur!
Turn the computer off!

Vocabulaire Extra!

télécopier
to send a fax

envoyer un courriel
to send an e-mail

surfer le web
to surf the web

imprimer
to print

copier
to copy

jouer à un jeu vidéo
to play a video game

Activités

A **Your teacher will say at random the words for 26 classroom objects in French. After you hear the first word, find it in the list below and write "1" in the space provided. Mark the second word you hear with a "2," etc.**

7 un tableau
13 une règle
22 un CD
20 un stylo
6 un livre
26 une carte
12 une corbeille à papier
24 une imprimante
4 un drapeau
18 un clavier
16 une peinture
10 une chaise
21 un ordinateur
8 une feuille de papier
14 un feutre
5 un crayon
17 un cahier
1 une souris
15 une horloge
11 une bibliothèque
2 un effaceur
19 une fenêtre
23 un écran
3 un bureau
25 un pupitre
9 un DVD

B **Look around your own classroom in order to answer these questions.**

1. Do you have *une feuille de papier* on your desk?

Non

2. Where is *le drapeau*?

Je n'ai aucune idée

3. How many *fenêtres* does your room have?

6

4. Is the *imprimante* near the computer?

Oui

5. Are there many *livres* in the *bibliothèque*?

Je n'ai aucune idée

C **Écris en français le nom de chaque objet. N'oublie pas l'article indéfini: "*un*" ou "*une*."** ***(Write the French name for each object. Remember to include the indefinite article:* un *or* une *before the noun.)***

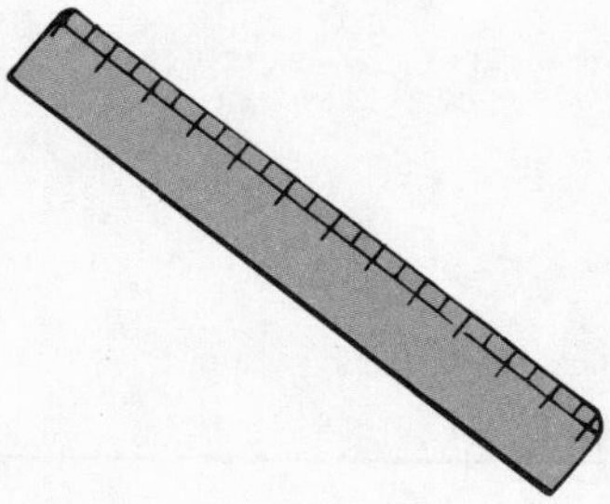

1. une règle

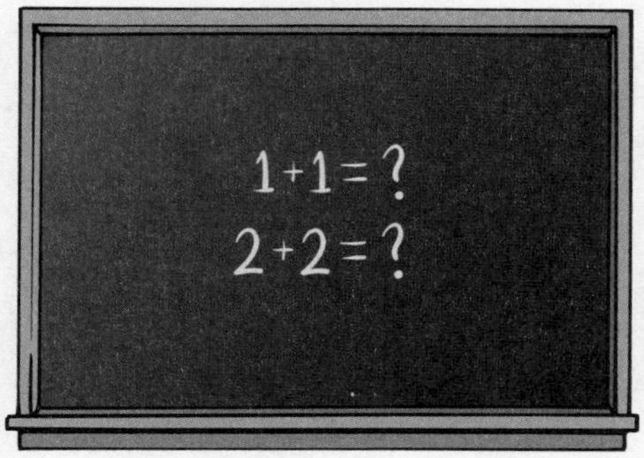
1+1=?
2+2=?

2. un tableau

3. une bibliothèque

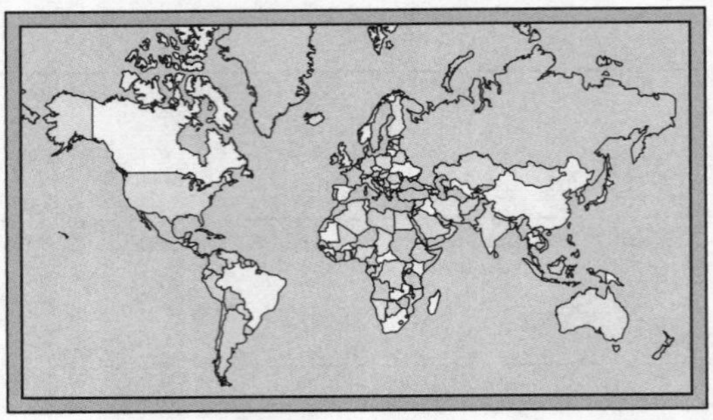

4. une carte

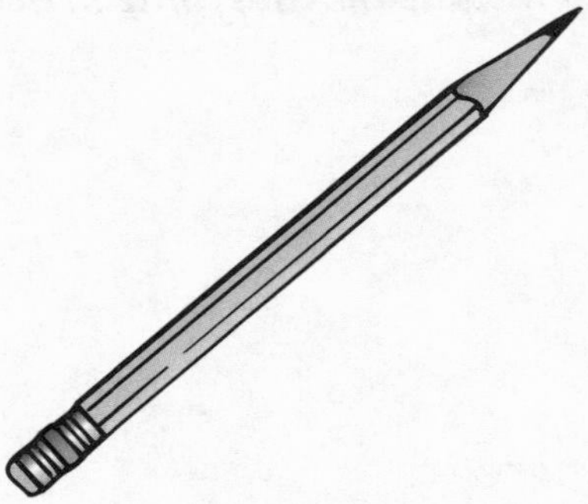

5. un crayon

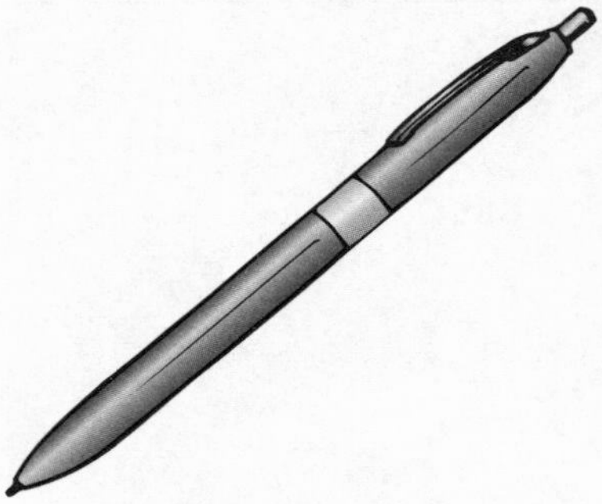

6. un stylo

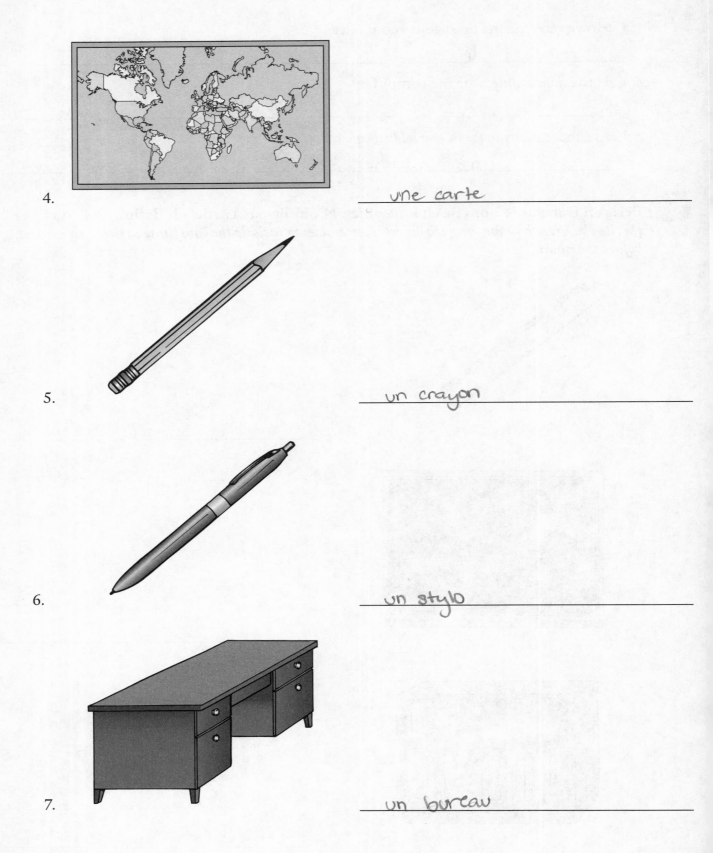

7. un bureau

8. 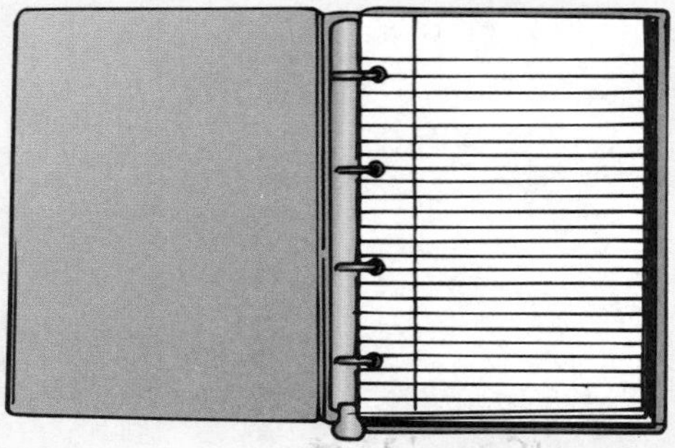

un cahier

9. 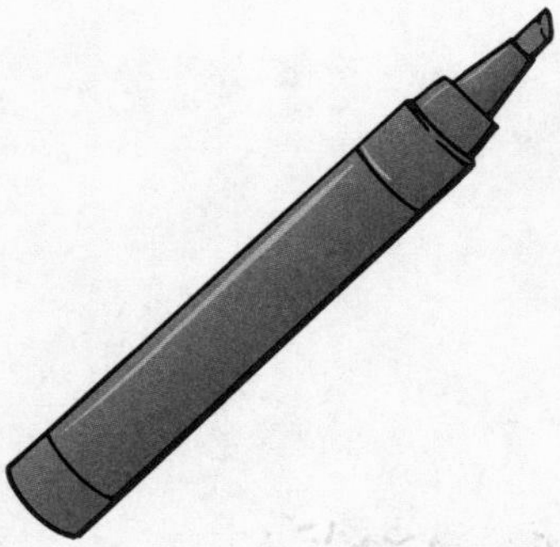

un feaûtre

10. 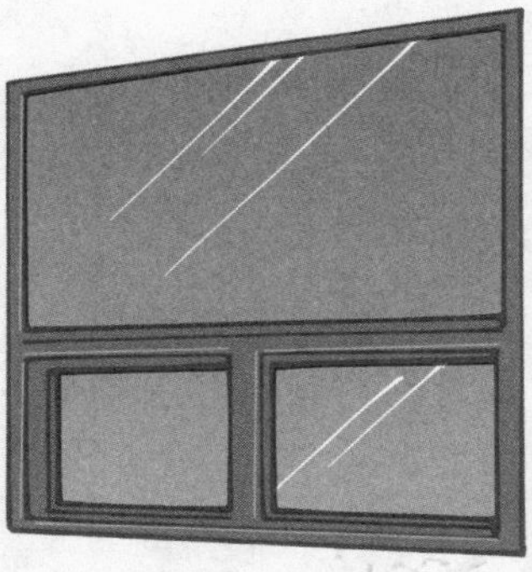

une fenêtre

11. 

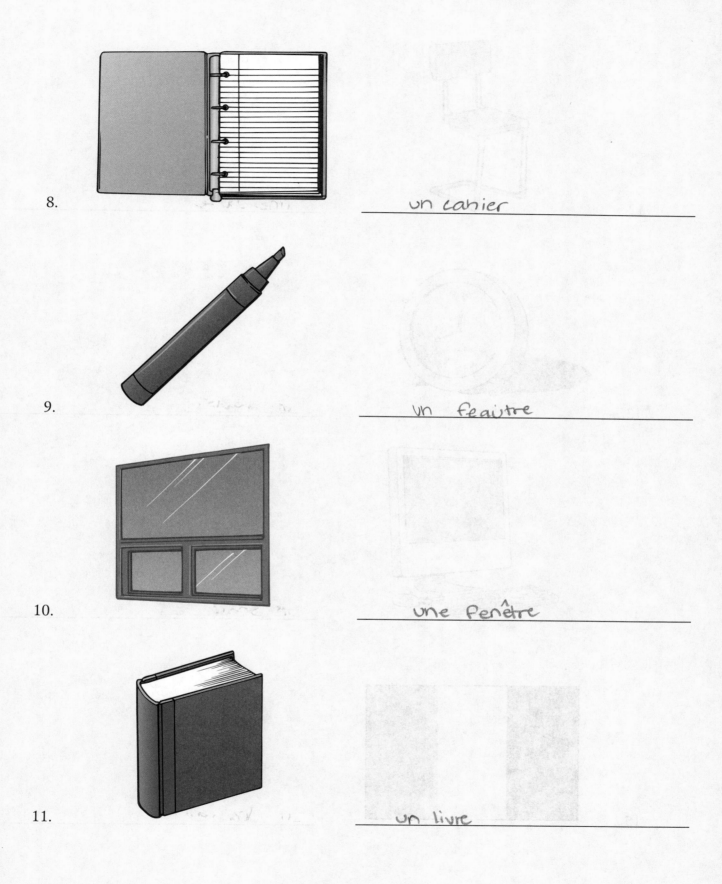

un livre

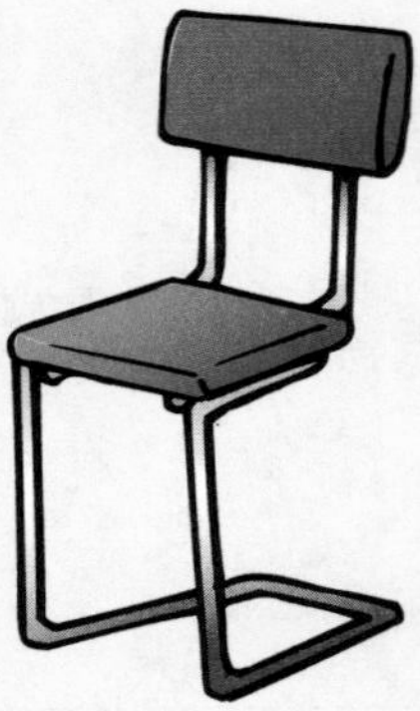

12. une chaise

12
3
9
6

13. une harloge

14. un ordinateur

15. un drapeau

D Complète les phrases. *(Complete the sentences.)*

1. Qu' est-ce que c'est?
2. C'est un stylo.
3. C'est une chaise.
4. C'est un livre.

E Do what your teacher commands.

F Complète les phrases en français, s'il te plaît. *(Complete the sentences in French, please.)*

1. Parle français! *(Speak)*
2. Dis -le en français! *(Say)*
3. Écoute! *(Listen)*
4. Étiens l'ordinateur! *(Turn off)*
5. ouvre le livre! *(Open)*

G Complète les phrases en français, s'il te plait. *(Complete the sentences in French, please.)*

1. Prends une feuille de papier!
2. Complète les phrases!
3. Ferme le livre!
4. Dessine une image!
5. Allume l' ordinateur!
6. Écris avec *(with)* un crayon!
7. Réponds à la question!

H Écris en français un ordre qui correspond à chaque image. *(Write a command in French for each illustration.)*

1. Va au tableau

2. Etiens l'ordinateur

3. Lève la main

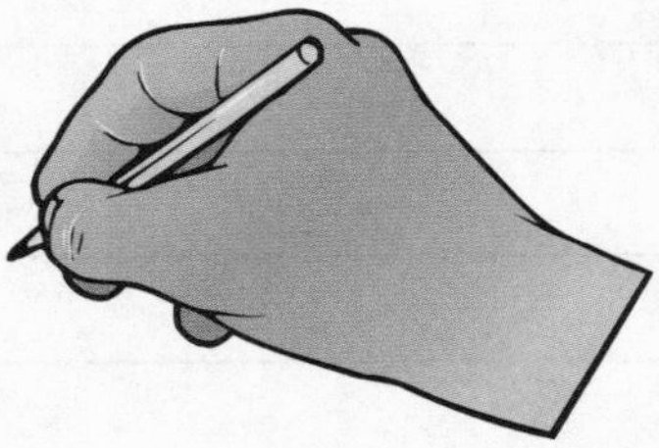

4. Écris

5. Lis

I **Which objects go together? Match each noun in column A with a related noun in column B.**

A		B
1. ______	une souris	A. un mur
2. ______	un bureau	B. un écran
3. ______	un effaceur	C. un cahier
4. ______	une feuille de papier	D. un tableau
5. ______	une peinture	E. une chaise

J **Parlons! Point to a classroom object, such as a ruler and ask, "*C'est une règle?*" Your speaking partner should answer, "*Oui, c'est une règle.*" Point to a window and ask, "*C'est un crayon?*" Your partner should answer, "*Non, c'est une fenêtre.*" Practice this type of patterned response for ten items in the classroom.**

K **Word associations. You and your speaking partner should each make a list of five words or expressions from the classroom commands. Then say one of the words or expressions for your partner, who gives a word or expression that is related to what you said.**

Modèles: **A:** la main
B: Lève
or
B: Dis-le. . .
A: . . .en français!

L **C'est à toi! With a partner, walk around your classroom. Point to ten different objects, and each time ask your partner "*Qu'est-ce que c'est?*" If he/she answers incorrectly, change places. Now it is his/her turn to ask you the name of each item. Keep going until ten objects have been correctly identified.**

Proverbe

"Les amis de nos amis sont nos amis.
A friend of yours is a friend of mine."

Langue vivante!

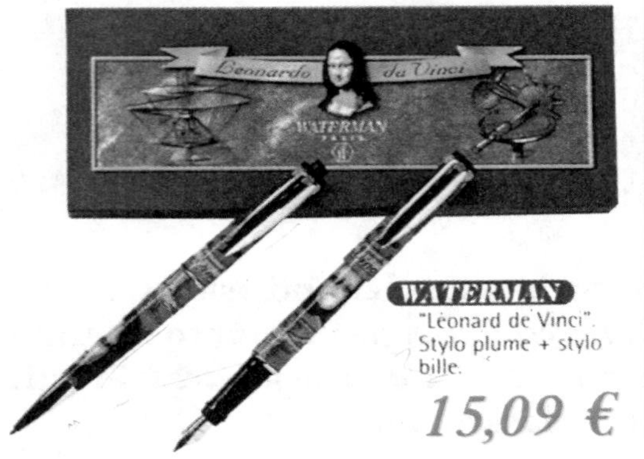
Leonardo da Vinci
WATERMAN
WATERMAN
"Léonard de Vinci".
Stylo plume + stylo bille.
15,09 €

Dictionnaire
HACHETTE
ENCYCLOPÉDIQUE
EN COULEURS
125 000 DÉFINITIONS
3 000 ILLUSTRATIONS

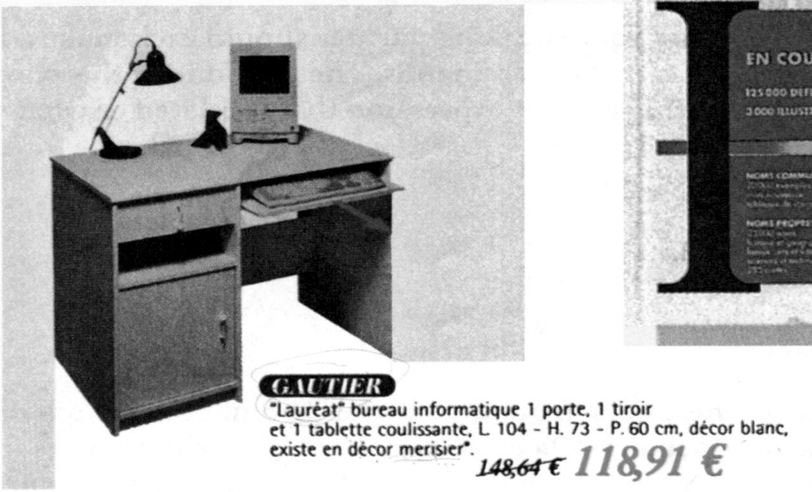
GAUTIER
"Lauréat" bureau informatique 1 porte, 1 tiroir
et 1 tablette coulissante, L. 104 - H. 73 - P. 60 cm, décor blanc,
existe en décor merisier*.
148,64 € 118,91 €

DE L'ORDINATEUR A LA PHOTO EN 14 SECONDES.
IMPRIME
SCANNE
COPIE
FAXE

M **Answer the following questions in French.**

1. Where can you find the definition of a word?

   Dictionnaire Hachette Encyclopédique

2. What word indicating a wide range of information describes this book?

   Encyclopédique

3. What words describe a special feature of this book?

   En couleurs

4. *Il y a combien de définitions?*

   125,000 définitions

5. *Il y a combien d'illustrations?*

   3000 illustrations

N **Answer the following questions.**

1. There are two kinds of pens. What are they? *(En français, s'il te plaît.)*

   stylo plume et stylo bille

2. Is there a price difference? *(En français, s'il te plaît.)*

   Non

3. What famous artist's works are portrayed on the pens?

   Leonardo de Vinci

4. On what piece of furniture can you use *l'ordinateur*? *(En anglais, s'il te plaît.)*

   un bureau

5. What two French words identify this item?

   Gautier, lauréat

6. Find the four commands on the page. Write what they mean in English.

   imprime

   scanne

   copie

   faxe

Symtalk

O **Écris le mot ou l'expression en français dans l'espace blanc.** ***(In the space, write the correct word or expression in French.)***

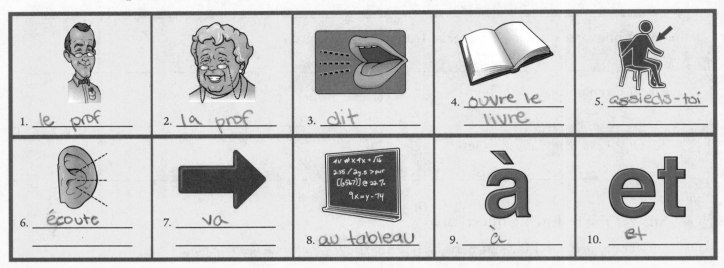

 1. le prof	 2. la prof	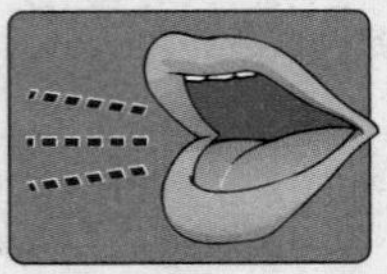 3. dit	 4. ouvre le livre	 5. assieds-toi
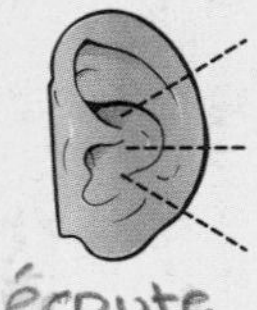 6. écoute	 7. va	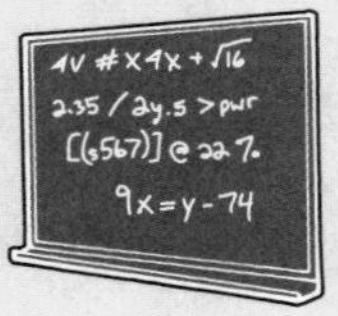 8. au tableau	**à** 9. à	**et** 10. et

P **Dis les phrases, puis-écris les en français.** ***(Say the sentences, then write them in French.)***

1.  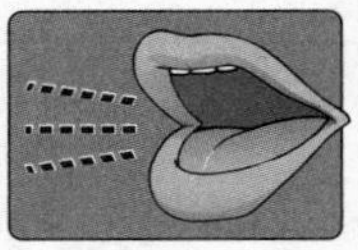 **à**  

Le prof dit a Brigitte assieds-toi

2.  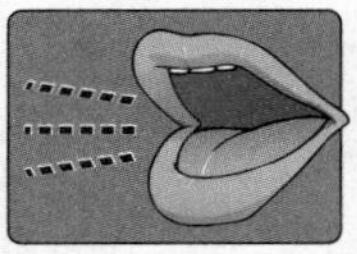 **à**   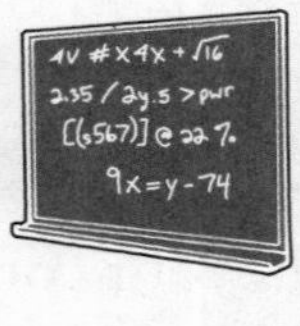

Le prof dit a Antoine va au tableau

3.  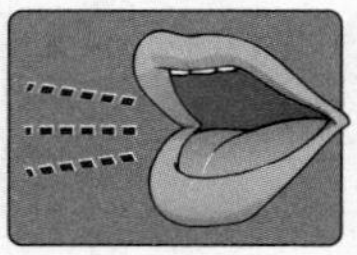 **à**  **et**  

La prof dit a Hiko et Gerard ouvre le livre

4. 
à
et

La prof dit a Sylvie et Brigitte ècoute

Q **En français, décris chaque scène par oral et par écrit.** ***(In French, say and write a description of each scene.)***

1. 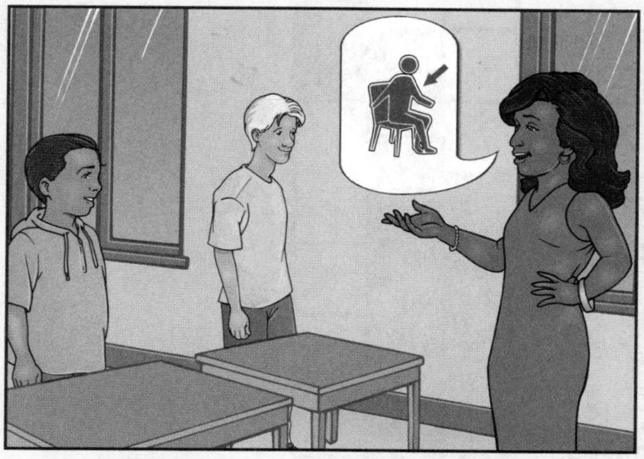

Assieds-toi

2. 

Ouvre le livre

3. 
23 + 25 - Y = ?
X (3) + 27

Ècoute

Mots croisés

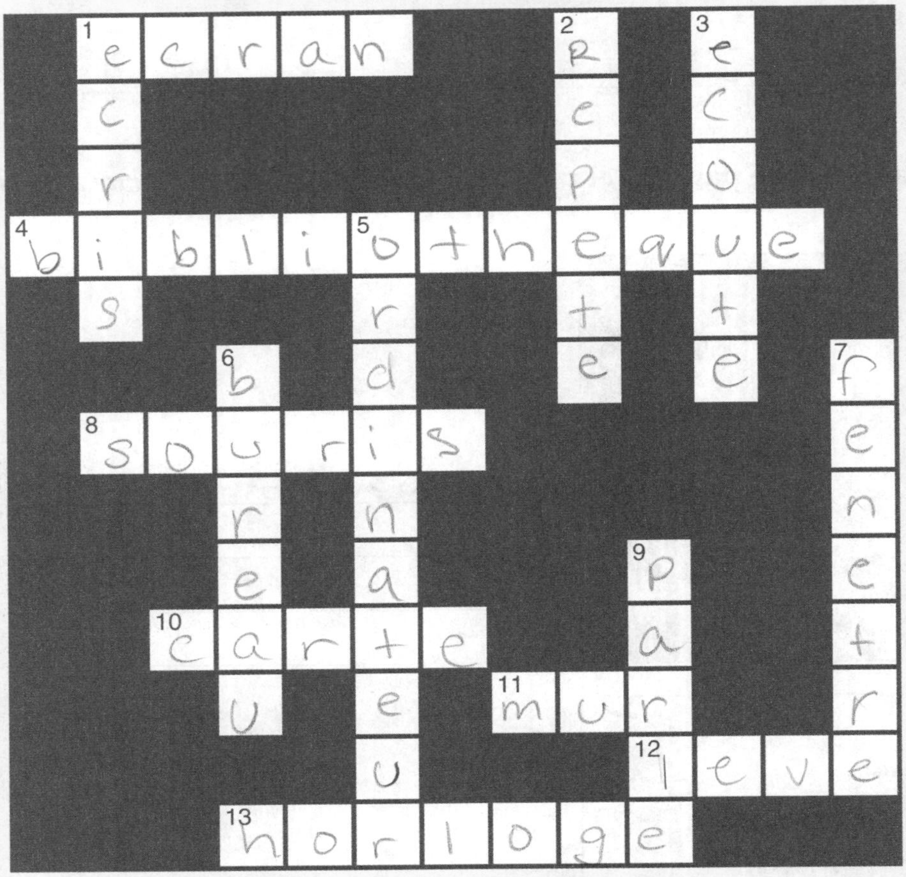
1 ecran
2 Repete
3 ecoute
4 bibliotheque
5 ordinateur
6 bureau
7 fenetre
8 souris
9 parler
10 carte
11 mur
12 leve
13 horloge

Horizontalement

1. screen
4. storage place for books
8. computer animal
10. shows continents and oceans
11. place to hang a picture
12. ____ *la main!*
13. It tells us the time.

Verticalement

1. Write!
2. Repeat!
3. Listen!
5. useful machine
6. large desk
7. opening in the wall for air and light
9. Speak!

Unit 3

Les nombres — Numbers

À 100m
D53
LA GRAVE 6
NICE 22
P
LA POSTE

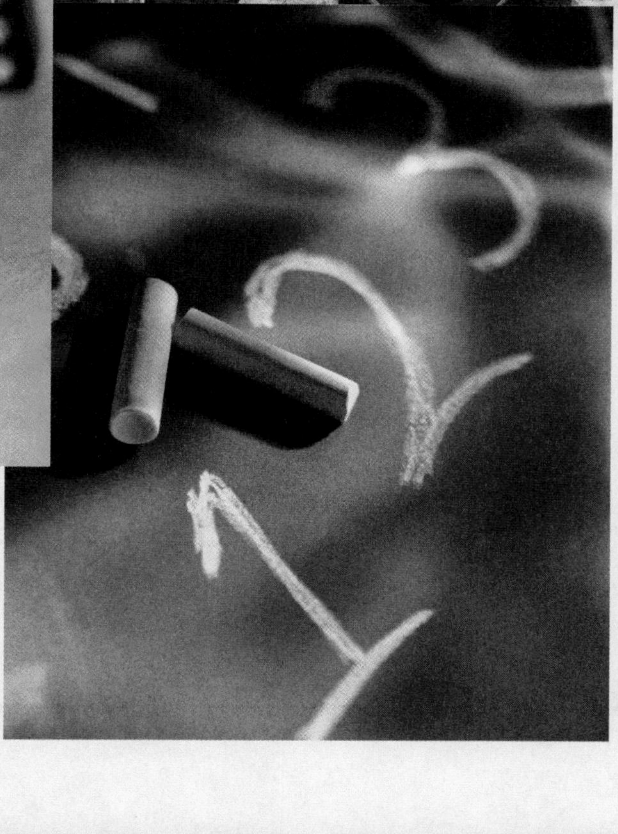

Vocabulaire

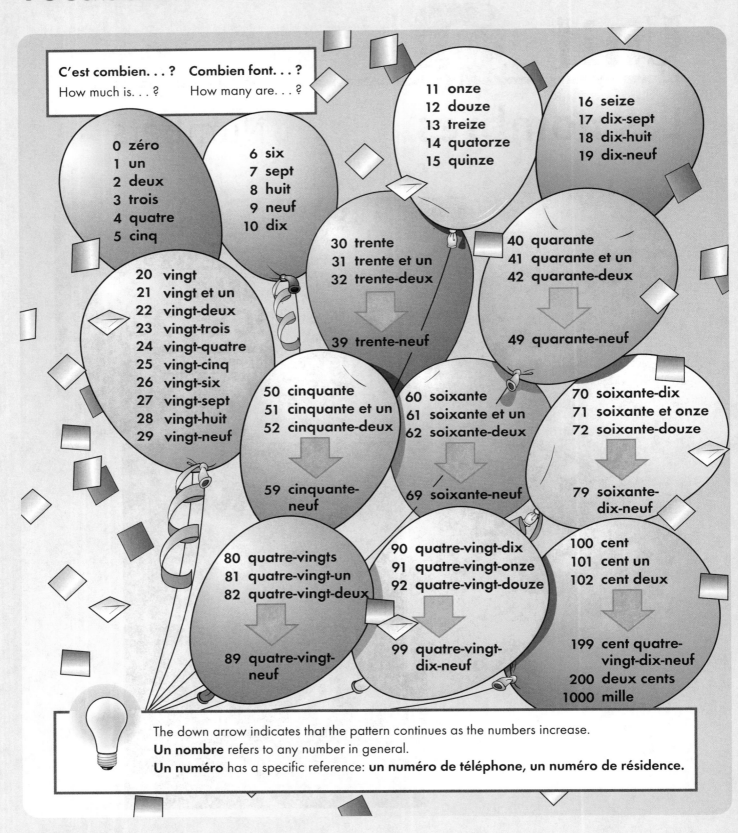

C'est combien. . . ?	**Combien font. . . ?**
How much is. . . ?	How many are. . . ?

0 zéro
1 un
2 deux
3 trois
4 quatre
5 cinq

6 six
7 sept
8 huit
9 neuf
10 dix

11 onze
12 douze
13 treize
14 quatorze
15 quinze

16 seize
17 dix-sept
18 dix-huit
19 dix-neuf

20 vingt
21 vingt et un
22 vingt-deux
23 vingt-trois
24 vingt-quatre
25 vingt-cinq
26 vingt-six
27 vingt-sept
28 vingt-huit
29 vingt-neuf

30 trente
31 trente et un
32 trente-deux
↓
39 trente-neuf

40 quarante
41 quarante et un
42 quarante-deux
↓
49 quarante-neuf

50 cinquante
51 cinquante et un
52 cinquante-deux
↓
59 cinquante-neuf

60 soixante
61 soixante et un
62 soixante-deux
↓
69 soixante-neuf

70 soixante-dix
71 soixante et onze
72 soixante-douze
↓
79 soixante-dix-neuf

80 quatre-vingts
81 quatre-vingt-un
82 quatre-vingt-deux
↓
89 quatre-vingt-neuf

90 quatre-vingt-dix
91 quatre-vingt-onze
92 quatre-vingt-douze
↓
99 quatre-vingt-dix-neuf

100 cent
101 cent un
102 cent deux
↓
199 cent quatre-vingt-dix-neuf
200 deux cents
1000 mille

The down arrow indicates that the pattern continues as the numbers increase.
Un nombre refers to any number in general.
Un numéro has a specific reference: **un numéro de téléphone, un numéro de résidence.**

Vocabulaire Extra!

Combien. . .?
How much. . .?

Combien de. . .?
How many. . .?

Il y a. . .?
Are there. . .? Is there. . .?

Combien coûte le livre?
C'est combien, le livre?
How much does the book cost?

Le livre coûte quinze euros.
C'est quinze euros.
The book costs 15 euros.

Il y a combien de cahiers?
How many notebooks are there?

Il y a douze cahiers.
There are 12 notebooks.

Combien font deux et un?
How much is two and one?

Ça fait combien?
How much does that make?

Ça fait trois.
That makes three.

coûter
to cost

il / elle coûte
it costs

ils / elles coûtent
they cost

+ = *et*	× = *fois*	— = *moins*	÷ = *divisé par*

The currency of France is the euro, *l'euro* (m.). It contains 100 *centimes* (cents).

Le CD coûte 18,50 euros. (18 euros and 50 centimes)

Notice how the French use commas where we use periods, and periods where we use commas.

$1,250.50 = 1.250,00 €

Activités

A **After you have studied the numbers 1-10 and practiced saying them, try to write the numbers in French from memory.**

1. un
2. deux
3. trois
4. quatre
5. cinq
6. six
7. sept
8. huit
9. neuf
10. dix

B **Rate yourself. How did you do? In France students are graded on a point system, with 20 points being the top score. Circle your evaluation.**

20	19	18	17	16
15	14	13	12	11
10	9	8	7	6
5	4	3	2	1

C Identify the French words by writing the corresponding Arabic numerals.

Modèle: deux 2

1. cinq 5
2. huit 8
3. un 1
4. neuf 9
5. sept 7

D Écris le mot français pour chaque nombre. *(Write the French word for each number.)*

3 trois
4 quatre
6 six
10 dix

E Tell whether the following equations indicate addition, subtraction, multiplication, or division.

1. Quatorze divisé par sept font deux.
   Division
2. Deux et dix font douze.
   Addition
3. Huit fois trois font vingt-quatre.
   multiplication
4. Dix-neuf moins treize font six.
   subtraction

F Try once more to write out the numbers in French.

8 huit
3 trois
10 dix
1 un
9 neuf
2 deux
5 cinq
4 quatre
7 sept
6 six

G

Combien d'objets sont représentés? Écris les réponses en français. N'écris pas les chiffres!
(How many objects are pictured? Write out the French numbers. Do not use numerals!)

1. deux

2. six

3. trois

4. un

5. quatre

H **Il y a combien d'objets en tout?** ***(How many objects are there all together?)*** 16

Écris la somme en français. ***(Now, write this sum in French.)***

seize

I **Écris les résultats en français.** ***(Write the answers to the math problems in French.)***

> **Modèle:** 6 − 4 = deux

1. 12 × 4 = vingt-quatre
2. 30 − 10 = vingt
3. 8 − 6 = deux
4. 12 + 18 = trente
5. 100 ÷ 2 = cinquante
6. 60 + 10 = soixante-dix
7. 30 − 15 = quinze
8. 80 ÷ 2 = quarante
9. 10 × 10 = cent
10. 15 + 4 = dix-neuf

J **Your teacher will say ten numbers in French. Write the corresponding Arabic numerals.**

> **Modèle:** **Teacher says:** dix-neuf
> **You write:** 19

1. 54
2. 25
3. 37
4. 44
5. 14
6. 66
7. 16
8. 29
9. 55
10. 70

K **How many interior angles are there in each design? Circle the number.**

1. 
quatre dix
huit trois

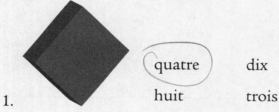

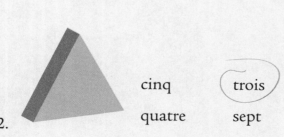

2. 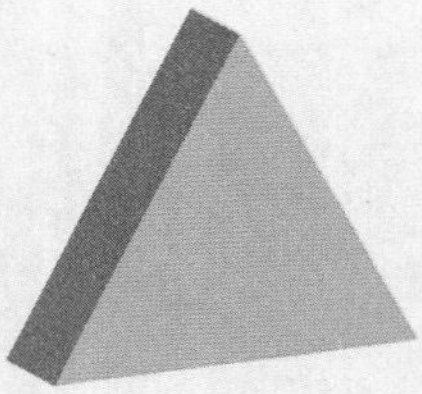
cinq trois
quatre sept

3. 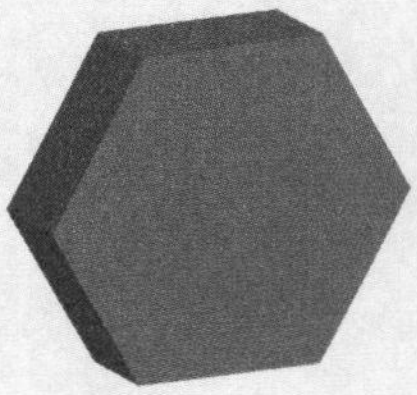
sept onze
six cinq

4. 
onze huit
neuf cinq

L

Lis le paragraphe. Encercle les bonnes réponses. ***(Read the paragraph. Then circle the correct completions.)***

> Dans la salle de classe il y a beaucoup d'objets: vingt-huit chaises, quatre fenêtres, dix-neuf cahiers, six effaceurs, et une carte. Une chaise coûte soixante-quinze euros. Un effaceur coûte un euro et une carte coûte quatre-vingts euros.

beaucoup	many	**euros**	currency used in France

coûte cost

1. Dans la salle de classe il y a ___ objets.
- A. peu de (*few*)
- B. beaucoup d'
- C. cinq
- D. dix

2. Il y a combien d'objets dans la salle de classe? *(Add.)*
- A. quarante et un
- B. cinquante-huit
- C. vingt-deux
- D. quatre-vingt-dix

3. Combien coûte une chaise?
- A. 75 euros
- B. 57 euros
- C. 37 euros
- D. 73 euros

4. Il y a combien de cahiers?
- A. 91
- B. 25
- C. 19
- D. 30

5. Il y a combien de fenêtres?
- A. 13
- B. 8
- C. 6
- D. 4

M

Parlons! **Find out about prices. With your speaking partner, select six objects in the classroom. Ask your partner how much the first three cost. Then your partner should ask you about the remaining three items and you will answer.**

Modèles: **A:** C'est combien, le stylo?
B: C'est deux euros.

A: Combien coûte le stylo?
B: Ça coûte deux euros.

N

C'est à toi! **With a classmate, count the number of books, windows, notebooks, pens, and computers in your classroom. After you have counted carefully, announce your findings to the class in French by saying "*Il y a. . .*" At the end add up all the items to find out the total number of things you have. Write all the numbers on the board.**

Modèle: **A:** Il y a combien de livres? *(How many books are there?)*
B: Il y a vingt livres. *(There are twenty books.)*

Langue vivante!

PHOTO VIDEO
phox
PAS D'INTOX
400 MAGASINS
PHOTO VIDEO
MORDUS
D'IMAGES
SPÉCIAL Rentrée
1 planche
de 4 photos
4,57 €
2 planches
de 4 photos
6,86 €
SUPER AFFAIRE
POINT VERT
VOS
PHOTOS
D'IDENTITÉ

VEDETTES
PONT-NEUF
SQUARE DU VERT-GALANT - PARIS 1er
Tél. : 46 33 98 38
Bus : 24-27-72-74
75-58-67-70
STOP : PONT-NEUF
Métro et parking :
PONT-NEUF ou LOUVRES
RER : CHATELET

Cette semaine
DVD n°1
Épisodes 1 et 2 - Durée 3h
5 €70*
seulement

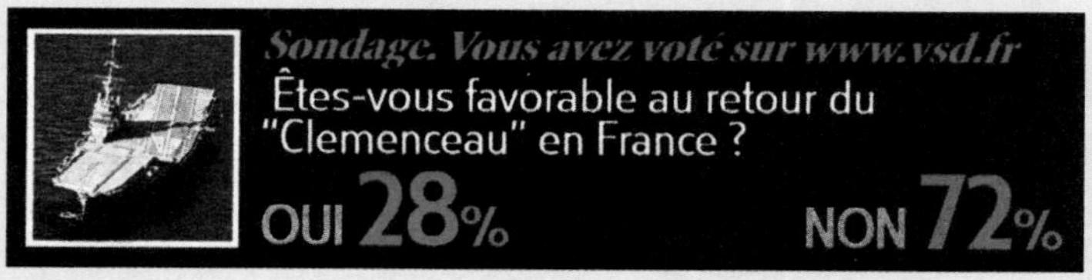
Sondage. Vous avez voté sur www.vsd.fr
Êtes-vous favorable au retour du
"Clemenceau" en France ?
OUI 28%
NON 72%

O

Study the clippings about *la rentrée* (back to school photo specials) and then answer the questions.

1. *Il y a combien de photos sur* (on) *UNE planche?*

____

2. *Une planche, ça coûte combien?*

____

3. *Il y a combien de planches?*

____

4. Which price is a better deal? (Write out.)

____

P

Review the clippings about the sight-seeing boats and poll and answer the following questions.

1. What does the abbreviation *Tél.* stand for?_______________________________
2. Write out the parts of the *Vedettes Pont-Neuf* telephone number in French:

   46 = ____________________ 98 = ____________________

   33 = ____________________ 38 = ____________________

3. Write out the following numbers found in the DVD advertisement:

   a. N° 1 = ____________________ c. 70 = ____________________ centimes

   b. 5 = ____________________ euros

4. Write out the following numbers found in the clipping about survey results.

   a. *Positif:* ____________________________ *pourcent*

   b. *Négatif:* ____________________________ *pourcent*

Proverbe

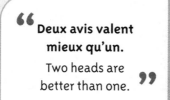

“**Deux avis valent mieux qu'un.**
Two heads are better than one.”

Symtalk

Q **Écris le mot ou l'expression en français dans l'espace blanc.** ***(In the space, write the correct word or expression in French.)***

				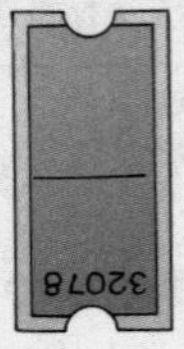		
1. Coûte/coûtent	2. le cd	3. le cahier	4. les bonbons	5. le billet	6. les lunettes de soleil	7. Combien

R **Dis les phrases, puis écris-les en français.** ***(Say the sentences, then write them in French.)***

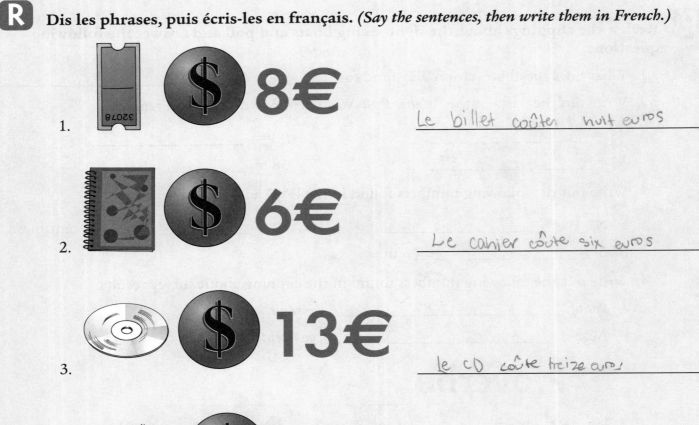

1. 
8€
Le billet coûter huit euros

2. 
6€
Le cahier coûte six euros

3. 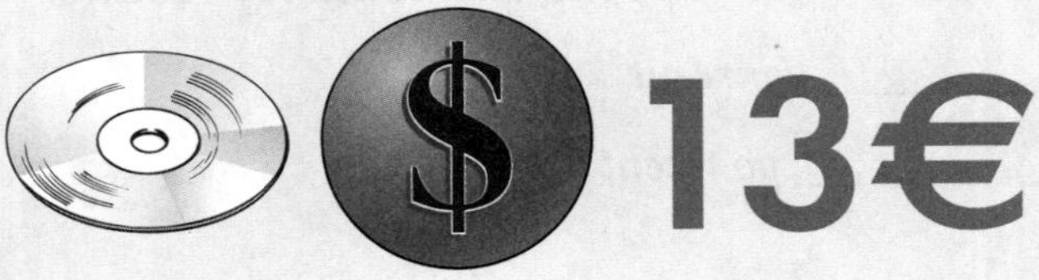
13€
le CD coûte treize euros

4. 
9€
Les bonbons coûtent neuf euros

5. 
24€
Les lunettes de soleil coûtent vingt-quatre euros

S **Travaille avec un partenaire. Pose la question ou donne la réponse. Puis, écris le dialogue.** ***(Work with a partner. Ask the question or give the answer. Then, write the dialogue.)***

> € l'euro les euros
> The euro is the currency of France and of most members of the European Union.

1. 

14 €

combien le coûte le cd ? — quatorze les euros

2. 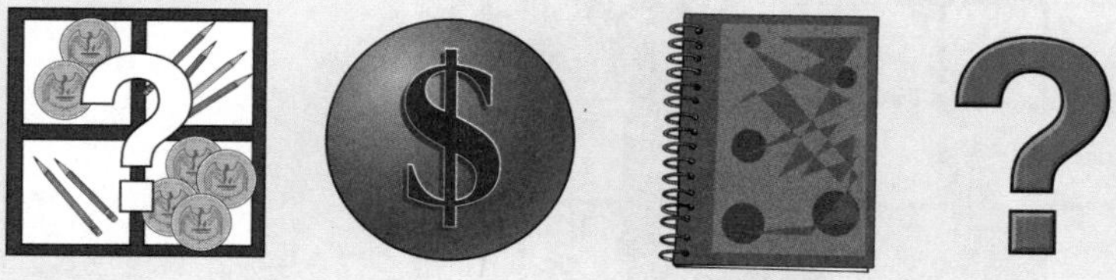

5 €

combien le coûte le cahier ? — cinq les euros

3. 

19 €

Combien le coûte les lunettes de soleil ? — dix-neuf les euros

4. 
32078

20 €

Combien le coûte les billet ? — vingt les euros

5. 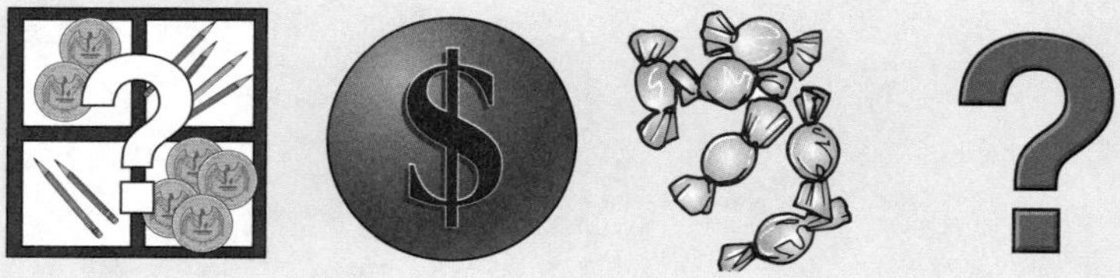

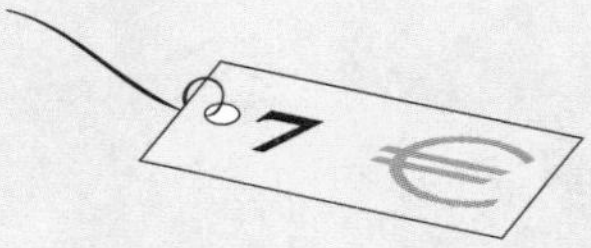
7 €

combien le coute les bonbons ? — sept les euros

Mots croisés

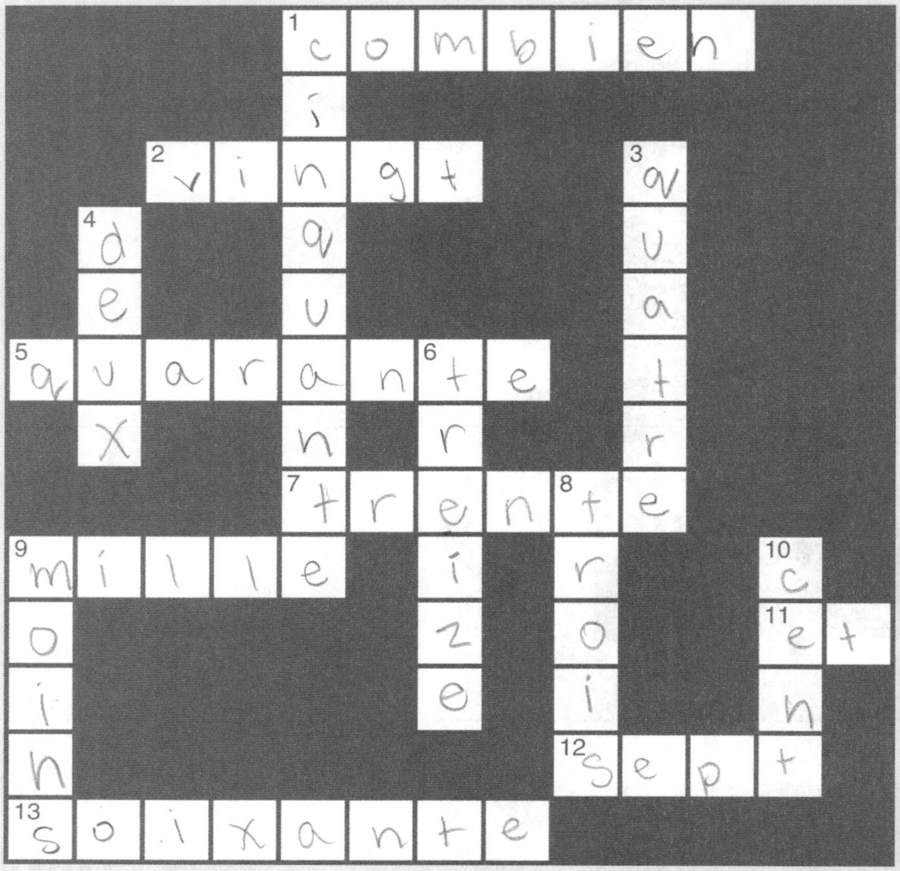
combien
cinquante
vingt
quatre
deux
quarante
treize
trente
trois
mille
moins
cent
et
sept
soixante

Horizontalement

1. How much?
2. *quatre fois cinq*
5. 100 − 60 = ____
7. number of days in June
9. 1001 − 1 = ____
11. word to indicate addition
12. number of days in a week
13. 30 × 2 = ____

Verticalement

1. half of *cent*
3. number of seasons in a temperate climate
4. the number of items in a pair
6. dozen plus one
8. between *deux* and *quatre*
9. word to indicate subtraction
10. 70 + 30 = ____

Unit 4

La géographie Geography

N49CB

France

Important Cities

Paris, an inland port, is the capital of France and the most populated city. It is the economic, industrial, and cultural center of the nation and an international fashion center. Some outstanding landmarks include *la tour Eiffel* (Eiffel Tower), *le Centre Georges Pompidou* (Pompidou Center of Modern Art), *le Louvre* (Louvre Museum), *l'Opéra* (the Opera), *l'arc de triomphe* (Arch of Triumph), the avenue called the *Champs-Elysées*, and *Notre-Dame* (the Gothic Cathedral of Our Lady). The Seine River divides the city into the right and left banks called *la rive droite* and *la rive gauche*. Two amusement parks nearby are *le Parc Astérix* (based on a Gallic cartoon character who fights against the Romans) and *Disneyland Resort Paris.*

The Eiffel Tower, completed in 1889, is located at the Champ-de-Mars, a popular park in Paris.

Lyon, the second largest city, is located on the site where the Saône and the Rhône Rivers join together. Two old Roman amphitheaters serve as stages for operas and rock concerts. In years past Lyon was a wealthy trade center for the silk industry. Today it houses banking, pharmaceutical, and textile industries. Lyon is also renowned for its culinary arts. For fun, people like to go to the parks for boating and picnics. They also enjoy the cycle rinks for skateboarding, roller-skating, and bike racing. For ice-skating and swimming there are other excellent facilities.

Tourists traveling by boat in the Mediterranean often sail into the port of Marseille.

Marseille, situated on the Mediterranean Sea, is France's third largest city and largest seaport, which welcomes ships primarily from North Africa, the Middle East, and the Orient. The city started as a Greek port and later became a Roman city. Today it is a melting pot of people of many races and national origins. Not far from the shore is *le château d'If*, a fortified prison, made famous by the writer Alexandre Dumas in his novel, *Le Comte de Monte-Cristo* (*The Count of Monte-Cristo*).

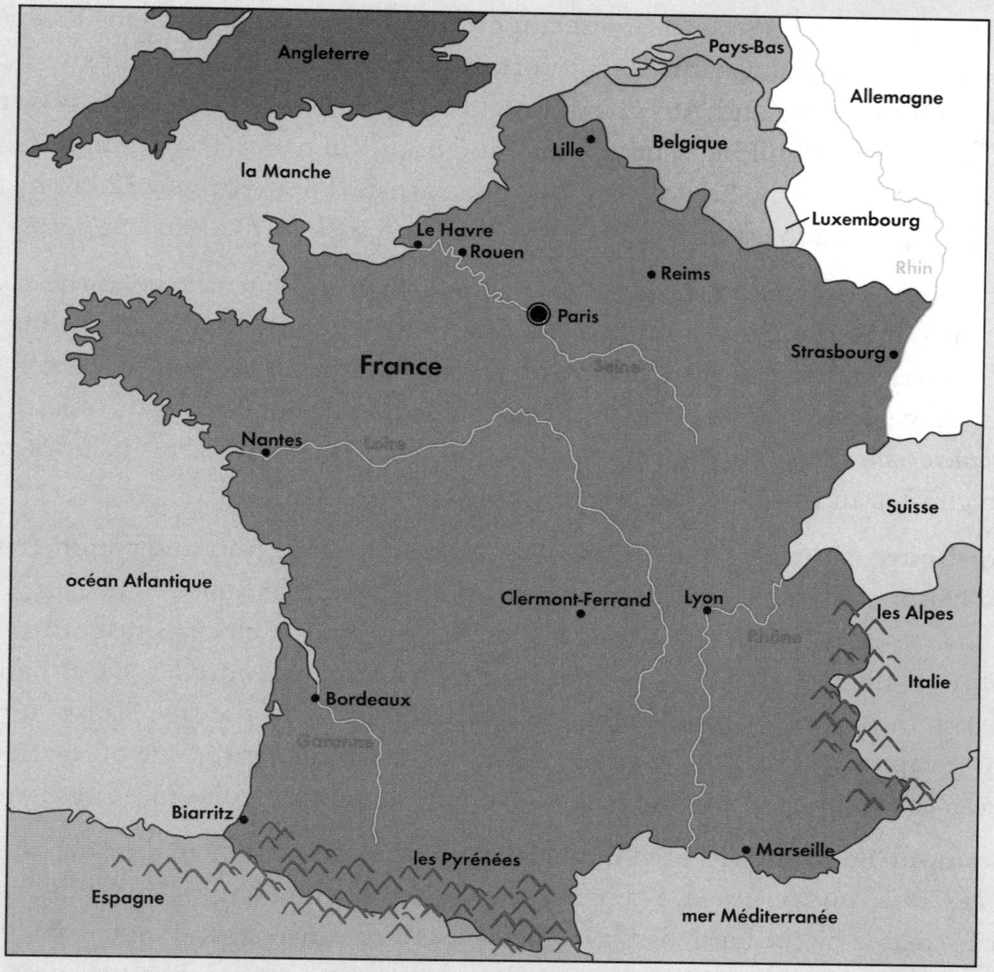
Angleterre
Pays-Bas
Allemagne
Belgique
Lille
la Manche
Luxembourg
Le Havre
Rouen
Reims
Rhin
Paris
France
Strasbourg
Seine
Nantes
Loire
Suisse
océan Atlantique
Clermont-Ferrand
Lyon
les Alpes
Rhône
Italie
Bordeaux
Garonne
Biarritz
les Pyrénées
Marseille
Espagne
mer Méditerranée

Lille, together with its suburbs, makes up the fourth largest urban area. Because it was once part of Belgium, Lille has an old Flemish quarter and a Flemish history. Traditionally it has been a major center for the production of cotton and linen fabrics, as well as industrial machinery. More recently it has developed a business quarter, *EuroLille*, which is a European center for high tech industries. Lille is only a short distance from the three headquarters of the European Union: Brussels, Belgium; Luxembourg City, Luxembourg; and Strasbourg, France. Lille has a zoo and a botanical garden.

Near Bordeaux, grapes are grown to make fine wines.

Bordeaux, the fifth largest city, is found in the southwest. Located on the Garonne River and very close to the Atlantic Ocean, its history is tied to the production of wine and to international trade. The city has a zoo and several museums. Not far from Bordeaux is *Tépacap,* a fun park in the woods where children can spend a day being acrobatic adventurers as they walk on rope bridges and play outdoor games. An aquatic theme park, *Aqualand,* is also not far away.

Le Havre is France's second largest seaport. It is found where the Seine River empties into the *la Manche* (English Channel). The port serves transoceanic cargo ships and car ferries en route to and from England. After its destruction in World War II, Le Havre was completely rebuilt. It now has new buildings, new streets, and beautiful parks. The fine arts museum contains many paintings by France's Impressionist artists. Located about 32 kilometers (20 miles) to the north are the spectacular seaside cliffs and rock formations of *Étretat*.

Nantes is a port city on the Loire River. A nearby historic landmark is the castle where Duchess Anne of Brittany was born in 1477. Many visitors to the city enjoy the maritime museum. Others take river cruises and go all the way up the Loire River to see the *châteaux.** The botanical garden features a chestnut tree that is over a thousand years old. Children like to visit *Planète Sauvage* (Wild Planet), an attraction not too far away that includes an animal park with giraffes and a marine show with sea lions.

Strasbourg, situated on the Rhine River, is a major river port and commercial center. In the old historic district there are many picturesque medieval houses. The large Gothic cathedral has a stained glass rose window and an astronomical clock. Strasbourg has a strong cultural alliance with its next-door neighbor, Germany. Indeed, the German influence is reflected in the food, language, and architecture of the city. Strasbourg is also one of three capital cities of the European Union, and as such, is the site of the European Parliament. The Council of Europe *(le Conseil d'Europe)* holds regular meetings here.

Clermont-Ferrand is located in the center of the country where the now extinct volcano, *Le Cantal,* once erupted. Many of the old churches and houses were built with the black rocks created by the hardened lava. Today it is a commercial and industrial center known for the production of Michelin tires. People interested in architecture come to see the beautiful houses built by merchants during the Renaissance period (14th – 17th centuries). Families today enjoy visiting *Vulcania*, an interactive attraction where they can have fun while learning all about volcanoes. Movie fans go to the annual short film festival.

Reims, located northeast of Paris, is noted historically for its Roman ruins and as the site where Clovis, King of the Franks, was baptized in the year 496. From the 11th century on, all French kings were crowned at the cathedral, giving Reims the nickname the "City of Coronations." At the conclusion of World War II, the Germans surrendered to the Allies in Reims. Today the city's economy is based chiefly on the annual grape harvest and on tourism to the museums and historical sites.

Biarritz is found along the southwestern Atlantic shore. Once a whaling port, it is now a resort with an aquarium, good beaches, scuba diving, and excellent surfing and windsurfing. Biarritz hosts one of the most popular international surfing contests every year. At the Basque Museum visitors can learn about the Basque people, who live in the region near Spain. At the Chocolate Museum, you can see how chocolate sculptures are made and even get free samples.

*The *châteaux* are also discussed in the section on France's important rivers.

Boats of all shapes and sizes can be found in France's five most navigable rivers.

Five Important Rivers

La Seine is the most navigable of all French rivers. That means it is deep enough for barges and ships. As a result, it is the most important commercial river of France. It empties into the English Channel at *Le Havre*.

La Loire is the longest river in France. It is a popular tourist attraction due to the *châteaux* that are found scattered throughout the Loire Valley. The *châteaux* are the fortresses, castles, and palaces that in years past belonged to the royal family, aristocrats, and wealthy merchants.

La Garonne, the shortest river of France, is a major source of hydroelectric power. It starts in the *Pyrenées* Mountains and empties into the Atlantic Ocean.

Le Rhône, which starts as a glacial stream in Switzerland, flows southward to the Mediterranean Sea. It also is an important hydroelectric power source.

Le Rhin (the Rhine), which starts in Switzerland and flows through the Netherlands into the Atlantic Ocean, serves as a natural boundary with Germany. It provides France with a vital link to other parts of Europe and helps expedite the transfer of merchandise into and out of France.

Important Facts

- The English Channel is called *la Manche* in French. There is a train and motor tunnel underneath *la Manche*, enabling travelers between England and France to cross at great speed and convenience.
- There are five major mountain ranges: 1) the Pyrenees *(les Pyrénées)*, which form a natural boundary with Spain, and 2) the Alps *(les Alpes)*, which lie on France's borders with Italy and Switzerland. *Le Massif Central* is located in the southern center of the country around Clermont-Ferrand. Near Strasbourg by the German border are *les Vosges. Le Jura* is situated on the border between France and Switzerland and France and southern Germany.
- The Mediterranean island of Corsica is also part of France.

Activités

A **Write the letter of each city next to its name.**

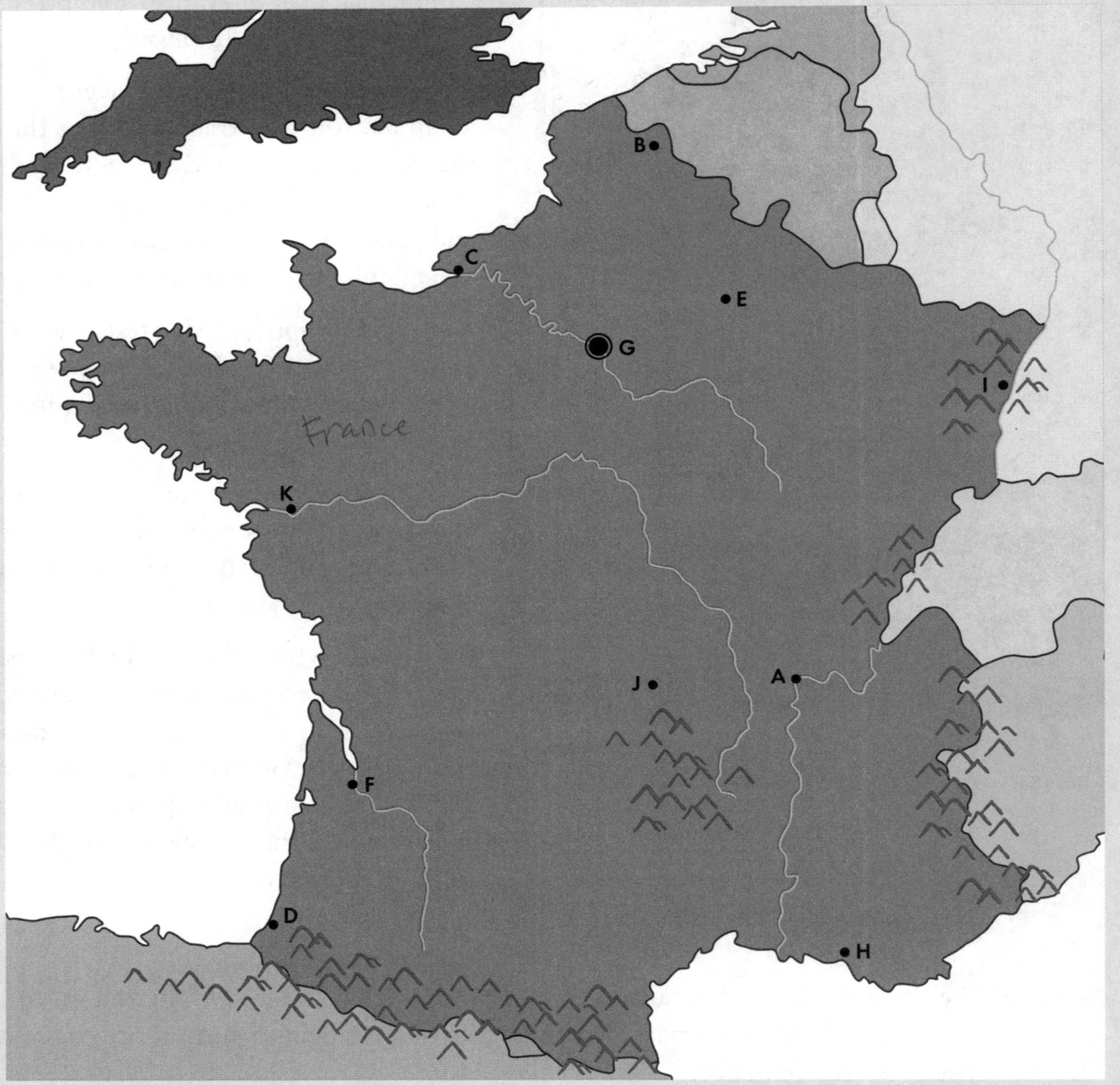
B
C
E
G
I
France
K
J
A
F
D
H

1. D Biarritz
2. J Clermont-Ferrand
3. C Le Havre
4. H Marseille
5. K Nantes
6. B Lille
7. A Lyon
8. G Paris
9. E Reims
10. I Strasbourg
11. F Bordeaux

B Identify the cities described in the information below.

1. Ocean vacation site: Biarritz
2. High tech center: Lille
3. City with an extinct volcano: Clermont-Ferrand
4. City where silk was made: Lyon
5. Center of the Council of Europe: Strasbourg
6. Chief port on the English Channel: Le Havre
7. Capital city divided into two banks by a river: Paris
8. City of Coronations: Reims
9. City on the Garonne River: Bordeaux
10. City settled by the ancient Greeks and Romans: marseille
11. Birthplace of Duchess Anne of Brittany: Nantes

C Study the map on page 43 carefully so that you can identify the following items.

1. The mountain range separating France from Spain: les Pyrénées
2. The river dividing France and Germany: le Rhin
3. The ocean bordering France on the west and northwest: l'océan Atlantique
4. The country bordering France on the north: Belgique
5. The longest river of France: la Loire

D Match Column A with Column B.

A

1. G Reims
2. F Strasbourg
3. J Nantes
4. I Biarritz
5. H Clermont-Ferrand
6. B Marseille
7. D Lyon
8. A Paris
9. C Le Havre
10. E Lille

B

A. international fashion center
B. Mediterranean seaport
C. port on the English Channel
D. city with two Roman amphitheaters
E. city historically and culturally tied to Belgium
F. city with cultural alliance with Germany
G. city of French kings
H. city of black volcanic rock
I. place for good surfing
J. gateway to many châteaux

E **Écris le nom de la ville indiquée par chaque image.** ***(Name the city associated with each illustration.)***

1. 
Le Conseil
de l'Europe
Strausbourg

2. 
Clermont-Ferrand

3.  Paris

4.  Reims

5.  Biarritz

F **Encercle la réponse correcte.** ***(Circle the correct answer.)***

1. The most populated city of France is B.
   A. Lille
   B. Paris
   C. Nantes
   D. Marseille

2. The shortest river of France is D.
   A. the Seine
   B. the Rhône
   C. the Loire
   D. the Garonne

3. The site of a chocolate museum is ____.
   A. Biarritz
   B. Paris
   C. Lyon
   D. Strasbourg

4. Lyon's history is linked to ____.
   A. cotton
   B. nylon
   C. silk
   D. linen

5. France's most navigable river is the ____.
   A. Garonne
   B. Seine
   C. Loire
   D. Rhône

6. A port city on the Loire River is ____.
   A. Paris
   B. Le Havre
   C. Nantes
   D. Bordeaux

7. Switzerland borders France on the ____.
   A. east
   B. north
   C. south
   D. west

8. Two major sources of hydroelectric power are the Garonne River and the ____.
   A. Seine
   B. Loire
   C. Rhine
   D. Rhône

9. The *Pyrénées* separate France from ____.
   A. Luxembourg
   B. Italy
   C. Spain
   D. Switzerland

10. The Alps mountain range separates France from Switzerland and ____.
   A. Belgium
   B. Italy
   C. Spain
   D. Germany

les Alpes

G **Write in each blank the geographical answer that makes each statement correct.**

France is shaped like a hexagon, a six-sided figure. (1) ___3___ (a number) sides border the water and (2) ___3___ (a number) sides have land boundaries with other countries. The longest international border is with the country of (3) ___Espagne___. In addition, two mountain ranges create natural boundaries for France. The (4) ___Pyrénées___ Mountains separate France from Spain, while the (5) ___les Alpes___ divide France from Italy and Switzerland. Of the important rivers, only the (6) ___Le Rhône___ flows southward. Starting as a glacial stream in Switzerland, it passes through the city of (7) ___Lyon___ and empties into the Mediterranean Sea. The (8) ___Seine___ River flows into the English Channel. It is considered France's most (9) ___navigable___ river. In Paris, merchandise for transoceanic export is either loaded into barges and shipped to (10) ___Le Havre___, or transported overland to that city. Another busy commercial river is the (11) ___Rhin___, a natural water border with Germany. Although of little value in terms of transportation, the (12) ___Garonne___ River is invaluable as a source of hydroelectric power. It begins in the Pyrenees Mountains and passes through the port city of (13) ___Bordeaux___. A pleasure cruise on the (14) ___Loire___ River or one of its tributaries offers spectacular views of the historic residences called *châteaux*. At the mouth of this river (where the river empties into the ocean), one may take a swim in the (15) ___Atlantic___ Ocean.

H **Imagine that you are a French official trying to convince a group of American business people to establish companies in France. List five cities the Americans should consider and explain why.**

I **Imagine that your family is taking a trip to France. Name six places you would enjoy visiting and tell what you would like to see and/or do there.**

J **Maze.** **Alain and Marie-France are ready to travel. Trace their vacation route to find out where they will be spending the summer. Name their destination in the space provided.**

Places they'll visit:

____

____

____

____

____

____

____

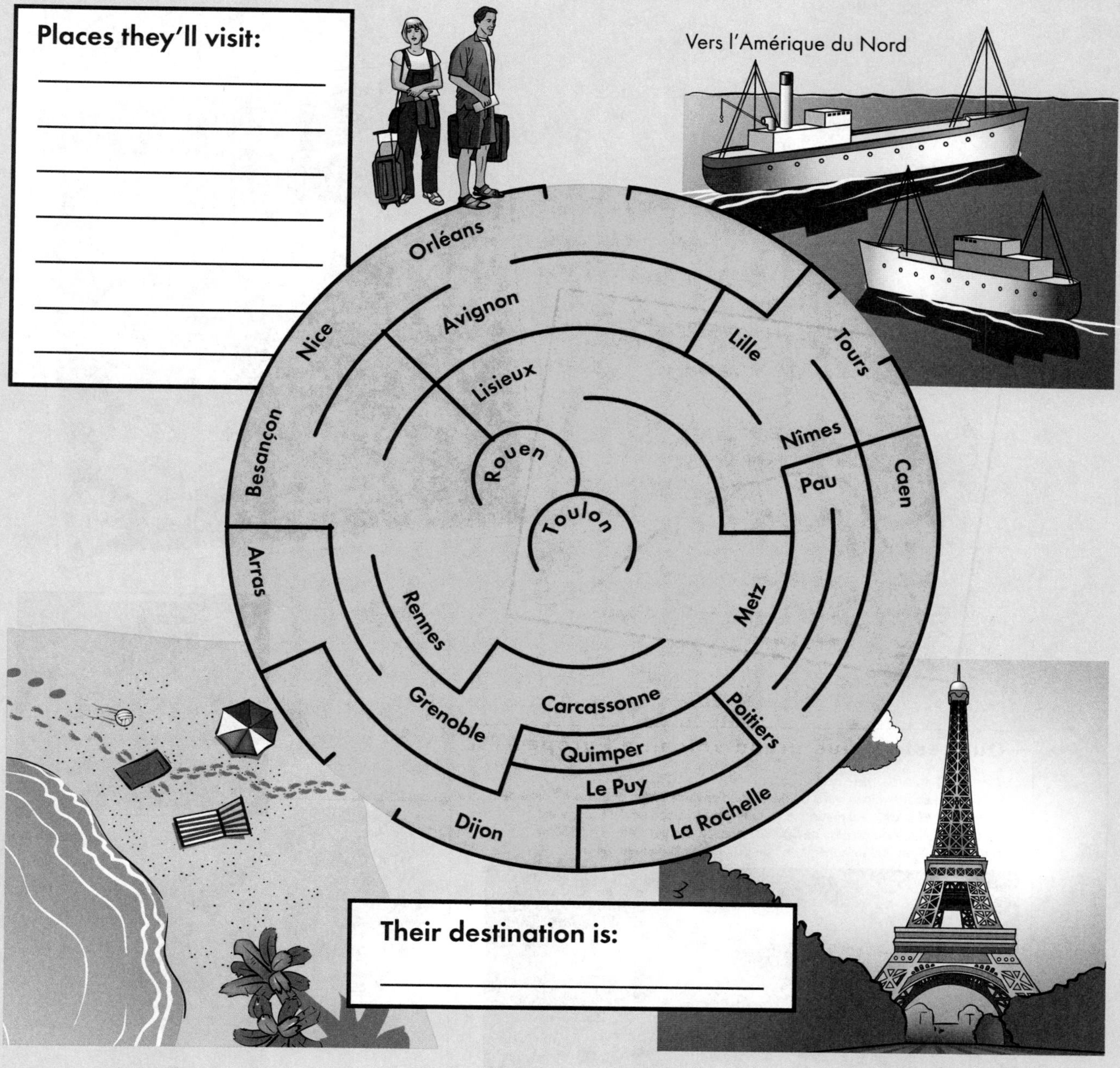
Vers l'Amérique du Nord
Orléans
Nice
Avignon
Lille
Tours
Lisieux
Besançon
Rouen
Nîmes
Pau
Caen
Toulon
Arras
Metz
Rennes
Grenoble
Carcassonne
Poitiers
Quimper
Le Puy
Dijon
La Rochelle

Their destination is:

____

K **C'est à toi! Travel Agency Role-play! Pretend that you are going on a trip to a French city. Ask for recommendations of places to visit. Your partner will play the part of the travel agent and make several suggestions. Be sure to use French greeting and leave-taking expressions.**

Langue vivante!

NORD PAS-DE-CALAIS
PICARDIE
NORMANDIE
PARIS ÎLE-DE-FRANCE
CHAMPAGNE ARDENNE
LORRAINE
ALSACE
BRETAGNE
PAYS DE LA LOIRE
CENTRE
BOURGOGNE
FRANCHE-COMTÉ
POITOU-CHARENTES
LIMOUSIN
AUVERGNE
RHÔNE-ALPES
AQUITAINE
MIDI-PYRÉNÉES
LANGUEDOC-ROUSSILLON
PROVENCE-ALPES CÔTE-D'AZUR
RIVIERA
CORSE

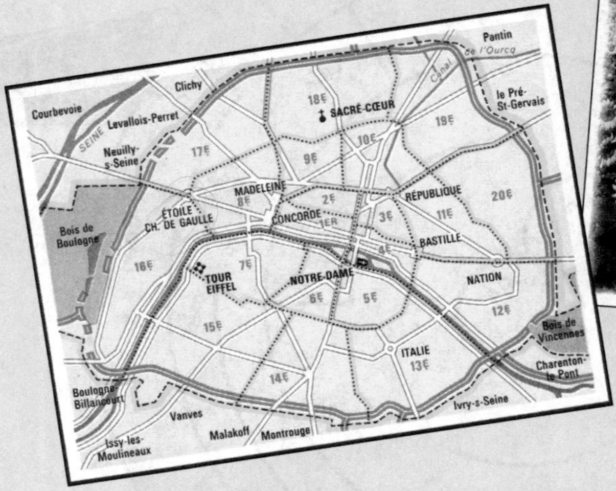

Pantin
Clichy
Courbevoie
Levallois-Perret
le Pré-St-Gervais
Neuilly-s-Seine
SEINE
SACRÉ-CŒUR
MADELEINE
RÉPUBLIQUE
ÉTOILE CH. DE GAULLE
CONCORDE
BASTILLE
Bois de Boulogne
TOUR EIFFEL
NOTRE-DAME
NATION
Bois de Vincennes
ITALIE
Charenton-le Pont
Boulogne-Billancourt
Ivry-s-Seine
Vanves
Malakoff
Montrouge
Issy-les-Moulineaux

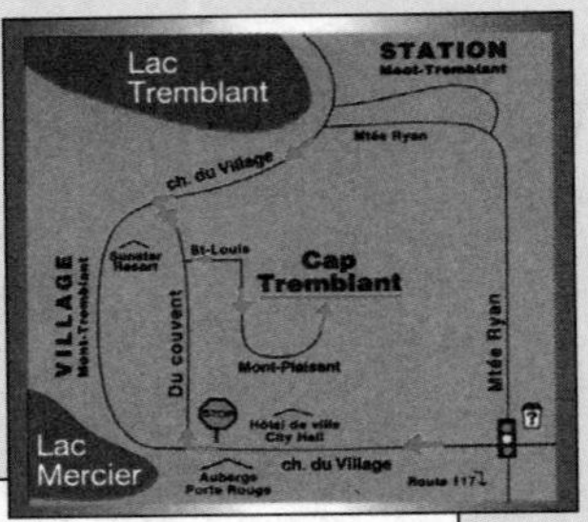

Lac Tremblant
STATION
ch. du Village
Cap Tremblant
VILLAGE
Du couvent
Mtée Ryan
Lac Mercier
ch. du Village

Quel est le plus grand volcan d'Europe ?

Le Cantal en Auvergne (France) est le plus grand volcan d'Europe !
Il s'agit d'un strato-volcan qui a un diamètre d'environ 70 km et une superficie de l'ordre de 2 600 km2. En revanche, le plus grand volcan actif d'Europe est l'Etna, en Sicile. Agé de plus de 500 000 ans, ce dernier s'élève à 3350 m et rejette environ 300 millions de m3 de produits volcaniques par an.

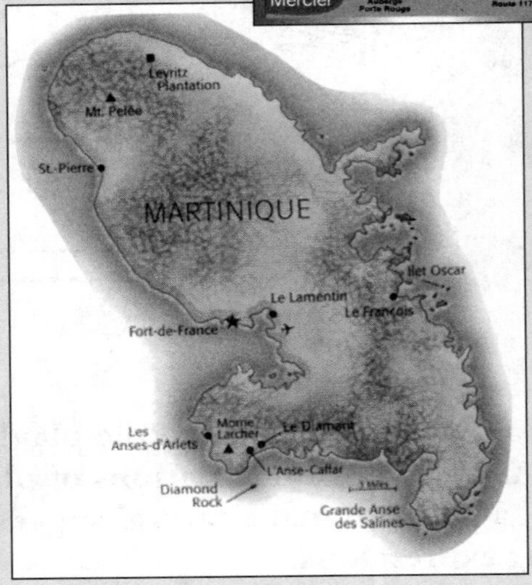

Leyritz Plantation
Mt. Pelée
St-Pierre
MARTINIQUE
Ilet Oscar
Le Lamentin
Le François
Fort-de-France
Les Anses-d'Arlets
Morne Larcher
Le Diamant
L'Anse-Caffard
Diamond Rock
Grande Anse des Salines

L Answer the following questions about Paris, France's volcano, and Quebec.

1. To what metropolitan area does the term *Île de France* refer? Paris
2. Is the *Notre-Dame* cathedral located on an island? Oui
3. Is the *Étoile Ch. De Gaulle* located in the east of Paris? Non
4. Is the Basilica of the *Sacré-Coeur* located in the 20th district? Non
5. Is the *tour Eiffel* located in the 7th city district? oui
6. What is the name of the highest volcano in Europe? Le Cantal
7. In which province is it located? Auvergne
8. About how many kilometers is the crater's diameter? 70Km
9. Where is *Etna*, the highest active volcano in Europe? en Sicile
10. What two lakes are near Québec's ski resort, *Cap Tremblant*? Lac Tremblant et Lac mercier

M The map shows the names of 22 provinces in France. Using the direction words "north," "south," "east," "west," and "center," locate the following provinces:

1. *Poitou-Charentes* west (l'ouest)
2. *Midi-Pyrénées* South (le sud)
3. *Picardie* north (le nord)
4. *Auvergne* center
5. *Franche-Comté* east (l'est

N Martinique is an overseas territory in the Caribbean Sea.

1. What is the name of its capital? Font-de-France
2. Where is the airport? sud de le Lamentin
3. In what part of the island is *Mt. Pelée*, Martinique's own volcano? North (le nord)

Proverbe

"**Autre pays, autre coutume.**
When in Rome, do as the Romans do."

Symtalk

O **Écris le mot ou l'expression en français dans l'espace blanc.** ***(In the space, write the correct word or expression in French.)***

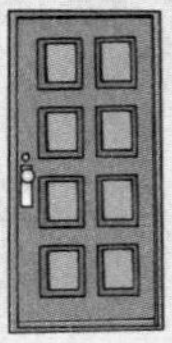

1. ____________________

2. ____________________

3. ____________________

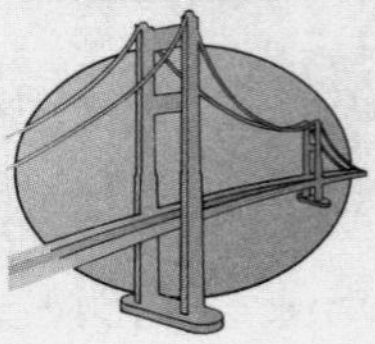

4. ____________________

5. ____________________

P **Dis les phrases, puis écris-les en français.** ***(Say the sentences, then write them in French.)***

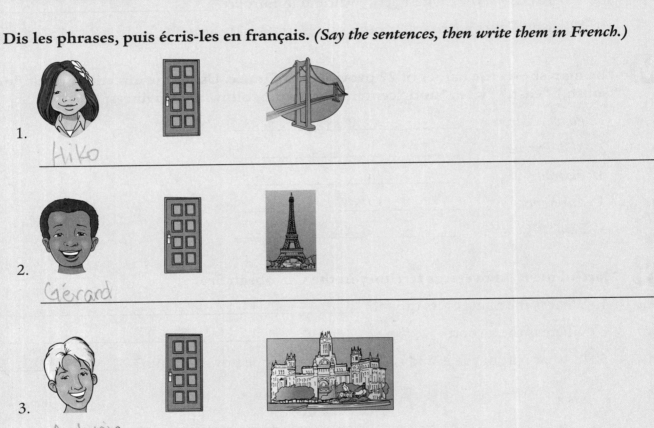

1.   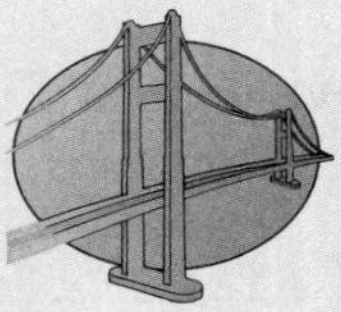

Hiko ____

2.  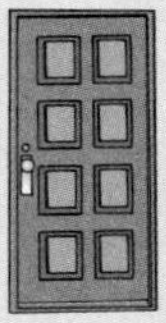 

Gérard ____

3.  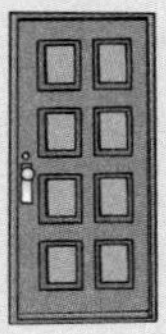 

Antonie ____

4.  **et**   

Gérard et Sylvie ____

5. 
et

Antonie et Brigitte

Q **Travaille avec un partenaire. Pose la question ou donne la réponse. Puis, écris le dialogue.** ***(Work with a partner. Ask the question or give the answer. Then, write the dialogue.)***

1. 

Brigitte? ______________________

2. 

Sylvie? ______________________

3. 
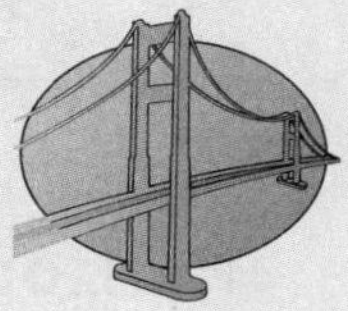

Hiko? ______________________

4. 
et

Brigitte et Antonie? ______________________

5. 
et

Sylvie et Gérard ______________________

Mots croisés

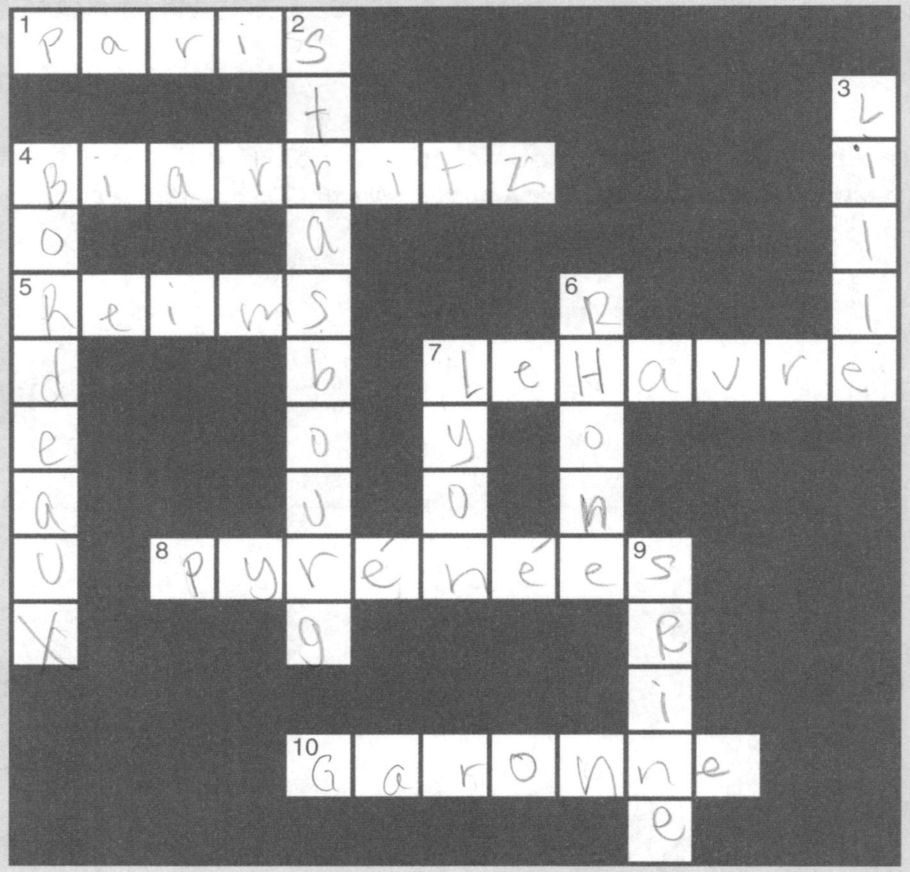
1 Paris
2 Strasbourg
3 Lille
4 Biarritz
Bordeaux
5 Reims
6 Rhône
7 LeHavre
Lyon
8 Pyrénées
9 Seine
10 Garonne

Horizontalement

1. city where you can see *l'arc de triomphe*
4. town with a famous aquarium
5. where Clovis was crowned
7. port city on *la Manche*
8. natural southern boundary near Spain
10. shortest river

Verticalement

2. city in the northeast
3. city with high tech industry
4. fifth largest city
6. French river that starts as a glacier
7. city with two Roman amphitheaters
9. northern river

Unit 5

La maison — House

Vocabulaire

ANNETTE:	**Où habites-tu?**	Where do you live?
BRIGITTE:	**J'habite dans une maison à Bordeaux.**	I live in a house in Bordeaux.
GEORGES:	**Où est le jardin?**	Where is the garden?
GUILLAUME:	**Le jardin est là-bas.**	The garden is over there.
ABDUL:	**Où est le garage?**	Where is the garage?
ALI:	**Il est derrière le jardin.**	It's behind the garden.
LISETTE:	**Il y a combien de pièces dans ta maison?**	How many rooms are there in your house?
MARIANNE:	**Il y a cinq pièces.**	There are five rooms.

There are four ways to write "the":
- **le** (in front of a masculine singular noun)
- **la** (in front of a feminine singular noun)
- **l'** (in front of noun that begins with a vowel)
- **les** (in front of a plural noun)

The word **jardin** can mean "yard," as well as "garden."

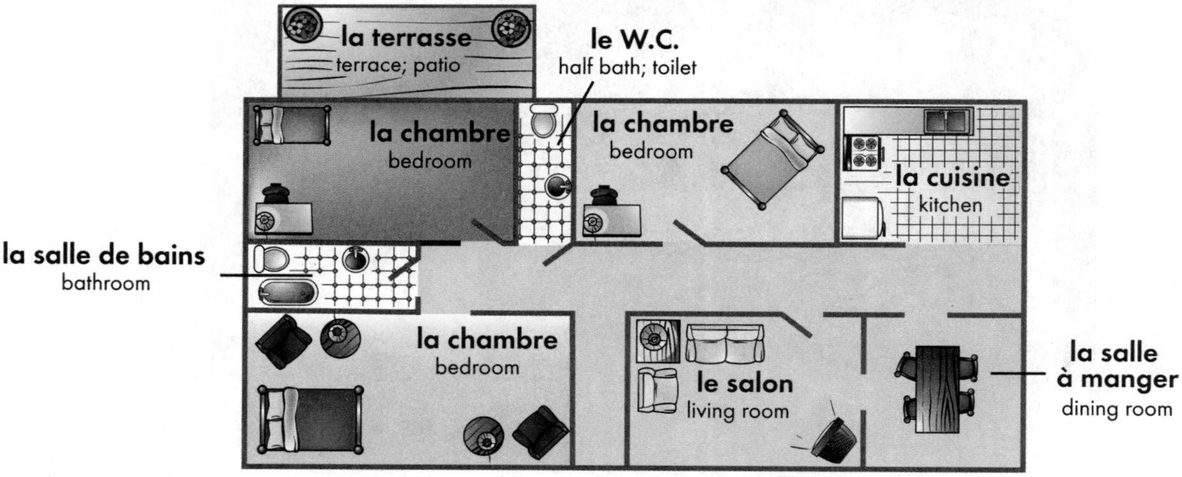
la terrasse
terrace; patio
le W.C.
half bath; toilet
la chambre
bedroom
la chambre
bedroom
la cuisine
kitchen
la salle de bains
bathroom
la chambre
bedroom
le salon
living room
la salle
à manger
dining room

Hospitality is part of French culture. Being gracious to one's guests includes making them feel at home.
La pièce refers to a room in a house.
La salle de séjour is another way to say "living room."

Vocabulaire Extra!

le château

2B
2C

l'appartement (m.), le condominium

la maison individuelle

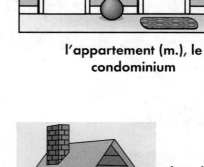

la cabane

la résidence, l'immeuble (m.)

la tente

Activités

A **Écris le mot français pour chaque pièce.** ***(Write the French word for each room.)***

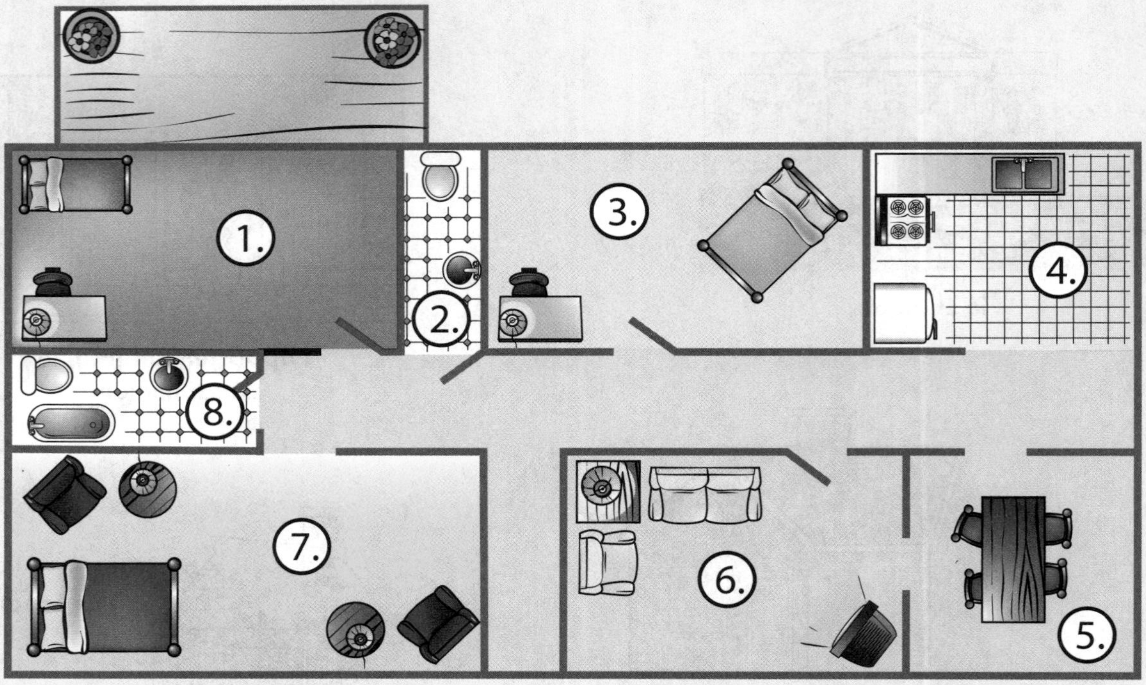
1.
2.
3.
4.
5.
6.
7.
8.

1. le chambre
2. le W.C.
3. le chambre
4. la cuisine
5. la salle à manger
6. le salon / la salle de séjour
7. le chambre
8. la salle de bains

B **Complète les phrases en français.** ***(Complete the sentences in French with house-related vocabulary.)***

1. Je fais la cuisine (*cook*) dans la cuisine.
2. Je me couche (*go to bed*) dans le chambre.
3. Je mange (*eat*) dans la salle de manger.
4. Je me lave (*wash*) dans la salle de bains.
5. Je joue (*play*) dans la jardin / la terrasse.
6. Je me distrais (*relax*) dans le salon ou sur (*or on*) la salle de séjour.

C Choisis la bonne pièce. *(Circle the meaning of the French expression on the left.)*

1. la salle à manger:	*bedroom*	*kitchen*	*dining room*
2. la cuisine:	*bathroom*	*kitchen*	*bedroom*
3. la chambre:	*bedroom*	*bathroom*	*living room*
4. la salle de bains:	*dining room*	*kitchen*	*bathroom*
5. le salon:	*living room*	*bathroom*	*dining room*

D Dans quelle pièce se trouve. . .? En français, s'il te plaît! *(In which room would you find a. . .? In French, please!)*

1. dining table la salle à manger
2. refrigerator la cuisine
3. alarm clock la chambre
4. piano le salon
5. shower la salle de bains
6. stove la cuisine
7. sofa le salon
8. tablecloth la salle à manger
9. toilet le W. C. / le toilet
10. dresser le chambre

E Écris l'expression pour un/une. . . *(Write the French expression for a(n). . .)*

1. place to sleep at a camp site la tente
2. renter's residence in a building l'appartement / le condominium
3. homeowner's residence la maison individuelle
4. millionaire's residence le château
5. automobile's parking place le garage

F Écris les mots correctement. *(Unscramble the words.)*

1. NOMSIA la MAISON
2. BRAMCHE le CHAMBRE
3. NALSO le SALON
4. INISUCE le CUISINE
5. ABNISDESAELL la SALLE DE BAINS

G **Lis le paragraphe et complète chaque phrase correctement.** ***(Read the paragraph; then, complete each sentence with the correct word or phrase.)***

Ma maison est *belle*. J'habite ici *avec* ma famille. J'adore ma maison et ma famille. Ma maison *a* sept pièces. Il y a beaucoup de fleurs dans le jardin. Il y a une terrasse.

la maison

la famille

belle	beautiful	**a**	has
avec	with	**(les) fleurs**	flowers

1. Ma maison est ____________.
   - combien
   - belle
   - nouvelle
   - grande
2. J'habite ____________.
   - avec mes parents
   - à Paris
   - derrière le jardin
   - dans le garage
3. La maison a ____________ pièces.
   - huit
   - six
   - sept
   - cinq
4. Les fleurs sont (*are*) dans ____________.
   - la maison
   - la famille
   - la pièce
   - le jardin

H **Parlons! Point to an illustration of a room in a house. Ask your speaking partner in French: "*C'est la chambre?*" He/she should answer: "*Oui, c'est la chambre*" or "*Non, c'est la cuisine.*" Take turns asking and answering questions about all the rooms in the house.**

I **Parlons! Point to one of the types of residences shown in your book. At the same time, ask your classmate where an imaginary student lives. Follow the model.**

Modèle: A: *(pointing to an apartment)* Où habite Jean-Paul?
B: Jean-Paul habite dans un appartement.

J **C'est à toi! To find out where certain famous people live, make a list with five names. Then ask your classmate in French: "*Où habite. . .* (+ name)?" Your classmate should answer by writing down the name of the city or country in his/her notebook.**

Proverbe

" **Ma maison est mon château.**
My home is my castle. "

Langue vivante!

À vendre en France

St-Tropez : appartement de charme sur jardin, centre-ville, 2/3 P. 2e étage, bon état. 475.000 €. (011 33) 6.20.83.28.40.

Date de publication: *Annonce #5586*

A 2 minutes du métro Frontenac, l'appartement est illuminé de tous côtés. Chambres spacieuses, un salon confortable, une cuisine avec grand plan de travail et une salle de bain agréable. Excellente boulangerie, IGA, pharmacie, pressing à 4 minutes.

virginie

Sur le plateau du Luberon

Pour des vacances de charme et de quiétude, venez découvrir ce magnifique mas provençal de 250 m² entouré de 1 hectare de terrain. Nombreux lieux de vie dont 4 chambres. Belles prestations. Réf. : 1763 - Prix nous consulter.

Luberon Investissements Immobilier

Vincent BŒUF

LUBERON INVESTISSEMENTS IMMOBILIER

La Combe - 84220 GORDES

Tél. : +33 (0)4 90 72 07 55 - Fax : +33 (0)4 90 72 08 97

E-mail : immo@lubinvest.com - www.lubinvest.com

Ateliers Poivre d'âne

MANOSQUE

Cuisines - Meubles - Décoration

MANOSQUE
Les Grands Jardins - 04220 SAINTE-TULLE
Tél. : 04 92 79 79 79
www.atelierspoivredane.com

© Raison Bleue

TOULOUSE	*LUBERON*
Hangar n°7 - COLOMIERS	*Hameau de Coustellet*
Tél. : 05 61 15 40 30	*Tél. : 04 90 71 71 71*
CÔTE D'AZUR	*ALLEMAGNE*
799 av. de Tournamy - MOUGINS	*Céramiques du Soleil*
Tél. : 04 93 75 17 00	*Tél. : 00 49 17 12 45 20 48*

Documentation sur simple demande contre 4 euros par chèque.

K **St.-Tropez is a town along the *Côte d'Azur,* an expensive resort area along the Mediterranean Sea. An apartment here is for sale.**

1. How is it described? Appartement de charme
2. What does it overlook? Sur jardin, centre ville
3. On what *étage* (floor) is it located? P. 2
4. What is the selling price? 475,000 €

L **Review *Annonce #5586* (Ad #5586) and answer the questions below.**

1. Is Virginia the landlady or the person looking for an apartment? Landlady
2. What French word describes the bedrooms? Spacieuses
3. What French word describes the living room? confortable
4. Is the kitchen small? Non

M **A Luberon real estate agency offers a renovated farm house for sale in the region of *Provence.***

1. What word describes this *mas provençal*?
   magnifique
2. What phrase suggests that this house could be a holiday home for someone?
   Pour des vacances
3. How many bedrooms does it have?
   quatre
4. What phrase suggests it is located in a peaceful place?
   de quiétude

N **Review the advertisement for *Ateliers Poivre d'âne* and answer the questions below.**

1. What can the store *Ateliers Poivre d'Âne* help furnish?
   Cuisines, meubles, Decoration
2. The store is located in France's southern Provençal region. What is the name of the town?
   manosque
3. Does the *cuisine* shown suggest a country-casual look or a contemporary urban look?
   country-casual

Symtalk

O

Écris en français le mot ou l'expression qui correspond à chaque image. ***(In French, write the word or expression that corresponds to each picture.)***

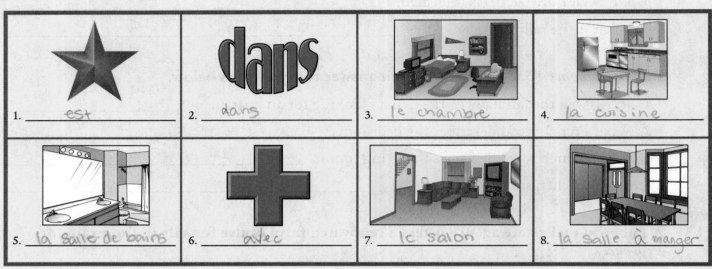

 1. est	dans 2. dans	 3. le chambre	 4. la cuisine
 5. la salle de bains	 6. avec	 7. le salon	 8. la salle à manger

P

Dis les phrases, puis écris-les en français. ***(Say the sentences, then write them in French.)***

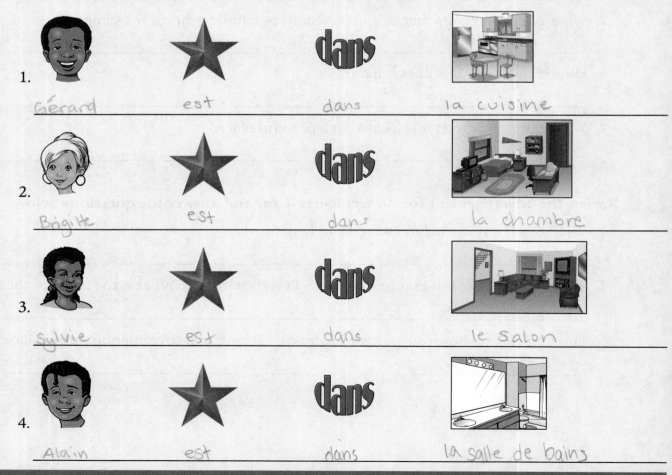

1.   
dans

Gérard est dans la cuisine

2.   
dans

Brigitte est dans la chambre

3.   
dans

Sylvie est dans le salon

4.   
dans

Alain est dans la salle de bains

Q **Travaille avec un partenaire. Pose la question ou donne la réponse. Puis, écris le dialogue.** *(Work with a partner. Ask the question or give the answer. Then, write the dialogue.)*

1.  

Combien est Gérard?

la salle de bains

2.  

Combien est Antoine?

le salon avec Brigitte

3.  

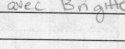

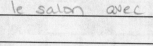

Combien est Sylvie?

la salle à manger avec Hiko

4.  

Combien est Alain?

le chambre

5.  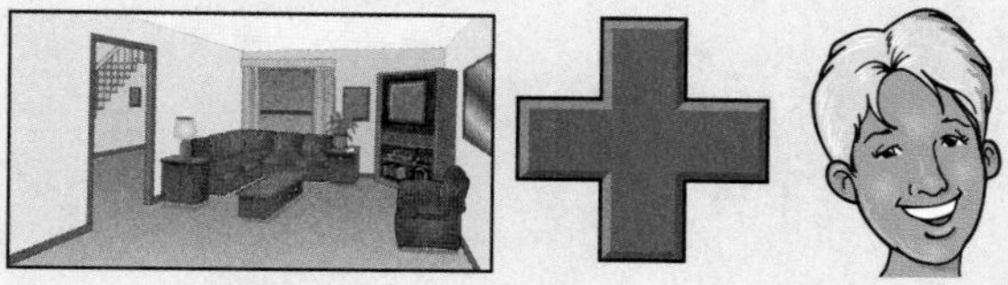

Combien est Brigitte?

le salon avec Antoine

Mots croisés

pièce
appartement
chambre
jardin
salle
maison
cabane
château
tente
cuisine
bain
garage
salon
ou

Horizontalement

2. room
5. rental unit
6. room for sleeping
10. yard or garden
11. ____ *à manger*
12. house

Verticalement

1. small house in the country or woods
3. luxurious residence
4. canvas camping shelter
6. where meals are made
7. *salle de* ____
8. the car's house
9. where guests are received
13. where

Unit 6

La famille

Family

Vocabulaire

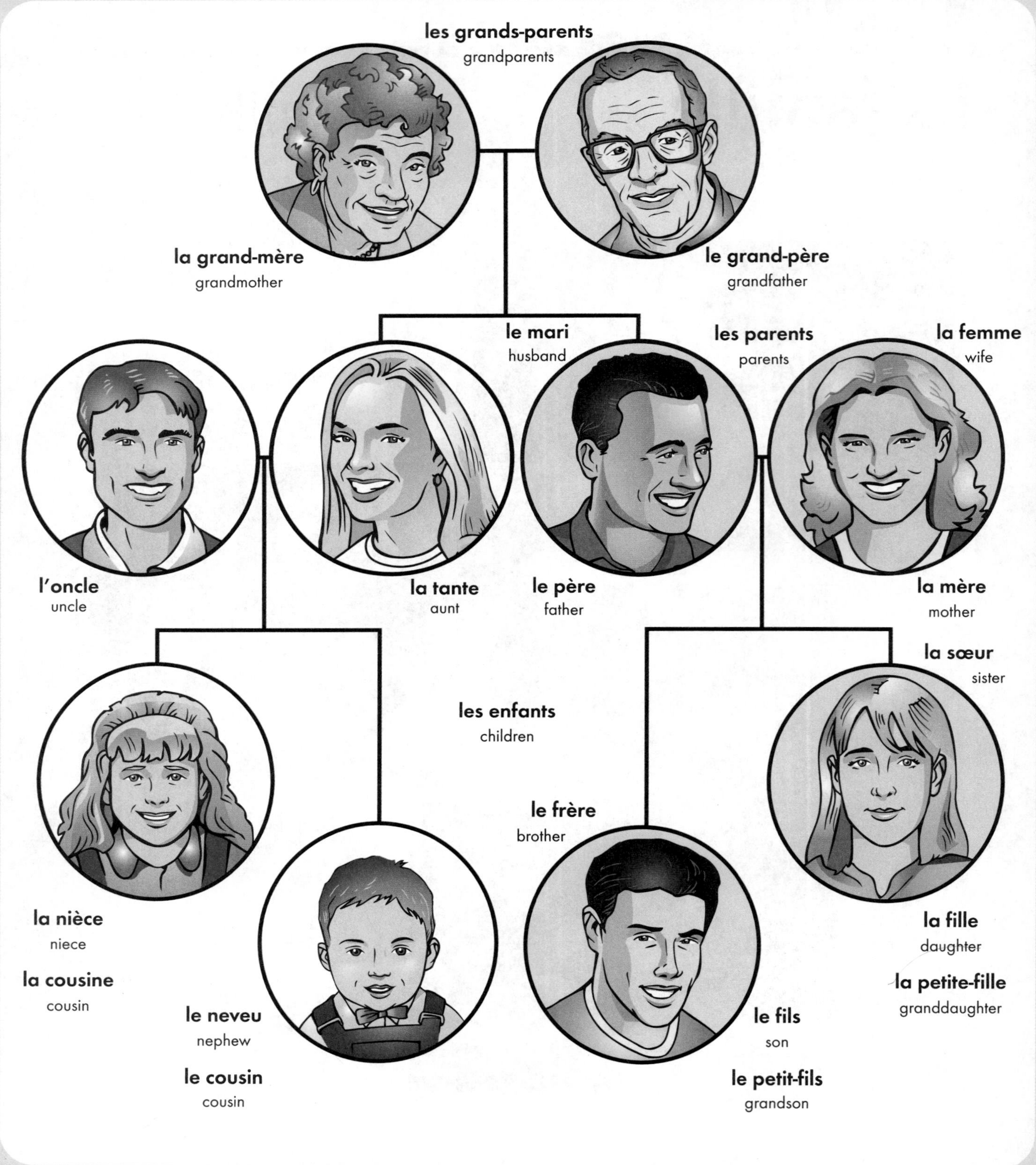

les grands-parents
grandparents
la grand-mère
grandmother
le grand-père
grandfather
le mari
husband
les parents
parents
la femme
wife
l'oncle
uncle
la tante
aunt
le père
father
la mère
mother
la sœur
sister
les enfants
children
le frère
brother
la nièce
niece
la cousine
cousin
le neveu
nephew
le cousin
cousin
le fils
son
le petit-fils
grandson
la fille
daughter
la petite-fille
granddaughter

Qui est-ce?
Who is this?
C'est mon frère.
It's my brother.
Ce sont tes parents?
Are they your parents?
Oui. Ma mère s'appelle Maryvonne et mon père s'appelle Gaston.
Yes. My mother's name is Maryvonne and my father's name is Gaston.
Qui sont les enfants?
Who are the children?
Ce sont ma petite-fille et mon petit-fils.
They're my granddaughter and my grandson.
Héloise, Marie, et Pierre sont sœurs et frère, n'est-ce pas?
Heloise, Marie, and Pierre are sisters and brother, aren't they?
Oui, et ce sont aussi mes cousins.
Yes, and they are also my cousins.

N'oublie pas:
Réunion de famille
Les invités:
Tante Danielle et
son mari
ma sœur et ses enfants
Oncle Bernard et sa femme
Fabienne et le bébé
Don't forget
Family Reunion
Guests:
Aunt Danielle and
her husband
my sister and her children
Uncle Bernard and his wife
Fabienne and the baby

PATRICE: **Où sont tes parents?**
Where are your relatives?

ALAIN: **Mes grands-parents sont à l'intérieur, et mes oncles et mes tantes sont dans le jardin.**
My grandparents are inside and my uncles and aunts are in the garden.

❀✿❀✿❀

ISABELLE: **Ta marraine et ton parrain, sont-ils ici?**
Are your godparents here?

ROBERT: **Bien sûr! Ma marraine parle avec mes tantes. Mon parrain est sur la terrasse.**
Yes, of course! My godmother is speaking with my aunts. My godfather is on the terrace.

Vocabulaire Extra!

l'enfant
(boy) child or (girl) child

le garçon
boy

l'enfant
(boy) child or (girl) child

l' homme
man

la jeune fille or fille
girl, daughter

la femme
woman

le bébé
baby

un/le beau-frère
stepbrother

une/la belle-sœur
stepsister

un/le beau-père
stepfather

une/la belle-mère
stepmother

un/le beau-fils
stepson

une/la belle-fille
stepdaughter

Godparents play an important part in a child's life. Their main role is to offer encouragement and spiritual guidance as the child grows. On special occasions they often remember their godchild with a small gift.

Activités

A **Indicate Véronique's, Maryvonne's and André's relationship to each family member listed.**

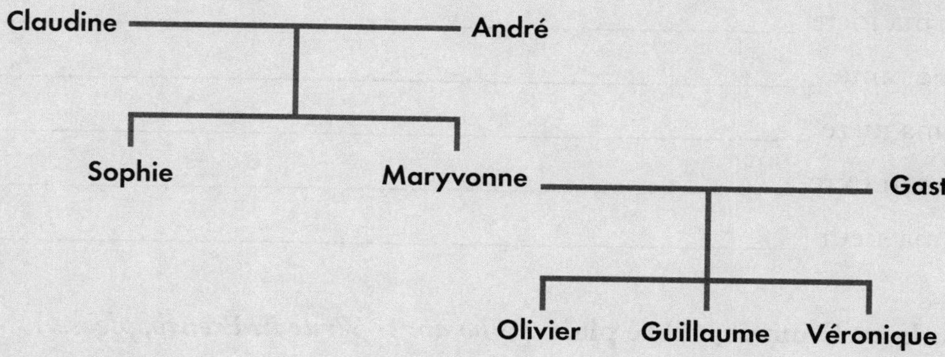
Claudine
André
Sophie
Maryvonne
Gaston
Olivier
Guillaume
Véronique

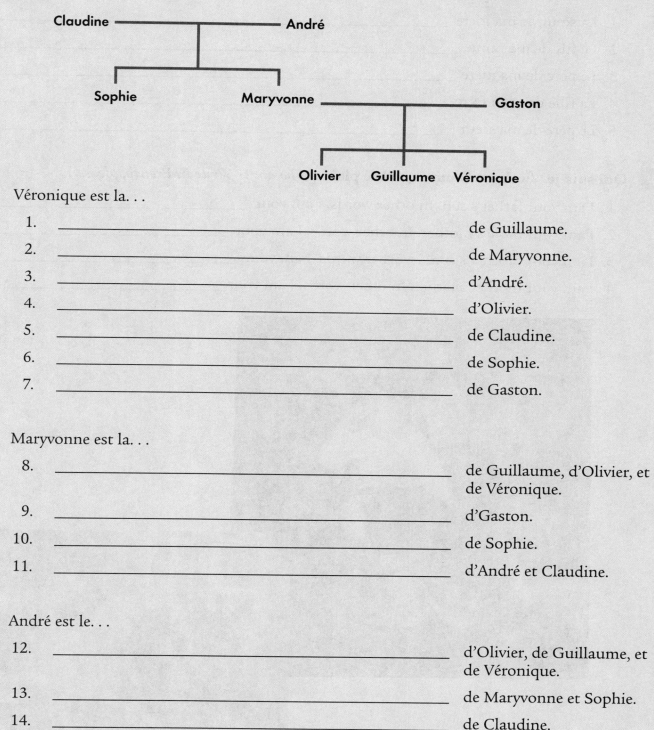

Véronique est la. . .

1. ______________________ de Guillaume.
2. ______________________ de Maryvonne.
3. ______________________ d'André.
4. ______________________ d'Olivier.
5. ______________________ de Claudine.
6. ______________________ de Sophie.
7. ______________________ de Gaston.

Maryvonne est la. . .

8. ______________________ de Guillaume, d'Olivier, et de Véronique.
9. ______________________ d'Gaston.
10. ______________________ de Sophie.
11. ______________________ d'André et Claudine.

André est le. . .

12. ______________________ d'Olivier, de Guillaume, et de Véronique.
13. ______________________ de Maryvonne et Sophie.
14. ______________________ de Claudine.

B Qui est-ce? Écris en français, s'il te plaît. *(Who is this? Write in French, please.)*

> **Modèle:** A: La fille de mon père et de ma mère est ma sœur.

1. La sœur de ma mère ______________________________.
2. Le fils de ma tante ______________________________.
3. Le père de ma mère ______________________________.
4. La fille de mon frère ______________________________.
5. Le père de ma sœur ______________________________.

C Qui suis-je? Écris en français, s'il te plaît. *(Who am I? Write in French, please.)*

1. I am your father's son. In other words, I am your ______________________.
2. I am your niece's mother. In other words, I am your ______________________.
3. I am your brother's son. In other words, I am your ______________________.
4. I am your mother's father. In other words, I am your ______________________.

D **Encercle la bonne réponse.** ***(Circle the correct answer.)***

1. Où sont les grands-parents?
   A. next to the crib
   B. in the crib
   C. in the foreground

2. Où sont les parents?
   A. on the bench
   B. in the crib
   C. in the foreground

3. Où est l'enfant?
   A. on the bench
   B. in the crib
   C. in the foreground

E **En anglais, s'il te plaît.** ***(What do these questions mean in English?)***

1. Qui est-ce? ______________________
2. Qui suis-je? ______________________
3. Qui est la femme? ______________________
4. Qui parle avec Tante Brigitte? ______________________

F **Réponds aux questions en français selon les indices en parenthèses.** ***(Complete the answers to the following questions in French, using the cues in parentheses.)***

1. Qui est le garçon? *(son)* C'est mon ______________________.
2. Qui est la jeune fille? *(cousin)* C'est ma ______________________.
3. Qui est l'homme? *(uncle)* C'est mon ______________________.

G **Read the passage and then write it in English. Try to figure out words you don't know from the context.**

J'ai une petite famille. Mon père *a* trente-sept ans. Ma mère a trente-huit ans. Ma sœur s'appelle Marie-France et elle a neuf ans. Mon frère s'appelle Alexandre et il a six ans. Je m'appelle Antoine et j'ai treize ans. Ma famille *habite* à Lille. *Nous avons* une maison. Mes grands-parents *habitent* à Nantes. Ils ont un appartement.

J'ai	I have	**habite**	lives
a	has	**habitent**	live
Nous avons	We have		

____
____
____
____
____
____
____
____
____
____

H **Parlons! Ask your speaking partner questions about five members of his/her family, for example, the person's name and age. Then, he/she will ask you about your family and you will answer.**

Modèle:
A: Tu as un frère? *(Do you have a brother?)*
B: Oui, j'ai un frère.
A: Il s'appelle comment? *(What is his name?)*
B: Il s'appelle Michel.
A: Il a quel âge? *(How old is he?)*
B: Il a quinze ans.

I **C'est à toi! Find some family photographs and exchange them with a friend. Holding up your friend's photo first, ask him/her who is in the picture. He/she will identify each person with the correct relationship. Then, reverse roles.**

Modèle:
A: Qui est-ce? *(Who is this?)*
B: C'est ma grand-mère, Sylvie Moreau. *(That's my grandmother, Sylvie Moreau.)*

Proverbe

"**Tel père, tel fils.**
Telle mère, telle fille.
Like father, like son.
Like mother, like daughter."

Langue vivante!

fête de famille
les épisodes
L'histoire
A propos
Colette
Francis
Richard
Marc
Charlotte
Clotilde
Gérald
Odile
Betty
Blaise
Peggy
Britney
Lou
Crédits

A

B

C

D

E

F

J ***La fête de famille*** **is a television show. Identify these TV characters:**

1. les parents de Blaise, Peggy, et Britney es Gérald et Odile
2. la sœur d'Odile et Marc Charlotte
3. le premier mari *(first husband)* de Colette Francis
4. la grand-mère de Blaise, Peggy, et Britney Colette
5. la deuxième femme *(second wife)* de Gérald Clotilde
6. la cousine de Blaise, Peggy, et Britney Lou
7. l'oncle de Blaise, Peggy, et Britney marc/et Newton

K **Look at the six pictures on the bottom of the page. Write the letter of the matching picture next to each description.**

1. B Ce sont mes grands-parents.
2. A C'est ma sœur, Isabelle.
3. E C'est mon petit cousin, Étienne.
4. F C'est mon oncle, Jean-Philippe.
5. C C'est toute la famille.
6. D C'est moi, Nicolas.

L **Fill in the blanks with the correct number of family members on this page.**

1. Il y a *(There are)* un oncles.
2. Il y a un grand-mères.
3. Il y a dreux familles.
4. Il y a deux grands-parents.
5. Il y a deux filles.
6. Il y a deux pères.

Symtalk

M **Écris en français le mot ou l'expression qui correspond à chaque image.** ***(In French, write the word or expression that corresponds to each picture.)***

1. ______________

2. ______________

3. ______________

4. ______________

5. ______________

6. ______________

N **Dis les phrases, puis écris-les en français.** ***(Say the sentences, then write them in French.)***

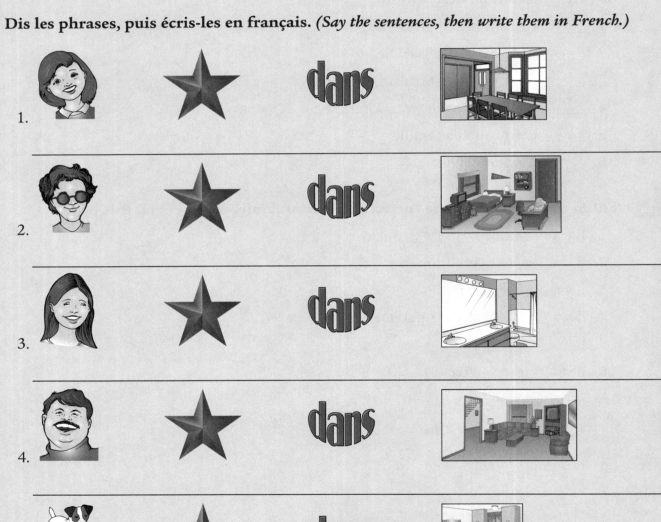

1.   dans 

____

2.   dans 

____

3.   dans 

____

4.   dans 

____

5.   dans 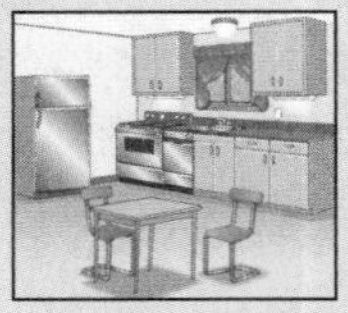

____

O **Travaille avec un partenaire. Pose la question ou donne la réponse. Puis, écris le dialogue.** *(Work with a partner. Ask the question or give the answer. Then, write the dialogue.)*

1. 
dans

______________________________ ______________________________
____

2. 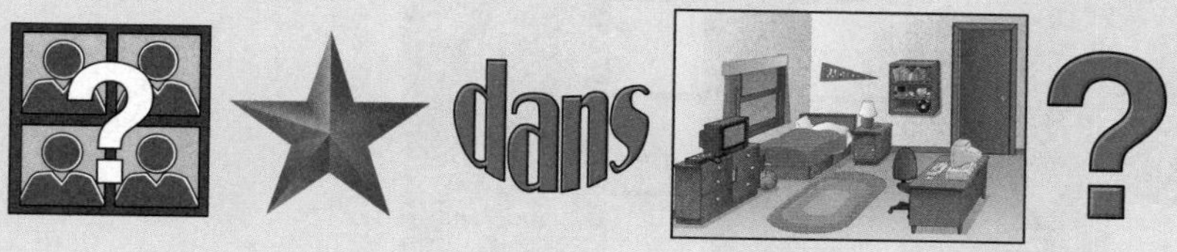
dans

______________________________ ______________________________
____

3. 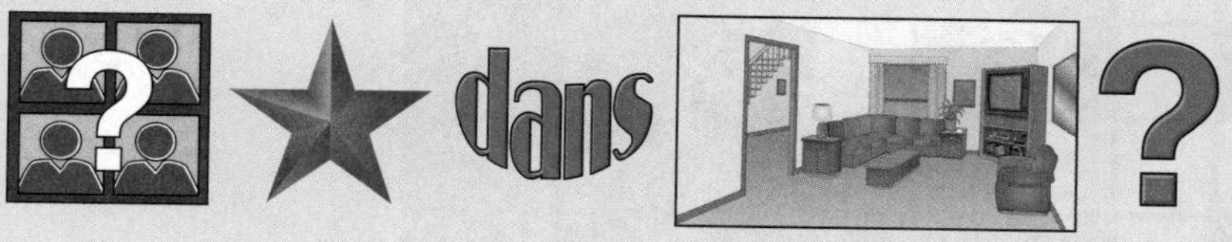
dans

______________________________ ______________________________
____

4. 
dans

______________________________ ______________________________
____

5. 
dans

______________________________ ______________________________
____

Mots croisés

Horizontalement

1. Mon ____ est le fils de mon père et de ma mère.
4. Mon ____ est le frère de mon père.
6. Mes oncles, tantes, cousins, et grands-parents sont mes ____.
7. Madame Beaufort est une ____.
10. Mon ____ est le fils de mon frère.
11. Mon ____ est le mari de ma mère.
12. Une mère, un père, et des enfants sont une ____.
13. Chantal est la ____ des ses *(her)* parents.

Verticalement

1. Jean-Marcel est le ____ de ses *(his)* parents.
2. Mon ____ est le père de mon père.
3. Monsieur Leduc est un ____.
5. Ma ____ est la mère de ma mère.
8. Ma ____ est la femme de mon père.
9. Ma ____ est la fille de ma tante et de mon oncle.

Unit 7

Les animaux

Animals

Promenade Touristiqu
Forfait :1, 2 ou 3 personnes 160F
par personne supplément

Vocabulaire

la vache
cow
l'âne (m.)
donkey
l'oiseau (m.)
bird
le canard
duck
le cochon
pig
le coq
rooster
la poule
hen
le chat (m.)
cat

YVETTE: **Bertrand, viens ici! Je donne à manger aux animaux. Je donne une pomme à Maurice.**
Bertrand, come here! I'm feeding the animals. I'm giving Maurice an apple.

BERTRAND: **Bien! Je voudrais t'aider.**
Great! I'd like to help you.

YVETTE: **Volontiers, Bertrand! Tu peux tenir le seau à la main.**
Of course you can, Bertrand! You can hold the pail.

BERTRAND: **Le chat, comment s'appelle-t-il?**
What's the cat's name?

YVETTE: **Il s'appelle Henri.**
That's Henri.

BERTRAND: **Il y a aussi des poules?**
Are there hens, too?

YVETTE: **Oui. Elles sont derrière la grange.**
Yes. They're behind the barn.

Tu peux ramasser les œufs.
You can collect the eggs.

le cheval
horse
le chien (m.)
dog

à la campagne
in the country
dans l'air
in the air
le perroquet
parrot
dans le pâturage
in the pasture
dans la grange
in the barn
l'animal
animal
la chèvre
goat
sur l'étang
on the pond
le lapin
rabbit
dans la stalle
in the stable
grand (m.)
grande (f.)
big
petit (m.)
petite (f.)
little

les œufs
eggs

CHANTAL: **Qu'est-ce que tu fais?**
What are you doing?

MARTIN: **Je ramasse les œufs.**
I'm collecting the eggs.

MICHEL: **Qu'est-ce que tu fais?**

CLARA: **Je caresse mon lapin.**
I'm petting my rabbit.

Sounds that animals make:

La vache dit "meuh" (moo).
Le cheval dit "hiiiiii" (neigh).
Le chat dit "miaou" (meow).
Le chien dit "ouah ouah" *(woof)*.
Le cochon dit "groin groin" *(oink)*.
Le canard dit "coin coin" *(quack)*.
Le coq dit "cocorico" *(cock-a-doodle-doo)*.

Activités

A **Identifie chaque animal.** ***(Identify each animal in French.)***

1. C'est le canard.

2. C'est le vache.

3. C'est le chien.

4. C'est le cheval.

5. C'est le oiseau.

B Quel animal est. . .? *(Which animal is. . .?)*

1. dans le pâturage?
   la chevre
2. dans la stalle?
   le cheval
3. sur l'étang?
   le canard
4. dans l'air?
   le oiseau
5. dans la grange?
   la poule

C Où. . .? Qui. . .? Que (Qu'). . .? Quel. . .? Encercle la bonne réponse. *(Where. . .? Who. . .? What. . .? Which. . .? Circle the correct answer.)*

1. Où sont Yvette et Bertrand?
   A. sur l'étang
   B. dans le pâturage
   C. à la campagne
2. Où est le cheval?
   A. dans l'air
   B. dans la stalle
   C. sur l'étang
3. Qui a *(has)* une pomme pour *(for)* Maurice?
   A. Yvette
   B. Bertrand
   C. le cheval
4. Qui voudrait *(would like)* aider?
   A. Yvette
   B. Bertrand
   C. Manon
5. Yvette, qu'est-ce qu'elle a? *(What does Yvette have?)*
   A. une vache
   B. une chèvre
   C. un seau
6. Quel animal est petit?
   A. un oiseau
   B. un cochon
   C. une vache

D Complète les phrases correctement. *(Complete the sentences correctly.)*

Maurice   petit   grand   Henri   pâturage

1. Le chat s'appelle ______________________.
2. L'âne est ______________________.
3. La vache est dans le ______________________.
4. La pomme est pour ______________________.
5. Le canard est ______________________.

E Rearrange this group of animals from the smallest to the largest.

la vache   le lapin   la chèvre   l'oiseau

1. ______________________
2. ______________________
3. ______________________
4. ______________________

F What is each animal like? Indicate the size of each animal by choosing *grand(e)* or *petit(e)*. Write out the full sentence in French.

Modèle: **A:** Un cheval, comment est-il?
Un cheval est grand.

1. Un âne, comment est-il?

____

2. Le chat, comment est-il?

____

3. Une chèvre, comment est-elle?

____

4. Un cochon, comment est-il?

____

5. Un oiseau, comment est-il?

____

G

Choisis la phrase à droite qui traduit la phrase à gauche. ***(Choose the sentence on the right that translates the one on the left. Focus on the familiar words and guess the others in context.)***

1. ___F___ Je suis à la campagne.
2. ___A___ Je vois les animaux.
3. ___B___ Je voudrais t'aider.
4. ___E___ Je peux tenir le seau à la main.
5. ___D___ Je donne à manger au chat.
6. ___C___ Je peux ramasser les œufs.

A. I see the animals.
B. I would like to help you.
C. I can collect the eggs.
D. I'm feeding the cat.
E. I can hold the pail.
F. I am in the country.

H

Parlons! **Select four animals from this unit. Ask your speaking partner where each one is. He/she should answer logically. Then, your partner asks you where four other animals are, and you reply.**

Modèle: **A:** Où est le canard?
B. Il est sur l'étang.

I

C'est à toi! **Find out whether your classmate knows the names of the animals. Offer a clue for each animal, such as the sound it makes in French or something it does, for example, "It says *coin coin*" or "It swims." Make sure your classmate says *le* or *la* before the name of each animal. Next, your partner will give you a clue by saying a location, such as *dans la stalle*. You will say in French the name of the animal associated with each place.**

Proverbe

"Le chat parti, les souris dansent.
When the cat's away, the mice will play."

Langue vivante!

Animaux

800 ANIMAUX SAUVAGES EN LIBERTÉ

LA RÉSERVE AFRICAINE
21 espèces et plus de 100 spécimens d'herbivores et d'oiseaux africains. Zèbres, éléphants, girafes, rhinocéros, hippopotames, autruches, oryx, hypotragues évoluent sous vos yeux, sur un territoire où alternent les points d'eau, les bois et les clairières.

JARDIN DES PAPILLONS

Assistez au ballet multicolore de nombreuses espèces de papillons d'Asie, d'Afrique ou d'Amérique sous un même toit.

AQUARIUM

Plus de 20 espèces de poissons de notre région de la source au fleuve en passant par les étangs et les lacs.

Le monde **fabuleux**
des **poissons**
Du 1er au 13 septembre

16
La vache qui rit

POIDS NET 250 g A L'EMBALLAGE
CAMEMBERT
COEUR DE LION
FABRIQUÉ EN NORMANDIE
45% DE MATIERE GRASSE
LA COMPAGNIE DES FROMAGES 14 BP · 14500 VIRE FRANCE

LA CHOUETTE
Ouououououh, qu'elle est belle!

J Find the French words that mean:

1. wild animals animaux sauvages
2. zebras zèbres
3. elephants éléphants
4. ostriches autruches
5. hippopotami hypotragues
6. butterflies papillons
7. fish poissons

K Review all the images and clippings on page 92, then answer the questions below.

1. *Cœur de Lion* is a brand name of Camembert cheese. It means the "Heart of the. . . ."

   Lion

2. Another brand name of cheese is *La vache qui rit,* or in English, "The Laughing. . . ."

   Cow

3. What is the name of the aquatic show?

   Le monde des fabuleux poissons

4. How many days does this show last?

   quatorze

5. Can you find the French words for "river," "ponds," and "lakes"?

   feuve, passant + etangs et lac

6. How many species of fish are there?

   vingt

7. From what parts of the world do they come?

   notre régions

8. Where can you see butterflies?

   Jardin de papillon

9. *Chouette* is an adjective meaning "cool" or "neat." It is also the name of a bird. What kind of a bird is it?

   owl

10. Write in French: "I like animals."

    Je comme animals

Symtalk

L **Écris en français le mot ou l'expression qui correspond à chaque image.** ***(In French, write the word or expression that corresponds to each picture.)***

1. Qui
2. vache
3. cochon
4. aime
5. perroquet
6. chat

M **Dis et écris la question. Puis, donne la résponse.** ***(Say and write the question. Then, give the answer.)***

1. 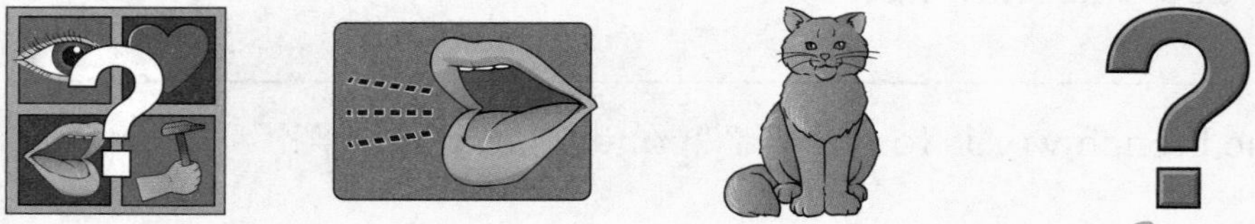

Qui parle chat ? cat (chat

2. 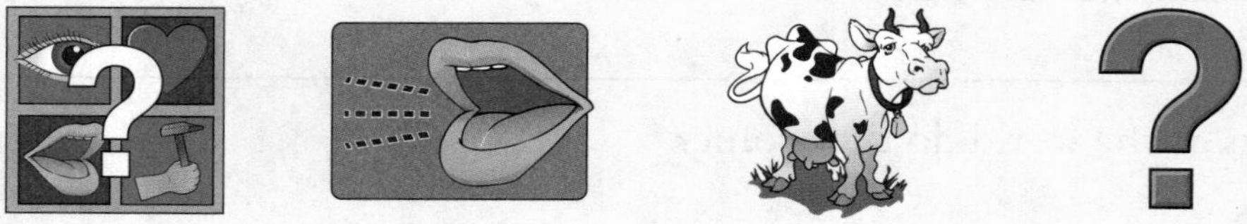

Qui parle vache ? cow (vache)

3. 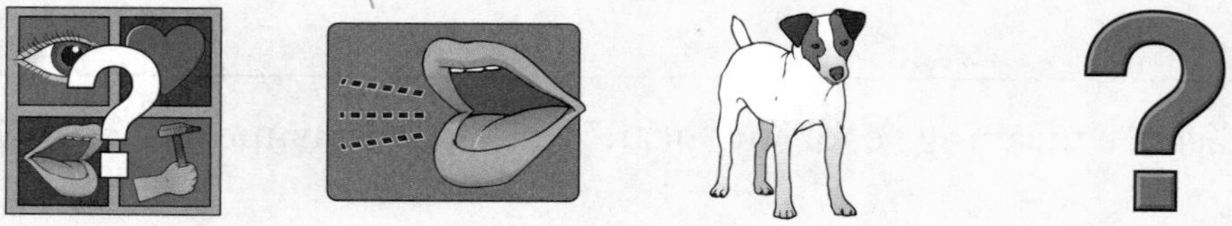

Qui parle chien ? dog (chien)

4. 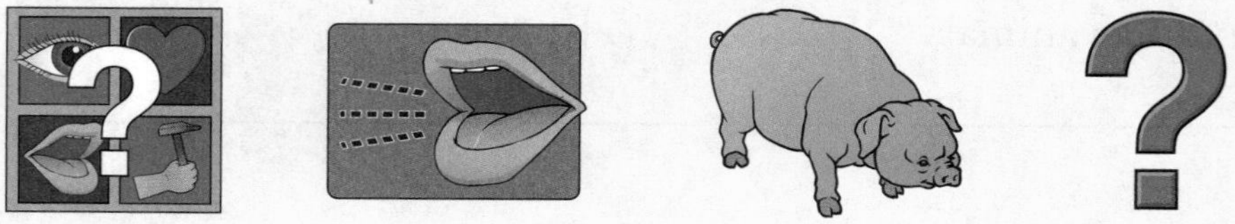

Qui parle cochon ? pig (cochon)

N **Work with a partner. After one of you asks the question, the other responds that no, the person likes a different kind of animal. Please write the dialogue in French.**

1.  

Gérard aime les chats?

Non, Gérard laime les chiens.

2.  

Brigitte aime les chiens ?

Non, Brigitte aime les chats.

3.  

Hiko aime les chats?

Non, Hiko aime les perroquets.

4.  

Antoinie aime les perroquets?

Non, Antoire aime les vaches,

5.  

Sylvie aime les vaches?

Non, Sylvie aime les cochons.

Mots croisés

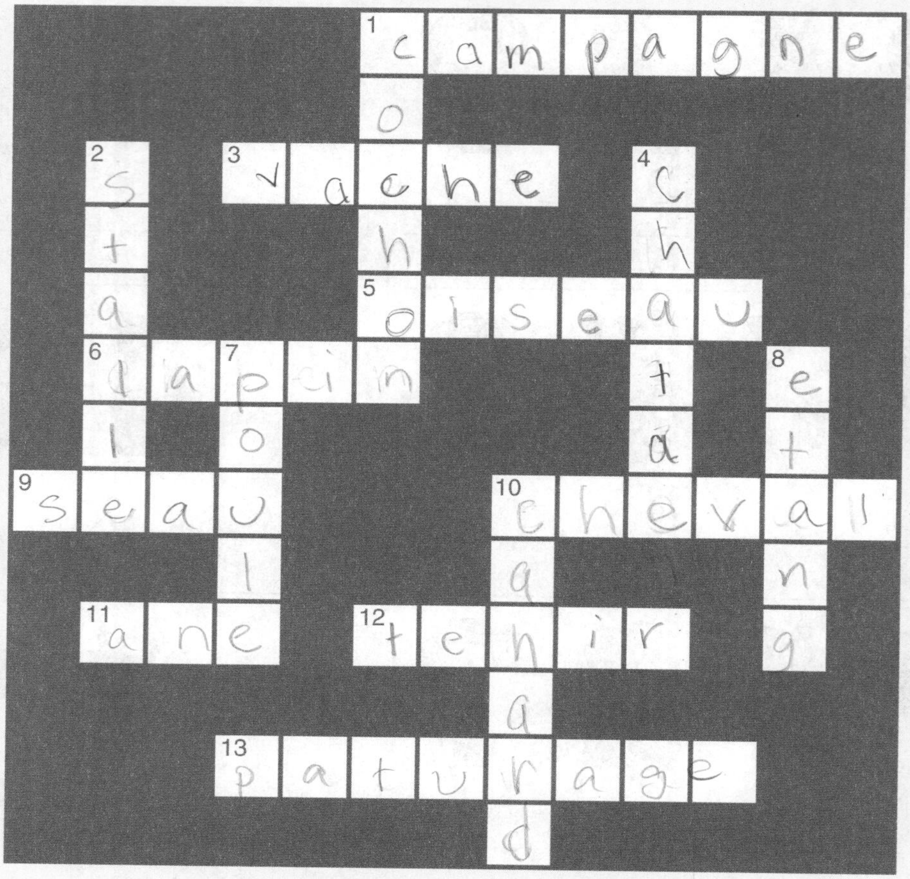

Horizontalement

1. country
3. gives us milk
5. sings and flies
6. has long ears and whiskers
9. pail or bucket
10. says *hiiiiii*
11. carries packs on its back
12. *Tu peux* ____ *le seau à la main.*
13. grazing area

Verticalement

1. says *groin groin*
2. horse's resting place in a stable
4. has kittens
7. gives us eggs
8. between the size of a puddle and a lake
10. swims and dives for food

Unit 8

Les professions et les métiers
Occupations

BYRRH

Vocabulaire

l'artiste (m. + f.)
artist

le commerçant
la commerçante
businessman, businesswoman

l'électricien
l'électricienne
electrician

le charpentier
la charpentière
carpenter

le cuisinier
la cuisinière
cook

l'infirmier (m.)
l'infirmière (f.)
nurse

le mécanicien
la mécanicienne
mechanic

le médecin
la femme médecin
physician

le musicien
la musicienne
musician

1+1=2

le prof
la prof
teacher

l'agriculteur (m.)
l'agricultrice (f.)
farmer

le facteur
la factrice
letter carrier

le plombier
la plombière
plumber

le programmeur
la programmeuse
computer programmer

Où est-ce que tu travailles?
Where do you work?

Je travaille à la campagne. Je suis agriculteur.
I work in the country. I am a farmer.

Une profession refers to a job or position requiring advanced academic or professional training. **Un métier** refers to a trade or a job requiring specific hands-on skills or technical training. **Un emploi** is a job.

Est-ce que tu aimes travailler?
Do you like to work?

Oui, j'aime travailler.
Yes, I like to work.

Que fais-tu pour gagner ta vie?
What do you do (for a living)?

Je suis actrice. Je travaille au théâtre.
I am an actress. I work at the theater.

Quelle est ta profession?
What is your occupation?

Je suis acteur.
I am an actor.

Activités

A **Number the professions or trades in order as your teacher says each one in French.**

_____ le médecin

_____ le mécanicien

_____ le facteur

_____ la cuisinière

_____ la commerçante

_____ l'électricien

_____ l'agricultrice

_____ la programmeuse

_____ l'artiste

_____ la musicienne

B **Qui travaille ici?** ***(Who works here? Write in an appropriate profession, either masculine or feminine.)***

1. restaurant _______________
2. wood shop _______________
3. post office _______________
4. school _______________
5. repair shop/service station _______________
6. dairy barn _______________
7. stage _______________
8. hospital _______________
9. retail shop _______________
10. art studio _______________

C **Écris les mots correctement.** ***(Unscramble the letters to show five occupations.)***

1. RUTECA _______________
2. DICEMÉN _______________
3. RATCUEF _______________
4. TARSETI _______________
5. ROGRAMMEESPU _______________

D Complète les phrases. *(Complete the sentences by putting the cues in parentheses into French.)*

1. Quelle est ta ____________________? *(occupation)*
2. Je ____________________ actrice. *(am)*
3. Je ____________________ au théâtre. *(work)*
4. Où est-ce que ____________________ travailles, Olivier? *(you, informal)*
5. Je travaille ____________________. *(in the country)*
6. Que ____________________ -tu, Valérie? *(do you do)*
7. Je suis ____________________. *(a cook)*
8. J' ____________________ travailler. *(like)*

E Comment dit-on. . .? *(How do you say this in English?)*

1. Ma mère est prof.

   ____

2. Elle enseigne *(teaches)* l'allemand et le portugais.

   ____

3. Mon père est musicien.

   ____

4. Il joue de la flûte.

   ____

5. Ma cousine est programmeuse.

   ____

6. Elle travaille avec un ordinateur.

   ____

7. Mon cousin est cuisinier.

   ____

8. Il prépare le dîner.

   ____

F **Devine qui c'est.** ***(Guess who it is.)***

1. *Le* ______________________ creates software.
2. *Le* ______________________ is in charge of (medical) operations.
3. *L'* ______________________ checks for faulty wiring.
4. *La* ______________________ installs wooden beams.
5. *L'* ______________________ paints portraits.
6. *La* ______________________ cooks food.
7. *La* ______________________ manages or owns a store.
8. *L'* ______________________ plants and harvests.
9. *Le* ______________________ delivers mail.
10. *La* ______________________ plays in a symphony orchestra.

G **Écris en français la profession ou le métier qui correspond à chaque image.** ***(Write in French the masculine and feminine name of the profession or occupation which corresponds to each picture.)***

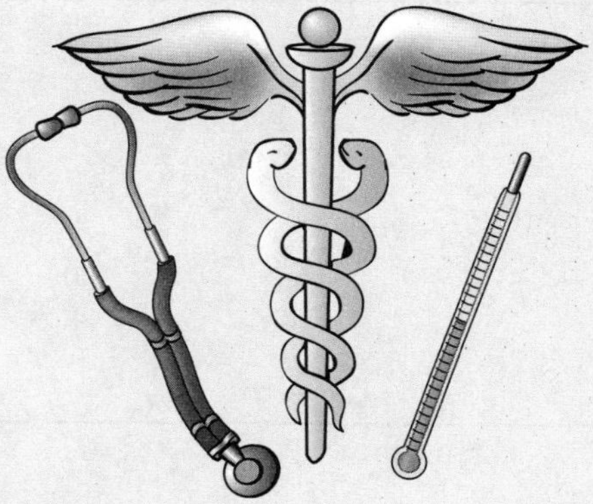

1. ______________________

____

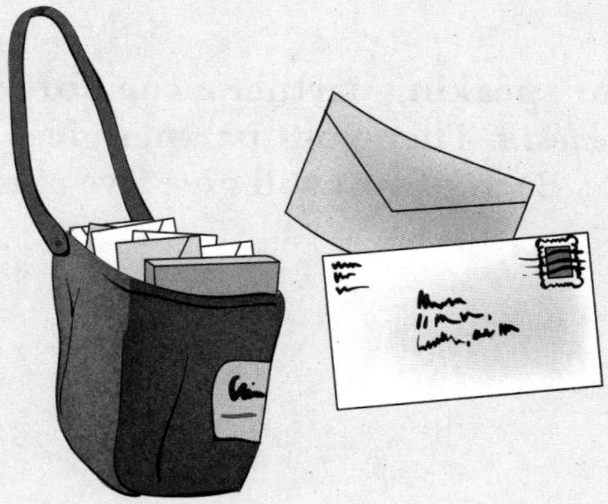

2. ______________________

____

3. ________________________________

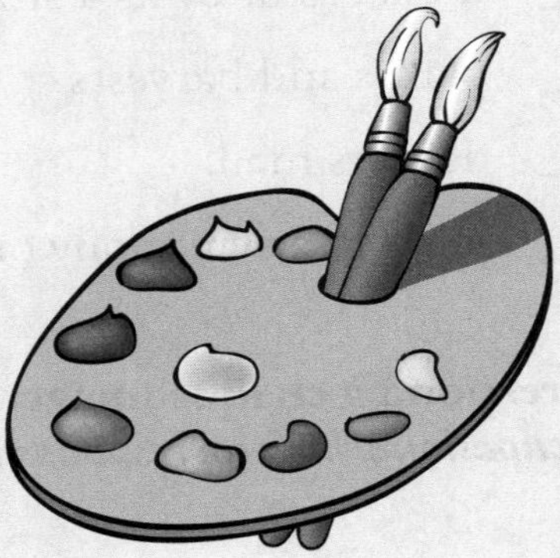

4. ________________________________

5. ________________________________

H **Parlons! Guess certain occupations. Give your speaking partner a cue, for example: You say "hospital" and your partner will say *le médecin.* Then your partner gives you a cue, such as "paintbrush" and you will say *l'artiste.* Each of you will give five cues to elicit five names of professions or occupations.**

I **C'est à toi!** **Help create a classroom bulletin board display about professions and occupations. Cut out pictures from magazines showing people doing the jobs listed in this unit. Label each one in French, for example, *M. Dupont est artiste* or *Mlle Lambert est commerçante.* Label the entire display as *Professions et métiers.***

Proverbe

“Les bons outils font les bons ouvriers.
Good tools make good workers.”

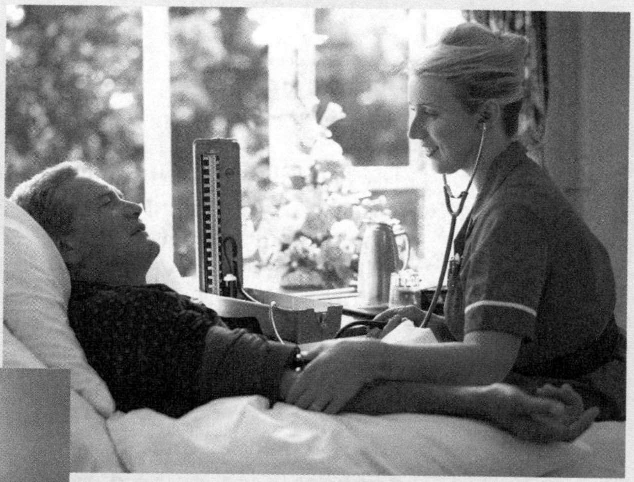

Langue vivante!

OFFRE

RECHERCHE VENDEUSE

Ville/Quartier: Nord | Lille | LILLE
Code postal: 59000 **Téléphone:**

Catégorie: Particuliers **Mail:**

Détail de l'annonce
RECHERCHE VENDEUSES DANS LE PRÊT-A-PORTER FEMININ, POSSIBILITÉ . D'ÉVOLUTION RAPIDE POUR UNE PERSONNE MOTIVÉE ET AMBITIEUSE

POSTE A POURVOIR AUSSI LE WEEK END POUR ÉTUDIANTE
AVEC OU SANS EXPERIENCES
CV AINSI DEMANDER

DEMANDES

Titre : URGENT jeune fille 18 ans...
Annonce : bonjour j'ai 18 ans et je recherche un petit emploi pour le mois de juillet.Sportive,cavalière,déterminée,motivée j'étudie tte proposition.

Titre : cuisinier qualifié
Annonce : recherche d'extra dans la région de manosque

Chauffeur parlant allemand, anglais

Détail de l'annonce
Chauffeur de grande remise parlant allemand, anglais, bonnes connaissances de Paris
et de son histoire. 20 ans d'expérience, étudie toutes propositions.

J **Review the ad titled *"Offre,"* and answer the questions below.**

1. What kind of position is vacant in this store?

___

2. Where is this position available?

___

3. Can you find two words that describe a well-qualified applicant?

___

4. What do these words mean in English?

___

K **Review the ad titled *"Demandes,"* which describes three people looking for jobs; then, answer the questions below.**

1. Who is looking for the first job?

___

2. How old is she?

___

3. When does she want a job?

___

4. She describes herself with four adjectives. What are these words?

___

5. Can you guess what these words might be in English?

___

6. The second job seeker is an experienced worker. What is his occupation?

___

7. Where would he like to find a job as a catering assistant *(un extra)*?

___

8. The third person seeks a job as a personal driver *(chauffeur)*. Other than driving a car, what can he do?

___

9. What are his other qualifications?

___

10. In your opinion, who might like to employ his services?

___

Symtalk

L **Écris en français le mot ou l'expression qui correspond à chaque image.** ***(In French, write the word or expression that corresponds to each picture.)***

 1. ______	 2. ______	 3. ______	 4. ______
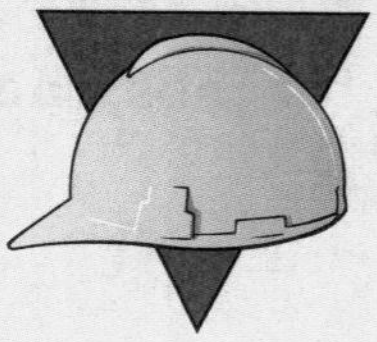 5. ______	 6. ______	 7. ______	 8. ______

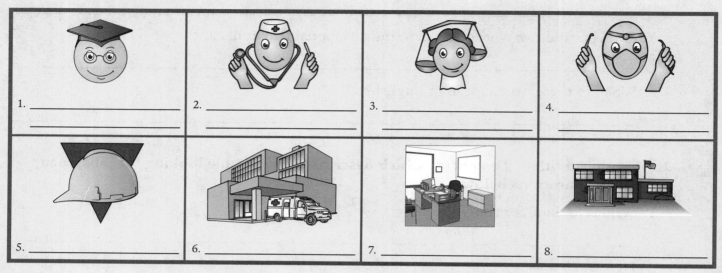

M **Dis les phrases, puis écris-les en français.** ***(Say the sentences, then write them in French.)***

1.   

____

2.   

____

3.   

____

4. 

____

N **Travaille avec un partenaire. Pose la question ou donne la réponse. Puis, écris le dialogue.** ***(Work with a partner. Ask the question or give the answer. Then, write the dialogue.)***

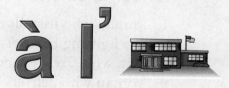

1. 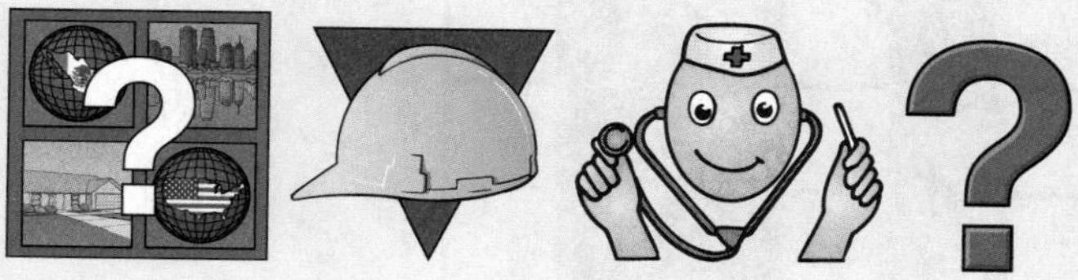 à l' 

______________________ ______________________

2. 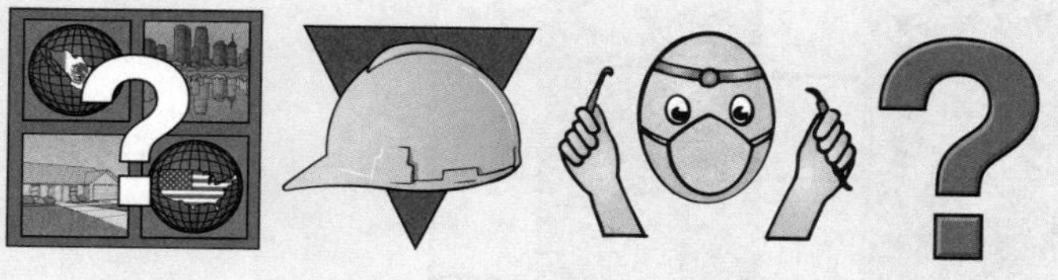 au 

______________________ ______________________

3. 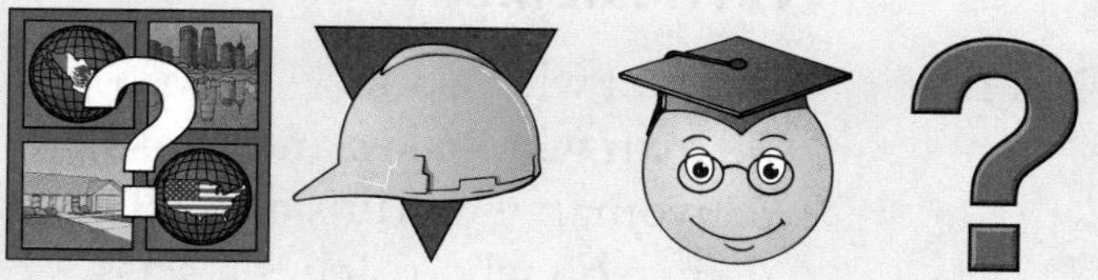 à l' 

______________________ ______________________

4. 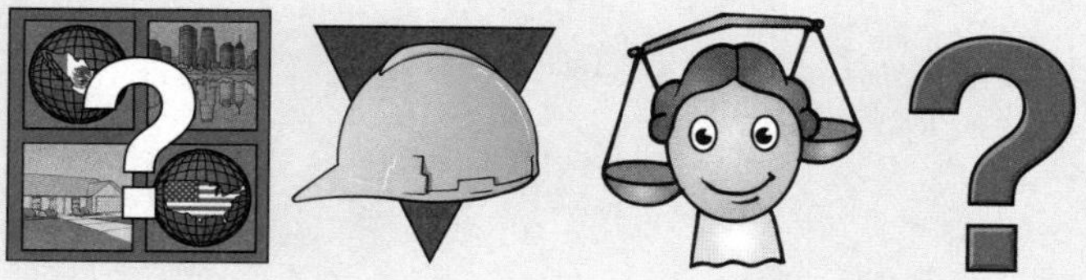 au 

______________________ ______________________

Mots croisés

1
2
3
4
5
6
7
8
9
10

Horizontalement

1. woman who installs electrical wires that run lighting fixtures
4. man who fixes motors
9. woman who delivers letters and magazines
10. woman who develops computer games

Verticalement

2. man who works with wood
3. man who bakes and cooks
5. woman who runs a small business
6. person who teaches a class
7. man who assists doctors in caring for sick people
8. woman who unclogs drain pipes

Unit 9

La nourriture — Food

Vocabulaire

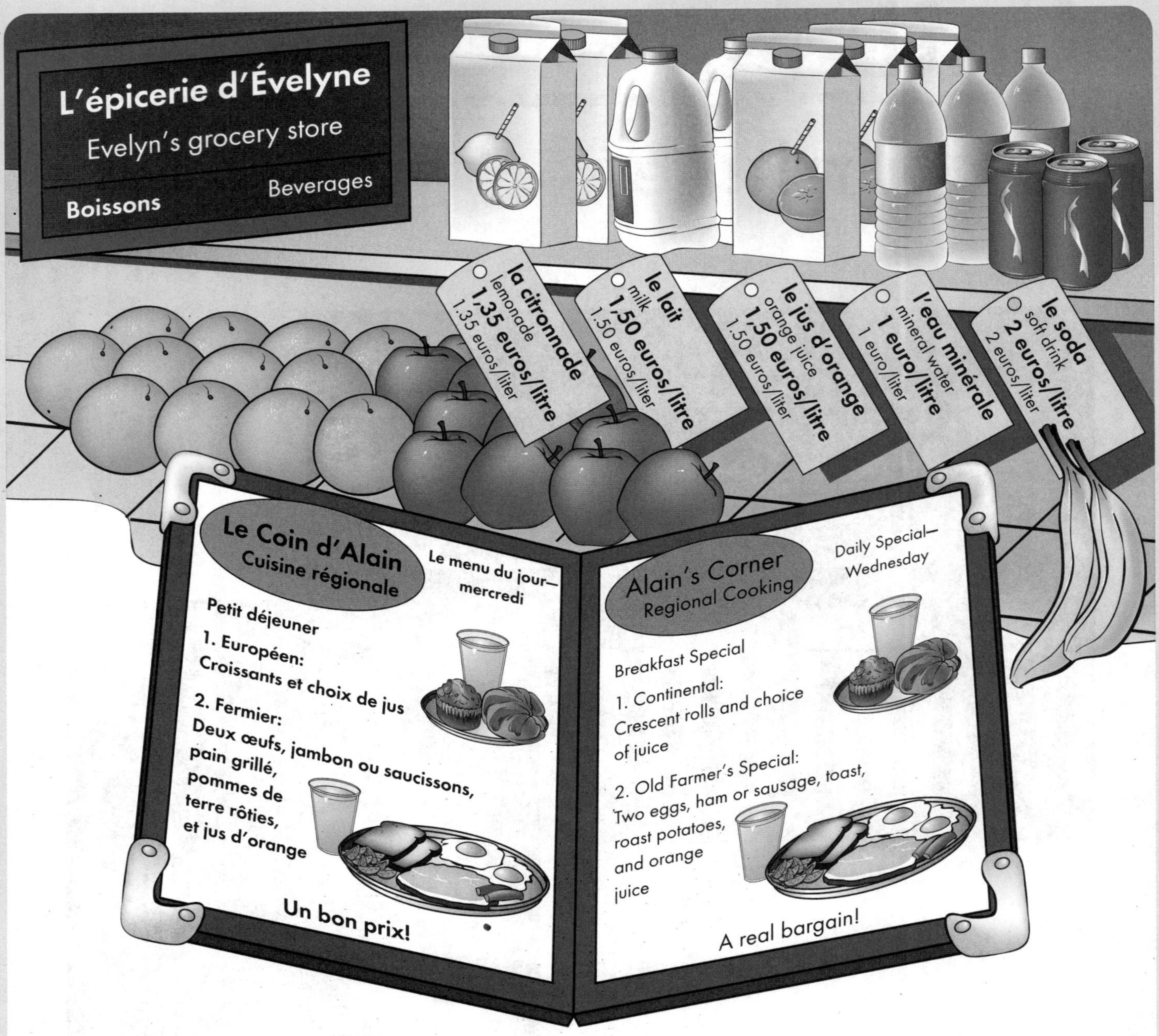
L'épicerie d'Évelyne
Evelyn's grocery store
Boissons
Beverages
la citronnade
lemonade
1,35 euros/litre
1.35 euros/liter
le lait
milk
1,50 euros/litre
1.50 euros/liter
le jus d'orange
orange juice
1,50 euros/litre
1.50 euros/liter
l'eau minérale
mineral water
1 euro/litre
1 euro/liter
le soda
soft drink
2 euros/litre
2 euros/liter
Le Coin d'Alain
Cuisine régionale
Le menu du jour—mercredi
Petit déjeuner
1. Européen:
Croissants et choix de jus
2. Fermier:
Deux œufs, jambon ou saucissons, pain grillé, pommes de terre rôties, et jus d'orange
Un bon prix!
Alain's Corner
Regional Cooking
Daily Special—Wednesday
Breakfast Special
1. Continental:
Crescent rolls and choice of juice
2. Old Farmer's Special:
Two eggs, ham or sausage, toast, roast potatoes, and orange juice
A real bargain!

Qu'est-ce qu il y a à manger?	What's there to eat?	**Qu'est-ce qu'il y a à boire?**	What's there to drink?
Il y de la soupe et de la salade.	There's soup and salad.	**Il y a du lait.**	There's milk.
As-tu faim?	Are you hungry?	**As-tu soif, Robert?**	Are you thirsty, Robert?
Oui. J'ai faim.	Yes. I'm hungry.	**Non. Je n'ai pas soif.**	No, I'm not thirsty.
Que manges-tu?	What are you eating?	**Que prends-tu à boire, Suzanne?**	What are you having to drink, Suzanne?
Je mange un sandwich.	I'm eating a sandwich.	**Je prends un verre de lait.**	I'm having a glass of milk.

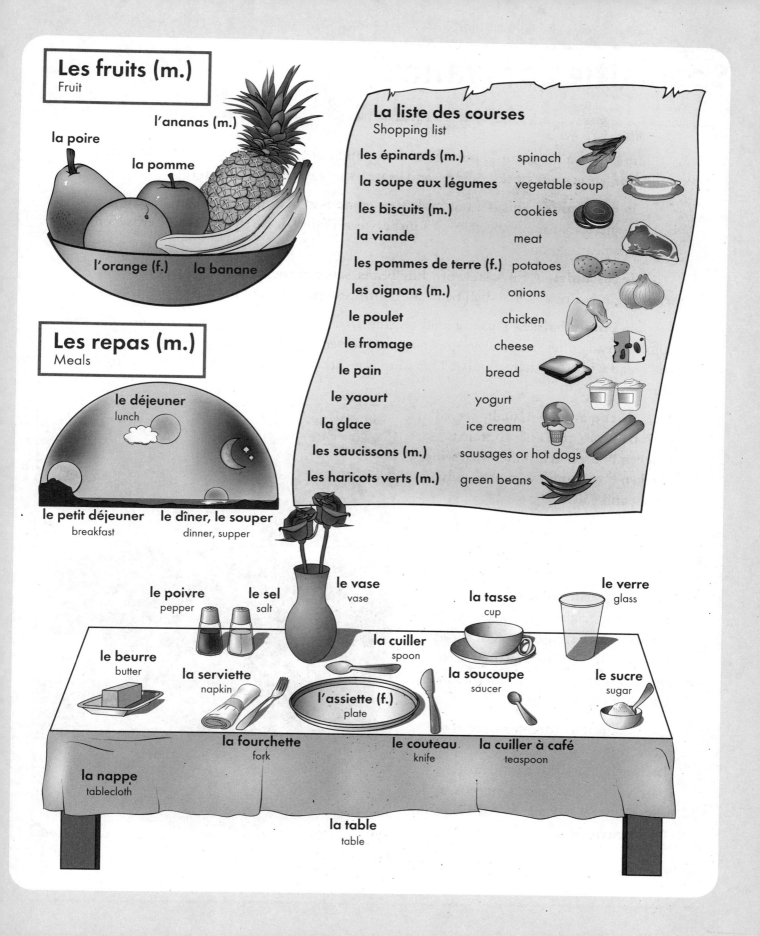

Les fruits (m.)
Fruit

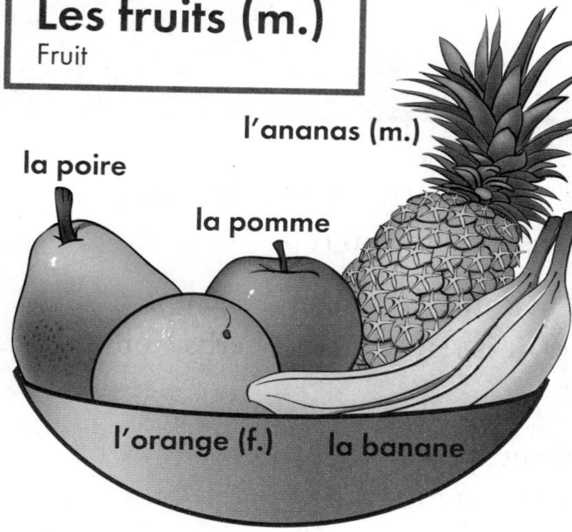
l'ananas (m.)
la poire
la pomme
l'orange (f.)
la banane

La liste des courses
Shopping list

les épinards (m.)	spinach
la soupe aux légumes	vegetable soup
les biscuits (m.)	cookies
la viande	meat
les pommes de terre (f.)	potatoes
les oignons (m.)	onions
le poulet	chicken
le fromage	cheese
le pain	bread
le yaourt	yogurt
la glace	ice cream
les saucissons (m.)	sausages or hot dogs
les haricots verts (m.)	green beans

Les repas (m.)
Meals

le déjeuner
lunch
le petit déjeuner
breakfast
le dîner, le souper
dinner, supper

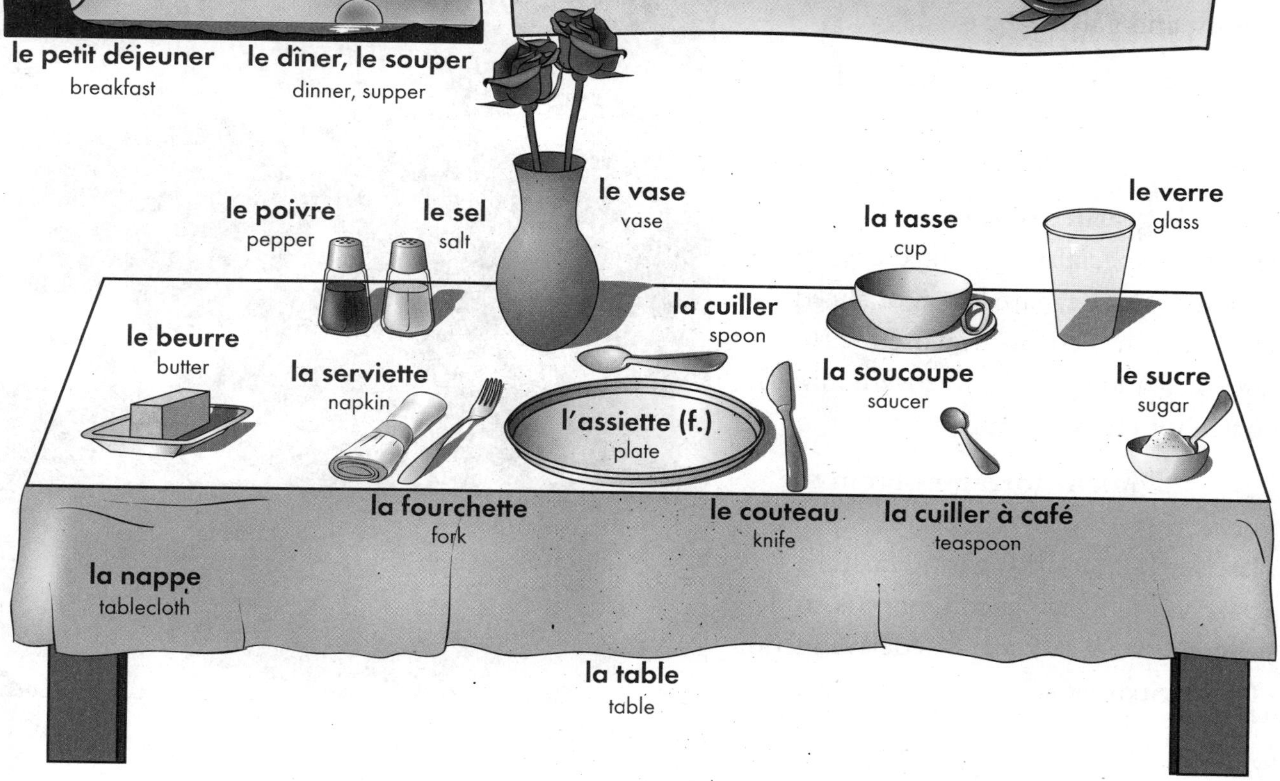
le vase
vase
le poivre
pepper
le sel
salt
la tasse
cup
le verre
glass
la cuiller
spoon
le beurre
butter
la serviette
napkin
la soucoupe
saucer
le sucre
sugar
l'assiette (f.)
plate
la fourchette
fork
le couteau
knife
la cuiller à café
teaspoon
la nappe
tablecloth
la table
table

Specialties of France

la soupe à l'oignon—This is French Onion Soup: light golden soup made with *consommé* (clear soup stock), onions, and grated white cheese melted on top.

la ratatouille—This is a vegetable stew composed mainly of eggplant, zucchini, onions, and tomatoes. A specialty of southeastern France, it is flavored with herbs from the Mediterranean region.

le cassoulet—A thick stew of white beans, sausage and meat (usually pork, duck, or mutton), it is a traditional dish from the southwestern region of France.

la bouillabaisse—This is a seafood stew that is flavored with tomatoes, olive oil, and spices. Bread either lines the soup tureen or is served separately. Many people like to spread the bread with spicy mayonnaise. This soup is a specialty from the southern port city of *Marseille.*

le coq au vin—Usually served with potatoes, this dish contains chicken braised in a skillet with wine, chicken broth, onions, mushrooms, herbs, and garlic.

le canard à l'orange—This is roast duck flavored with orange marmalade, vinegar, and soy sauce.

le gratin savoyard—This regional specialty is a baked casserole made with alternate layers of sliced potatoes and cheese, flavored with nutmeg and spices, and covered lightly with hot chicken soup.

la quiche lorraine—From the northeastern provinces of Alsace and Lorraine comes this round custard pastry filled with bacon, onions, and cheese. The word *quiche* is derived from the German word for cake, *Kuchen*.

le coq au vin

la charlotte aux framboises—This dessert has as a base a raspberry custard cream surrounded by sponge cake in the shape of "ladyfingers."

les crêpes bretonnes

les crêpes bretonnes—These are thin pancakes made with sliced apples, often served as dessert with fruit syrup, jam, or chocolate sauce. Crêpes are a specialty of the northwestern province of Brittany.

la tarte aux myrtilles

la tarte aux myrtilles—This is a pie-shaped dessert consisting of a shortbread crust and blueberry fruit filling.

Bon appétit! is a wish on the part of a friend or host for all guests to enjoy the meal and eat heartily.

La cuisine can refer to the kitchen or to cooking or a style or preparation of food in general, such as **cuisine régionale**.

Traditionally the large midday meal lasts two hours. It has several courses, often starting with soup and ending with cheese. Most people today, however, are not at home at this time. They eat out or take a bag lunch.

As an afternoon snack many children enjoy eating a **pain au chocolat**, a square roll filled with a bar of melted chocolate.

Evening meals are at a time when the whole family can sit down together.

Activités

A **Écris le nom français de chaque objet.** ***(Write the French name of each object.)***

1. la tasse

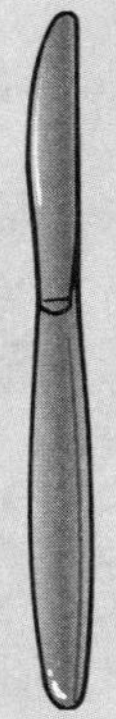

2. le couteau

3. un verre de lait
~~le verre / le lait~~

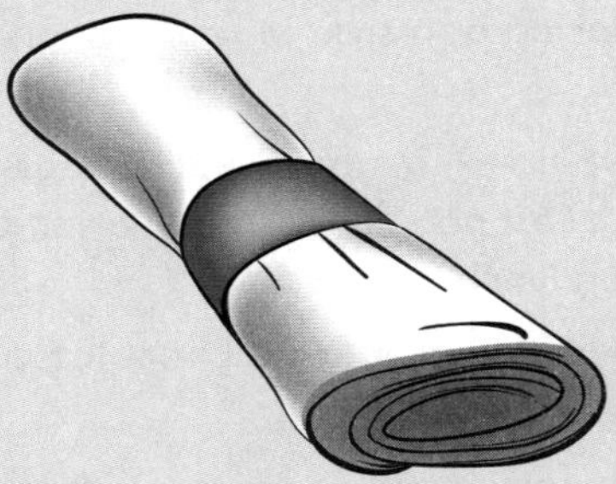

4. la serviette

5. le vase

6. la table

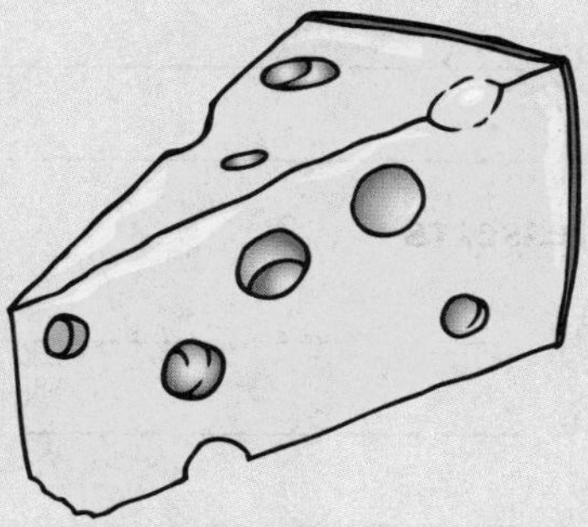

7. le fromage

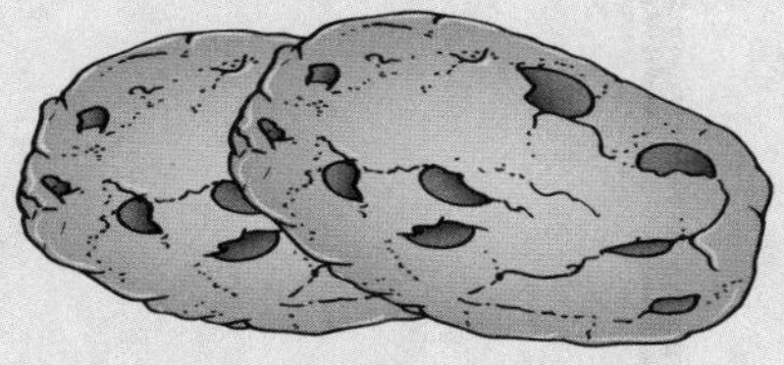

8. les biscuits

B **Complète chaque phrase selon tes connaissances de la cuisine régionale.** ***(Complete each sentence based on your new knowledge of regional French cuisine.)***

1. A famous chicken and wine dish is ______________________.
2. *Bouillabaisse* contains an assortment of ______________________.
3. *Cassoulet* is a specialty of ______________________ France.
4. A vegetable stew from southern France is ______________________.
5. A dish consisting of potatoes and cheese is ______________________.

C **Using your food vocabulary and the list of specialties, write three food items for each of the following categories.**

1. **meat**
   A. ______________________
   B. ______________________
   C. ______________________
2. **vegetables**
   A. ______________________
   B. ______________________
   C. ______________________
3. **dairy products**
   A. ______________________
   B. ______________________
   C. ______________________
4. **beverages**
   A. ______________________
   B. ______________________
   C. ______________________
5. **fruits**
   A. ______________________
   B. ______________________
   C. ______________________
6. **desserts**
   A. ______________________
   B. ______________________
   C. ______________________

D **Imagine you are opening a restaurant in France. From your food and specialty lists prepare a menu for lunch and dinner. At least three dishes or items for each meal should be offered.**

Menu à 14,48€
hors-d'œuvre
crudités
ou
escargots
viande ou poisson
côtelettes de porc
ou
saumon à la sauce hollandaise
desserts
mousse au chocolat
ou
crème caramel

E Prepare a poster using magazine pictures. Show a balanced breakfast and a balanced dinner. Label each food item with its French name.

F Prepare fifteen different flash cards with a picture of a food item on one side and its French name on the other. Select several of your flash cards and quiz a few classmates.

le coq au vin

G *Un jeu.* Play this game with a group that includes several of your classmates. List in French 20 words that name a food or beverage, then scramble each word. The student who unscrambles the most words correctly in the least amount of time is the winner.

H Parlons! Your classmate is in charge of the menu today. Tell him or her that you are hungry. You want to know what there is to eat today. He or she will name five foods and you will pick one. Next, your classmate will tell you that he or she is thirsty and ask you what there is to drink. Name five beverages so that he or she can order.

I C'est à toi! Imagine that you work at an elegant restaurant in France. A customer asks you about a regional specialty, such as *ratatouille.* Explain what the specialty is and how it is made.

Proverbe

"**On ne fait pas d'omelette sans casser des oeufs.**
You can't make an omelette without breaking eggs."

Langue vivante!

Perrier
330 ml

CRÈME BRÛLÉE
aux Pommes du Limousin

Hochepot à la flamande

Nord-Pas-de-Calais

Ingrédients 6-8 personnes

300 grammes d'oreille de porc
600 grammes de pieds de porc
125 grammes de queue de porc
250 grammes de lard salé
600 grammes de poitrine de bœuf
600 grammes d'épaule et de poitrine de mouton
200 gramme de carottes
200 grammes de chou
1 oignon
4 poireaux
3 pommes de terre
sel et poivre

FEUILLETÉ MARIN
SAUCE HOLLANDAISE

Recette pour 4 personnes :
- 300 g de pâte feuilletée
- 1 jaune d'œuf
- 500 g de filets de sole émincés
- 100 g de crevettes décortiquées
- 1 sachet de Sauce Hollandaise MAGGI
- 100 g de beurre
- 1/2 sachet de Court-Bouillon MAGGI
- 1 litre d'eau froide
- quelques feuilles d'épinard ébouillantées

Cuisson : 20 minutes

J'étale la pâte sur 1 cm d'épaisseur et découpe des carrés. Je les dore au jaune d'œuf et les fais cuire au four environ 20 minutes. Je fais pocher les filets et les crevettes dans le Court-Bouillon. Je prépare la Sauce Hollandaise. Je partage les feuilletés en 2 et les garnis des feuilles d'épinard, des filets de sole et des crevettes. Je les sers nappés de la Sauce Hollandaise.

Maggi
Fine Saveur
Sauce
Hollandaise

J Review the clippings and answer the following questions.

1. *Hochepot à la flamande* is a main dish from the Flemish/Dutch cultural region of northern France. Most of the ingredients can be sorted into two main groups. What are they?
____
2. What is a favorite French beverage? _______________
3. What is its brand name? _______________
4. What dessert has added fruit? _______________
5. What is the fruit? _______________
6. What is the word for "recipe"? _______________
7. The recipe shown is for seafood puff pastry. Besides shrimp (*crevettes*), it calls for a fish which has the same name in English. What is it?
____
8. Hollandaise sauce is made according to a Dutch recipe. It includes "one egg yolk." Find that term in French.
____
9. How much butter should one add? _______________
10. How much water should one add? _______________

le saumon (salmon) *à la sauce hollandaise*

Symtalk

K **Écris en français le mot ou l'expression qui correspond à chaque image.** ***(In the space, write the correct word or expression in French.)***

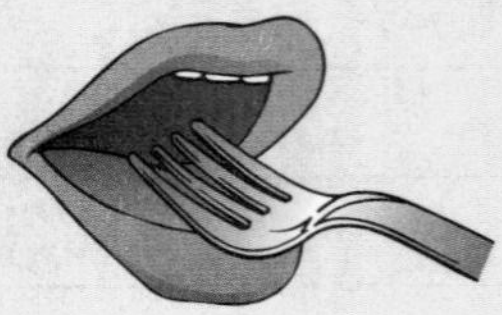

1. ______________________

2. ______________________

3. ______________________

4. ______________________

5. ______________________

6. ______________________

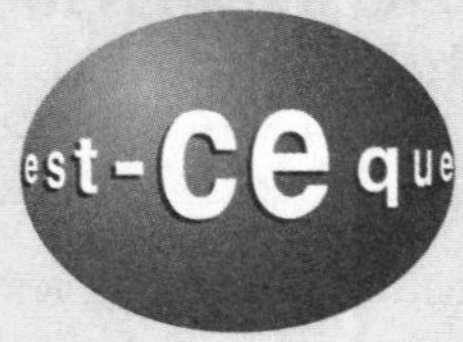
est-ce que

7. ______________________

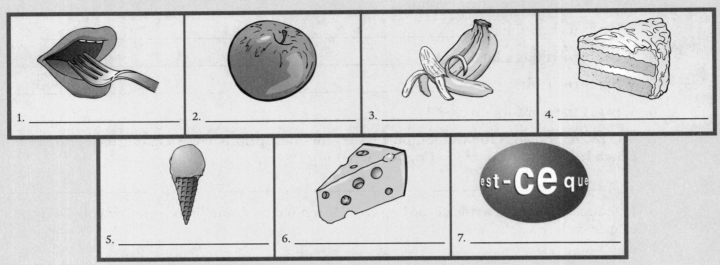

L **Dis les phrases, puis écris-les.** ***(Say the sentences, then write them.)***

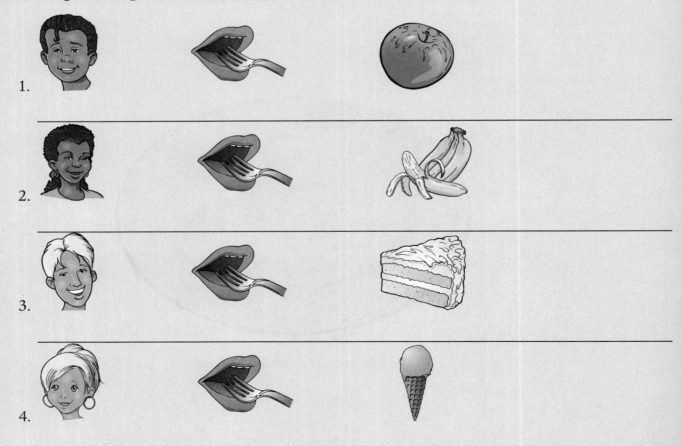

1.  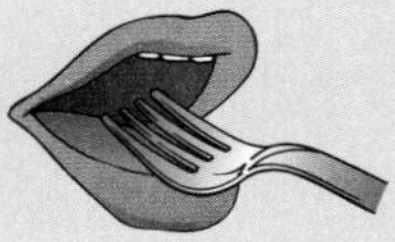 

____

2.  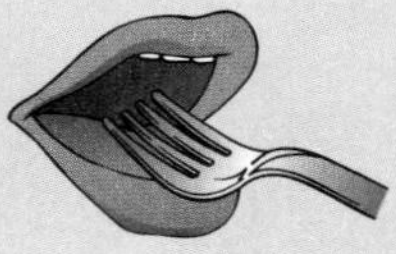 

____

3.  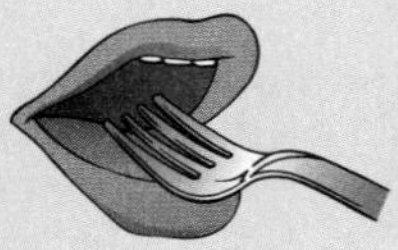 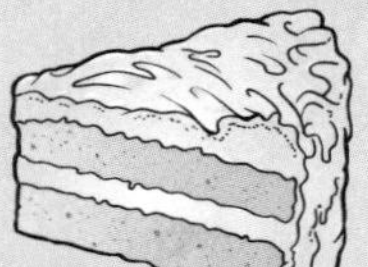

____

4.  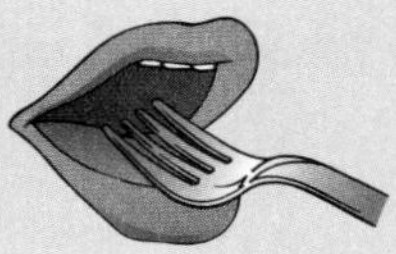 

____

5. 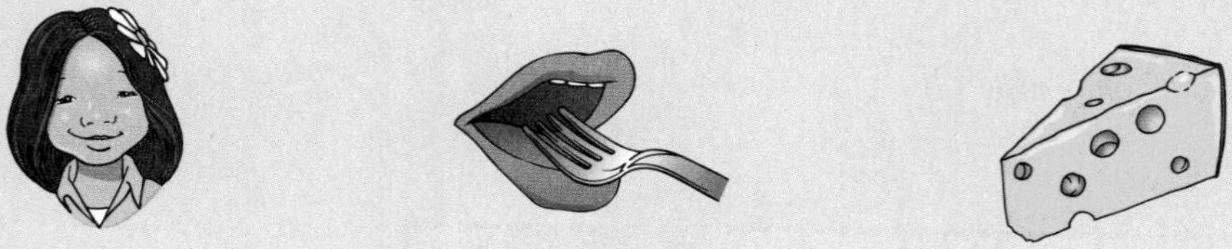

____

M **Travaille avec un partenaire. Pose la question ou donne la réponse. Puis, écris le dialogue.** ***(Work with a partner. Ask the question or give the answer. Then, write the dialogue.)***

1. 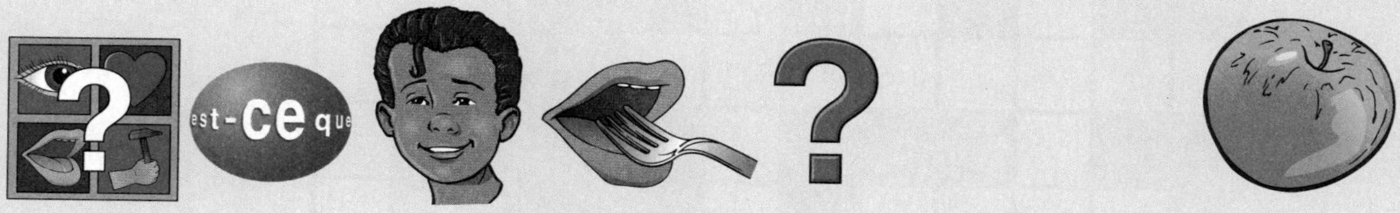
est-ce que

______________________ ______________________

2. 
est-ce que

______________________ ______________________

3. 
est-ce que

______________________ ______________________

4. 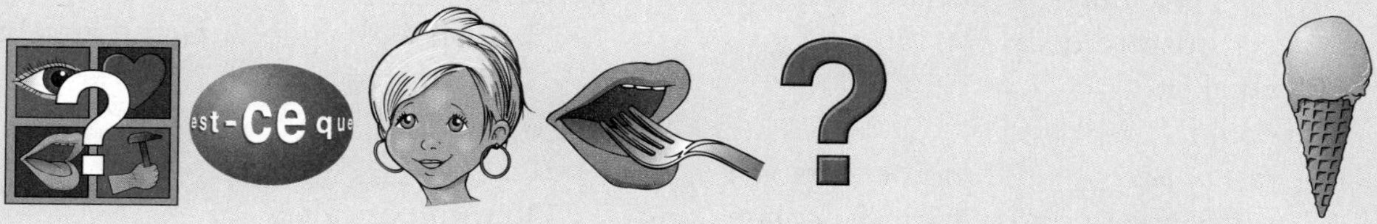
est-ce que

______________________ ______________________

5. 
est-ce que

______________________ ______________________

Mots croisés

Horizontalement

1. ____ *à l'orange,* a specialty game dish
4. egg custard dish
7. chicken
8. cookies
9. *Je n'ai pas* ____. ("I'm not thirsty.")
12. puffy cream pastry with chocolate icing
14. milk
15. a fruit
16. When you are thirsty, you might ask, *"Qu'est-ce qu'il y a à* ____*?"*

Verticalement

2. *Bon* ____*!*
3. dish with eggplants and zucchini
5. bean stew
6. water
10. *J'ai* ____. ("I'm hungry.")
11. thin pancakes
13. ____ *au chocolat,* a popular snack

Unit 10

L'art

Art

Des artistes merveilleux (Great Artists)

The Death of Socrates

(Oil on canvas, 1787) by Jacques-Louis David

The Metropolitan Museum of Art, New York (Wolfe Fund, 1931, Catherine Lorillard Wolfe Collection)

Jacques-Louis David (1748-1825) was born in Paris and studied under the famous artist François Boucher. He became known for his scenes of historical subjects. After winning the *Prix de Rome* (Prize of Rome) award in 1775, David was appointed official painter to the court of King Louis XVI. Unfortunately, he became involved in the political conflicts of his day and was imprisoned for siding with the Revolutionists. He was eventually reappointed, but this time as court painter of the next ruler, the emperor Napoléon.

David helped establish the movement of **Classicism** in French art. He admired ancient Greek art and created several paintings with Greek mythological and historical themes. He used clear lines to give the human body a realistic and natural appearance. Three of his Classical masterpieces are: *Oath of the Horatii, The Death of Socrates,* and the *Coronation* (of Napoléon.)

Moroccan Horsemen in Military Action

(Oil on canvas, 1832) by Eugène Delacroix

Musee Fabre, Montpellier, France

Eugène Delacroix (1799-1863) was born near Paris. After formal art study with the painter Pierre Guérin, Delacroix experimented with a new theory of art. He believed that the Classical artists of his time had removed feeling from art, making it lifeless and cold like a stone sculpture. He chose to use flowing lines to create the illusion of movement, varying shades of color to portray feeling, and contrasts of color to produce liveliness. A painting, he strongly believed, must be *felt* as well as viewed. He and his friends joined the new European cultural trend that promoted freedom in the arts. It was called **Romanticism.**

Delacroix's paintings titled *Dante and Virgil* and *The Fall of Constantinople* reflect his interest in history. The painting *Moroccan Horsemen in Military Action* was inspired by his travels to North Africa. It depicts a traditional Arabic show featuring armed warriors and fast horses.

On the Beach

(Oil on canvas, 1873) by Édouard Manet

Louvre, Paris, France

The Croquet Match

(Oil on canvas, 1873) by Édouard Manet

Städelsches Kunstinstitut, Frankfurt-am-Main, Germany

Édouard Manet (1832-83) was born in Paris and studied art under Thomas Couture. He was one of the founders of the French School of **Impressionism**, and has been referred to as the godfather of this art movement. He believed that a painting should create an immediate impression on the viewer. Whatever one sees or thinks he sees is important. Whatever one sees after some study of the painting is not at all important. Details are not needed to convey an impression. This type of art uses the techniques of ghost effect, blending and merging of color, and the joining of the foreground with the background. *On the Beach* and *The Croquet Match* are two examples of Manet's artwork.

Contemporary Artists

Recent artists include sculptors and painters with a variety of interests. **Catherine Mandron** sculpts objects out of marble, glass, and stone. Engraver and painter **Bernadette Planchenault** enjoys using animals in her etchings and paintings. **Françoise Gilot** creates oil paintings in a very modern style, influenced greatly by the Spanish painter, Pablo Picasso. Using a style called symbolism, **Françoise Dunesme** calls to mind an ancient culture through a layer of colorful images. She calls her picture *Egyptian Dream (Rêve égyptien)*. **Daniel Peccoux** uses groupings of stone and shadow to evoke shapes in a new way, as in *Pyramid (Pyramide)*.

Pyramide

(Oil on canvas, 2005) by Daniel Peccoux

Carel Gallery

Activités

A Name the painting that can be described as. . .

1. people playing an outdoor game.

____

2. a man surrounded by many people.

____

3. galloping horses.

____

4. the ocean at night.

____

B Name the artist whose works reveal. . .

1. a shadow or ghost effect.

____

2. a flowing line and contrasting color.

____

3. a clear line and Classical themes.

____

4. bright lighting effects.

____

5. symbols of an old culture.

____

C Match the item in column A with its description in column B.

A		B
1. ______	Paris	A. outstanding Romantic painting
2. ______	*Death of Socrates*	B. background absorbing foreground
3. ______	Delacroix	C. birthplace of David
4. ______	French Impressionist	D. masterpiece by David
5. ______	*Moroccan Horsemen in Military Action*	E. Édouard Manet
6. ______	a technique of Impressionists	F. Romantic artist

D **Complete the analogies.**

1. ______________________: Classicism = Delacroix: Romanticism
2. David: straight line = Delacroix: ______________________ line
3. the impression: ______________________ = reality: David
4. emotion: ______________________ = form: David
5. Mandron: sculptures = Planchenault: ______________________

E **Write the correct name of the artist associated with the idea represented by the image.**

1. 

____

2. 
PRIX
DE
ROME

____

3. 

____

F **Which artist would most likely. . .**

1. enjoy foggy and misty weather?

___

2. make a picture showing every exact detail?

___

3. show tree branches bending in a strong wind?

___

G **In your opinion. . .**

1. whose paintings appear fuzzy and unclear?

___

2. whose work shows the outlined figure of an ancient Eyptian?

___

3. whose work contrasts rest and motion?

___

4. who would like to create something out of metal or stone?

___

5. who might have a pet?

___

H **Which painting introduced in this unit do you like best? Who painted it? State in your own words what the picture is about and why you like it.**

____

____

____

____

____

____

____

I **Écris les noms qui manquent.** ***(Fill in the blanks with the missing names.)***

1. ____________________ was one of the founders of Impressionism.
2. ____________________ was a court painter for a king and an emperor.
3. ____________________ believed that a picture should portray emotion and movement.

J **C'est à toi. Choose an object or animal that you have learned the name for in this book, for example, a rabbit. On a sheet of paper or on the board, make your rabbit in two different styles: Classical and Modern (Expressionistic, abstract, or avant-garde). Label each as follows: *C'est un lapin.* Let the class see your drawings and vote twice: first on artistic style (which drawing is Classical and which one is Modern), and second on personal preference (which one the class prefers). Announce in French that you are an artist!**

Proverbe

« L'art est longue, la vie est courte.

Art is long-lasting but life is short. »

Langue vivante!

paris museum pass
carte musées-monuments
Valable pour 1, 3 ou 5 jours, la carte offre un accès libre et direct aux collections permanentes de 70 musées et monuments de Paris et de la région parisienne. En vente dans les musées, les monuments, les stations de métro et à l'Office de Tourisme de Paris.

RMN / HERVÉ LEWANDOWSKI

▲ *Le Jardin de Maubusson*, Paul Cézanne, Pontoise, 1877.

GALERIE D'ART YVON DESGAGNÉS

53, rue St-Jean-Baptiste, Baie St-Paul
Tél.: (418) 435-3429

Heures d'ouverture:
Mai à novembre: tous les jours de 9h30 à 20h00
Hiver: tous les samedis et dimanches de 10h00 à 18h00
Il est possible d'obtenir un rendez-vous après les heures d'ouverture normales

Bernadette PLANCHENAULT
55, rue de Montparnasse
75014 Paris

bernadette.planchenault@wanadoo.fr

Voir mes oeuvres

Peintre, Graveur - éditions d'estampes et de livres de bibliophilie.
Particicpe aux salons de livres de Bibliophilie et aux expositions de gravure ou d'art animalier.

SUITE DE LA PRÉSENTATION DE L'ARTISTE >

Prochaines manifestations:

Ville	Date	Adresse	Horaires	Invitation
Galerie Art et Lumières - Vannes (56)	01/04/2006 30/07/2006	18 Rue Emile Burgault	De 10 à 12h 30 et de14 h à 18 h du mardi au samedi -vernissage le 20 octobre	cliquez ici

K **Review the PASS CARTE card and answer the following questions.**

1. What does the PASS CARTE help you to do? ____________________
2. In what city can you use this card? ____________________
3. At what special place can a tourist obtain this card? ____________________
4. For how many days is it valid? ____________________

L **Look at the painting and answer the following questions.**

1. Who painted *Le jardin de Mauburon*? ____________________
2. In what year? ____________________

M **Review the clipping for the art gallery and answer the following questions.**

1. What would you see at the *Galerie d'Art*?

____

2. Who is the owner?

____

3. Where is the shop located?

____

4. In what city is it?

____

N **Review the final clipping and answer the following questions.**

1. What is the web address of artist Bernadette Planchenault?

____

2. What are two words that tell you the kind of artist she is?

____

3. What does she like to illustrate? *(En français, s'il te plaît.)*

____

4. What does she like to draw? *(En français, s'il te plaît.)*

____

Symtalk

O **Écris en français le mot ou l'expression qui correspond à chaque image.** ***(In the space, write the correct word or expression in French.)***

 1. ____________	 2. ____________	 3. ____________	 4. ____________
 5. ____________	 6. ____________	 7. ____________	 8. ____________

P **Dis les phrases, puis écris-les.** ***(Say the sentences, then write them.)***

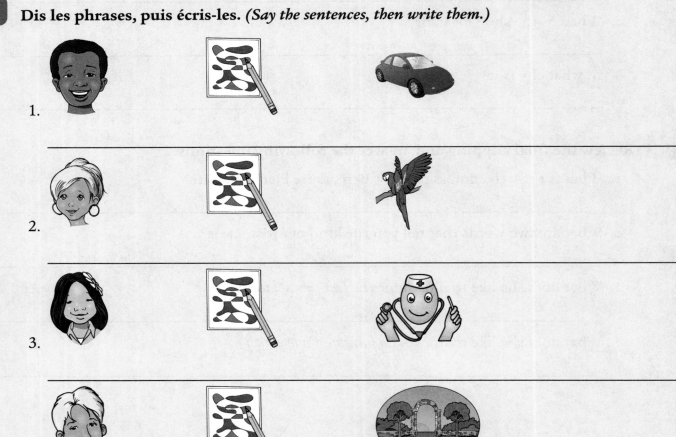

1.   

____

2.   

____

3.   

____

4.   

____

5. 

____

Q **Travaille avec un partenaire. Pose la question ou donne la réponse. Puis, écris le dialogue.** ***(Work with a partner. Ask the question or give the answer. Then, write the dialogue.)***

1. 
est-ce que

______________________ ______________________

2. 
est-ce que

______________________ ______________________

3. 
est-ce que

______________________ ______________________

4. 
est-ce que

______________________ ______________________

Mots croisés

Horizontalement

1. worked for a king, then an emperor
4. traveled to North Africa
7. what Delacroix tried to show
9. what is created out of stone, metal, or wood
10. painted *Moonlight (Clair de lune)*
11. art movement favored by David

Verticalement

2. art movement favored by Manet
3. one of David's interests
5. art movement favored by Delacroix
6. painted *Pyramid (Pyramide)*
8. a painter with modern, Picasso-like style

Unit 11

Le corps et la santé
Body and Health

Vocabulaire

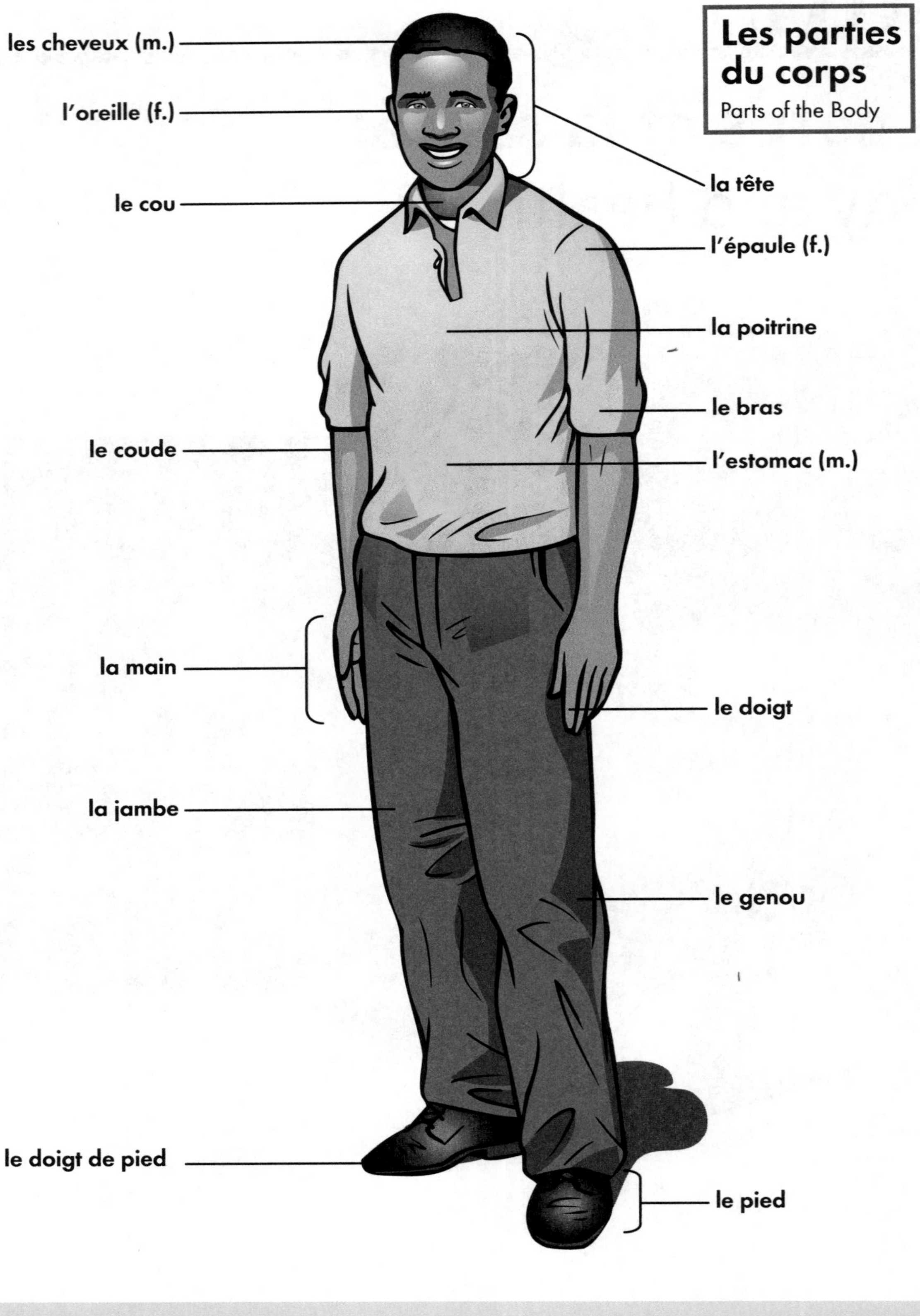

Les parties du corps
Parts of the Body
les cheveux (m.)
l'oreille (f.)
le cou
le coude
la main
la jambe
le doigt de pied
la tête
l'épaule (f.)
la poitrine
le bras
l'estomac (m.)
le doigt
le genou
le pied

La figure
Face

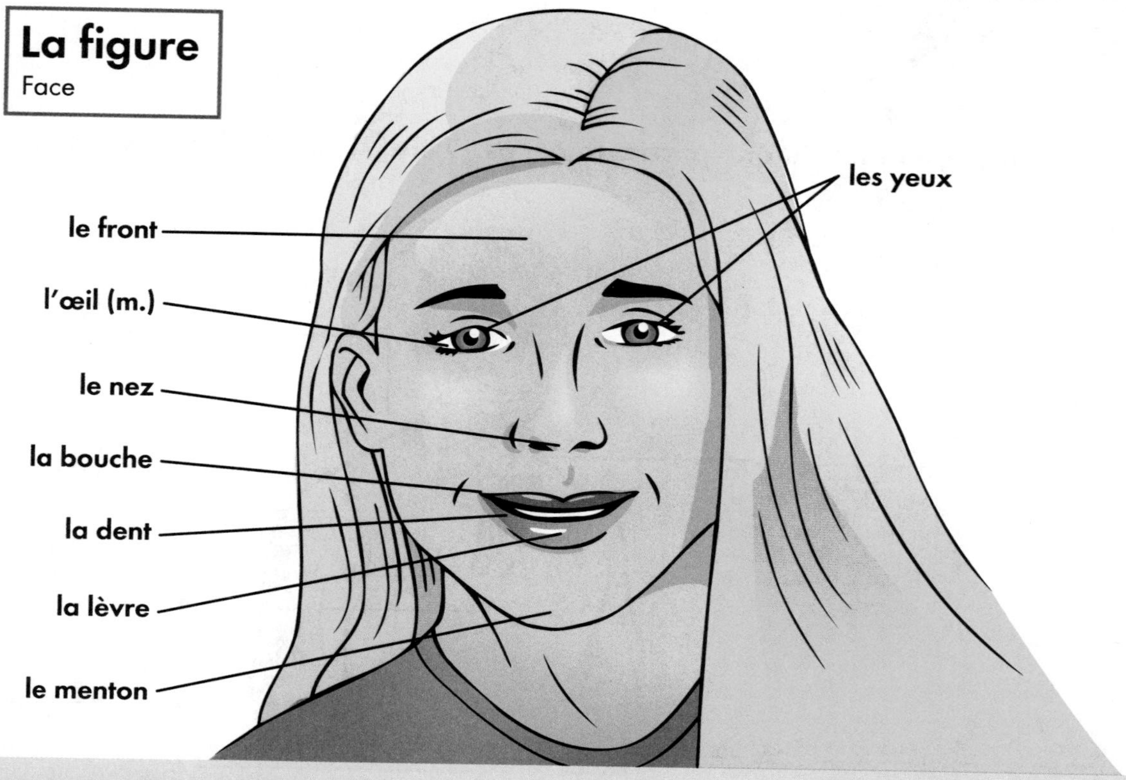
le front
l'œil (m.)
le nez
la bouche
la dent
la lèvre
le menton
les yeux

Vocabulaire Extra!

la santé
health

en bonne santé
healthy

en mauvaise santé
unhealthy

malade
sick, ill

bien
well, fine

triste
sad

heureux/heureuse
happy

PASCAL: **Salut, Fabienne! Comment vas-tu?**
Hi, Fabienne! How are you?

FABIENNE: **Je ne vais pas bien. Je me sens mal.**
I'm not doing well. I feel awful.

SYLVIE: **Tu travailles encore?**
Are you still working?

JEAN-PAUL: **Oui, j'ai une interro demain.**
Yes, I have a test tomorrow.

HALIMA: **Qu'est-ce que tu as?**
What's wrong with you?

AHMED: **J'ai mal à la tête.**
I've got a headache.

CHARLES: **Julie, est-elle malade aujourd'hui?**
Is Julie sick today?

DIDIER: **Oui. Elle a la grippe.**
Yes. She has the flu.

ALI: **Comment est-ce que tu te sens?**
How do you feel?

STÉPHANE: **Je me sens bien.**
I'm feeling well.

JEANNETTE: **Tu es triste, Raymond?**
Are you sad, Raymond?

RAYMOND: **Non. Je suis heureux!**
No. I'm happy!

Use **heureuse** to describe a girl: **Elle est heureuse**.
("She is happy.")
Use **heureux** to describe a boy: **Il est heureux**.
("He is happy.")

Activités

A **Écris le nom pour chaque partie du corps.** ***(Label the parts of the body in French.)***

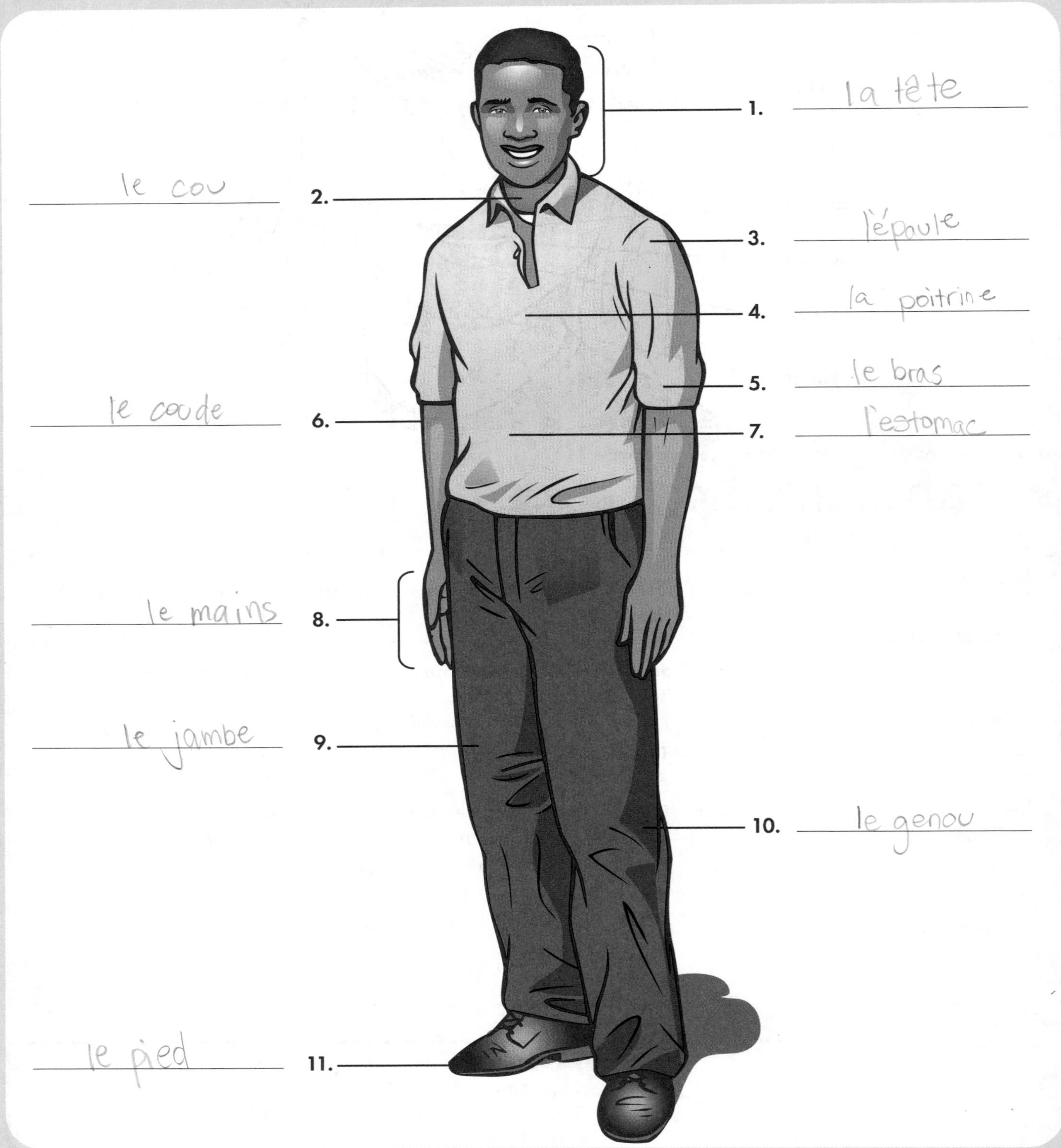
1. la tête
2. le cou
3. l'épaule
4. la poitrine
5. le bras
6. le coude
7. l'estomac
8. le mains
9. le jambe
10. le genou
11. le pied

B Écris le nom pour chaque partie du visage. *(Label the parts of the face in French.)*

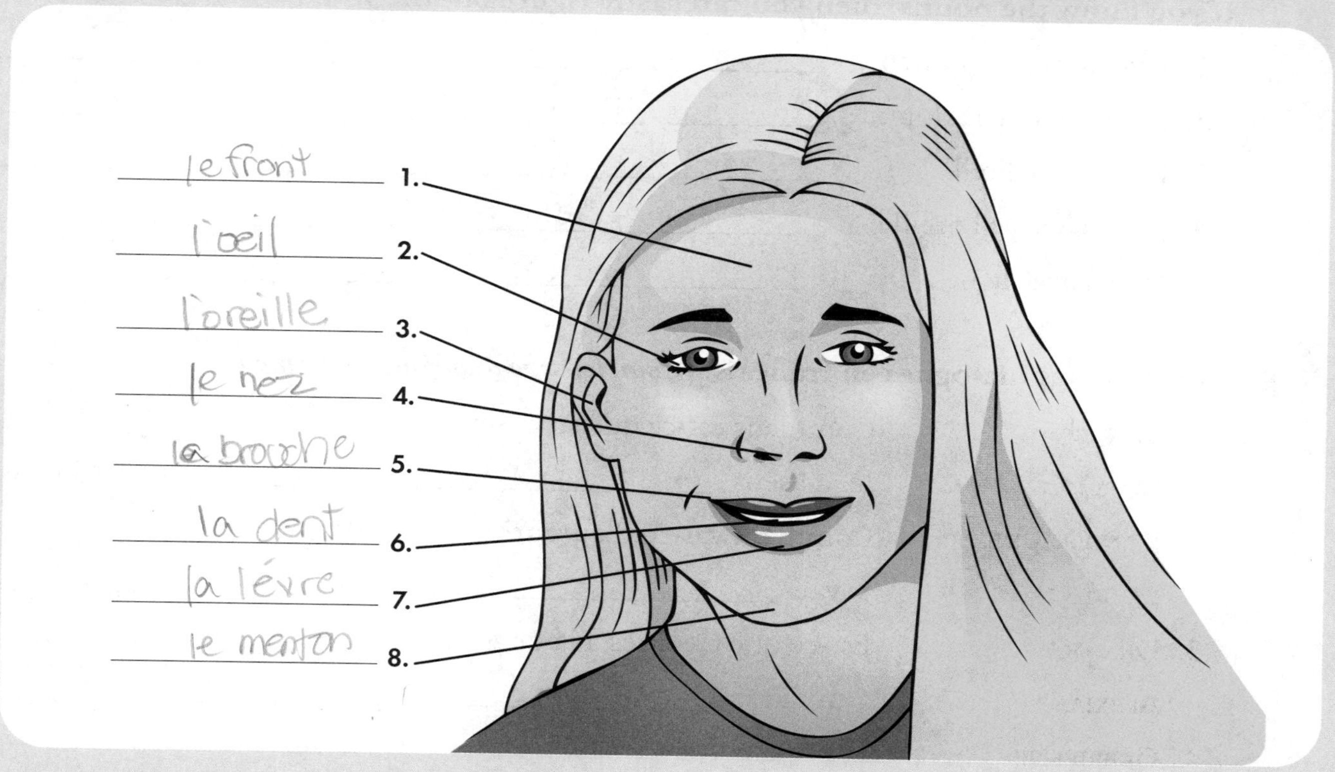
le front 1.
l'oeil 2.
l'oreille 3.
le nez 4.
la brouche 5.
la dent 6.
la lévre 7.
le menton 8.

C Complète les phrases en français. *(Complete each sentence in French.)*

1. We see with our yeux.
2. To speak I open my brouche.
3. An oreille is necessary for hearing.
4. You hold your pen in your main.
5. Your dents are needed to bite and chew food.
6. One pied has five toes.
7. We use the nez to smell a rose.
8. We play the guitar with our doigts.
9. The funny bone is located on the coude.
10. If you eat too much, your estomac will hurt.

D **What do you do with your senses? Guess the meaning of the italicized verbs in context. If you know the nouns, then you can easily figure out the verbs!**

1. Je *parle* avec la bouche. ___say___
2. Je *touche* avec le doigt. ___touche___
3. Je *vois* avec l'œil. ___blink cry___
4. J'*entends* avec l'oreille. ___hear___
5. Je *sens* avec le nez. ___smell___

E **Complète les dialogues en français.** ***(Complete the dialogues in French.)***

1. SYLVIE: Comment est-ce que tu te sens?
   MARC: Je me sens ___mal___. *(bad, awful)*
2. JEAN-CLAUDE: Comment vas-tu, Laurent?
   LAURENT: Je vais ___bien___. *(well)*
3. DIMITRA: Est-ce que Georges a la grippe?
   ALEXIA: Oui. Il est ___malade___. *(sick)*
4. GABRIELLE: Est-ce que tu es triste?
   THÉODORE: Non. Je suis ___heureux___. *(happy)*

F **Name the part of the body associated with each item.** ***En français, s'il te plaît.***

1.  ___les yeux___

2.  ___le nez___

3. les dents

4. la fête

5. le main

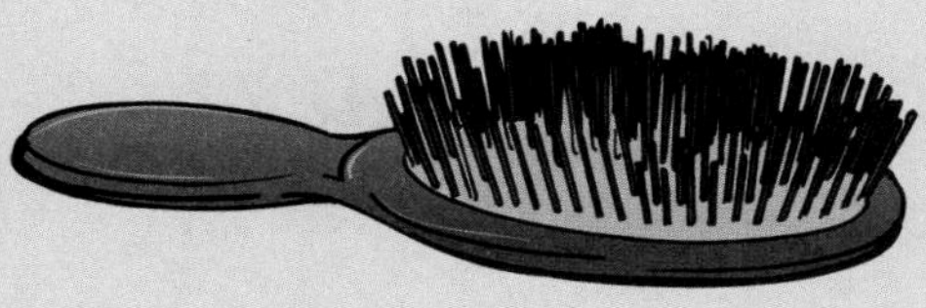

6. le cheveux

7. 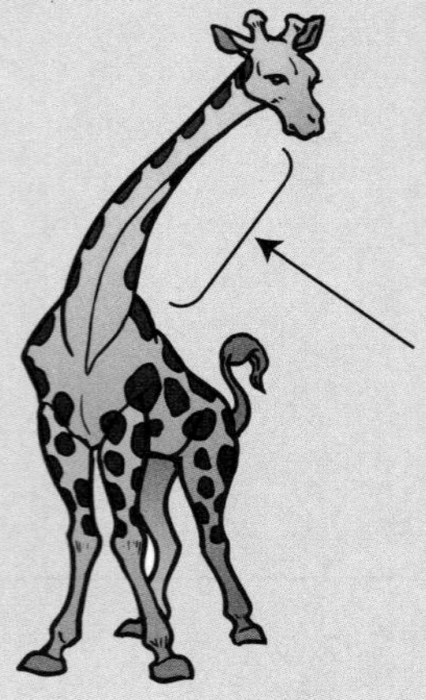

le cou

8. 

la brouche

9. 

l'oreille

10. 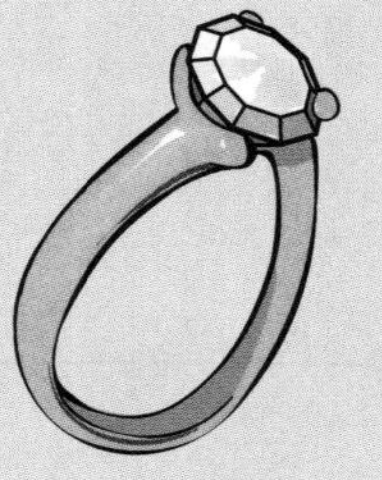

les draigts

G Match each part of the body to the activity associated with it.

A		B	
1. __H__ la main	6. __G__ l'estomac	A. running	F. thinking
2. __A__ le pied	7. __J__ la bouche	B. smelling	G. digesting
3. __E__ les yeux	8. __C__ le bras	C. carrying	H. writing
4. __B__ le nez	9. __F__ la tête	D. listening	I. touching
5. __D__ les oreilles	10. __I__ les doigts	E. seeing	J. speaking

H Lis le paragraphe. Choisis les réponses correctes. *(Read the paragraph. Choose the correct answers.)*

Je m'appelle Pierre. J'ai quatorze ans. Je vais très bien et je suis en bonne santé. *Avec* la tête je *pense*. Avec la bouche je parle français. Avec la main j'écris. Je *marche* au collège avec les jambes et les pieds. Avec les yeux j'admire les peintures de Manet. Avec le nez je *sens* les fleurs du jardin. Avec les dents je mange mon dîner. Le corps est fantastique, n'est-ce pas?

avec	with	**marche**	walk
pense	think	**sens**	smell

1. Pierre est _____.
   - (A.) un garçon
   - B. un homme
   - C. une fille
   - D. une femme

2. Pierre a _____ ans.
   - A. 11
   - B. 9
   - C. 12
   - (D.) 14

3. Pierre parle avec _____.
   - A. la main
   - B. la jambe
   - (C.) la bouche
   - D. l'oreille

4. Avec les jambes Pierre _____.
   - (A.) marche au collège
   - B. écrit à Manet
   - C. admire les peintures de Manet
   - D. sent les fleurs

5. Pierre est _____.
   - A. triste
   - (B.) heureux
   - C. en mauvaise santé
   - D. malade

I **Parlons!** Ask your classmate in French where a part of the body is. Your classmate will point to a part of the body. Take turns until you have identified ten parts of the body.

Modèle: A: Où est le nez? *(Where is the nose?)*
B: Voici le nez. *(Here is the nose.)*

J **C'est à toi!** Find magazine pictures showing people in different states of health. Paste these pictures on a poster and write a caption about each one. For example, under a picture of a sick girl, you could write *Elle est malade.*

Langue vivante!

Musculation EXPRESS

Futuristes, ludiques et terriblement efficaces, ces engins permettent de se tonifier sans trop se faire mal.

4. LE KINÉSIS : LA FLUIDITÉ. Imaginez un mur duquel sortirait un système de câbles et de poulies. De quoi effectuer deux cent cinquante exercices, en accomplissant à chaque fois des gestes naturels et fluides. Debout, assis, allongé sur un ballon, on pratique avec un coach qui surveille constamment votre position. *Infos : Thermes marins de Monte-Carlo, au (00) 377.98.06.69.00 ; Ken Club, à Paris, au 01. 46. 47.41.41 (1 000 € les 5 séances découverte du Club) ; autres lieux au 01.34.58.25.85.*

Votre corps est fait pour bouger !
MOVING

UNE ENFANCE SANS VIOLENCE

lactel
Lait Bio
DEMI-ÉCRÉMÉ
AB
6x1L
(3) Lait bio demi-écrémé U.H.T. LACTEL
6 x 1 L.
Soit le L : 1,08 €
ORIGINE FRANCE
6€48

K Review the clippings and answer the following questions.

1. What do you suppose *musculation* means?

   Muscle Excersize

2. A certain fitness training program uses a system of cables and pulleys. How many exercises are possible using this equipment?

   Deux cent cinquante

3. What two parts of the body can be toned with this program? *(En français, s'il te plaît.)*

   le kinésis et la fluidité

4. What are two places where you can get more information about the equipment?

   Monte Carlo et Ken Club à Paris

5. Find and write down the French words that say "Your body is made to move."

   Votre corps est fait pour bouger

6. Do the people in the picture appear to be *en mauvaise santé* or *en bonne santé*?

   en bonne santé

7. What do healthy people like to do? Use a French verb.

   bouger

8. Find the French words that describe a healthy childhood.

   une enfance sans violence

9. What do you suppose *sans* means?

   Feel/nose

10. What is the price of *lait*?

    € 48

Proverbe

"Il faut tourner la langue sept fois dans la bouche avant de parler.
Think before you speak."

Symtalk

= est

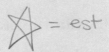

L **Écris en français le mot ou l'expression qui correspond à chaque image.** ***(In the space, write the correct word or expression in French.)***

1. content(e) / heureux/heureuse

2. triste

3. malade

4. fatigué/fatiguée

5. fâché/fachée

6. comment

7. Il/elle

M **Dis les phrases, puis écris-les en français.** ***(Say the sentences, then write them in French.)***

1. Brigitte est malade

2. Alain est fatigué

3. Hiko est triste

4. Sylvie est heureuse

5. 

Antoine est faché

N

Travaille avec un partenaire. Pose la question ou donne la réponse. Puis, écris le dialogue. ***(Work with a partner. Ask the question or give the answer. Then, write the dialogue.)***

1. 

comment est Bob ? — Il est heureux

2. 

Comment est Sarah ? — Elle est fatiguée

3. 

comment est Margaux ? — Elle est heureuse

4. 

Comment est Richard ? — Il est malade

Mots croisés

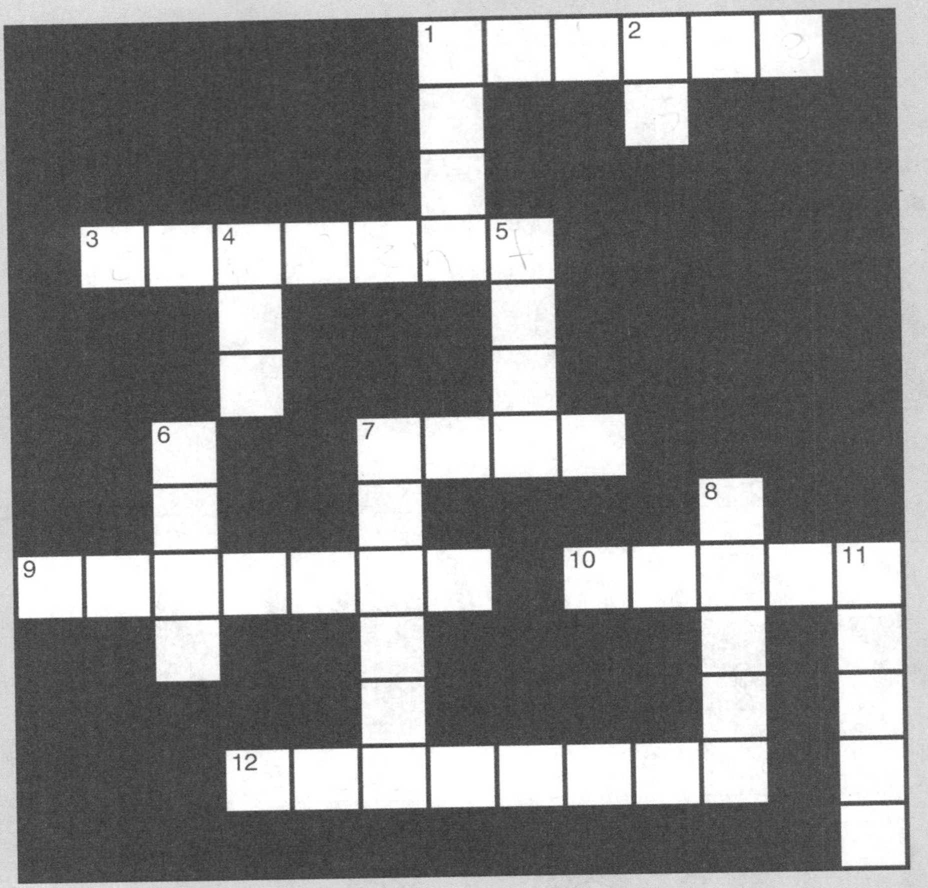

Horizontalement

1. Pascal ne va pas bien. Il est ____.
3. ____ vas-tu?
7. Je suis heureuse. Je vais ____.
9. Alain n'est pas triste. Il est ____.
10. On marche au tableau avec les ____.
12. On écoute avec les ____.

Verticalement

1. On écrit avec la ____.
2. Qu'est-ce qu tu ____?
4. Je me sens ____. Je suis malade.
5. J'ai mal à la ____.
6. On *(People)* voit *(see)* avec les ____.
7. On parle avec la ____.
8. On mange avec les ____.
11. La ____ est très importante.

Unit 12

Les vêtements — Clothing

Vocabulaire

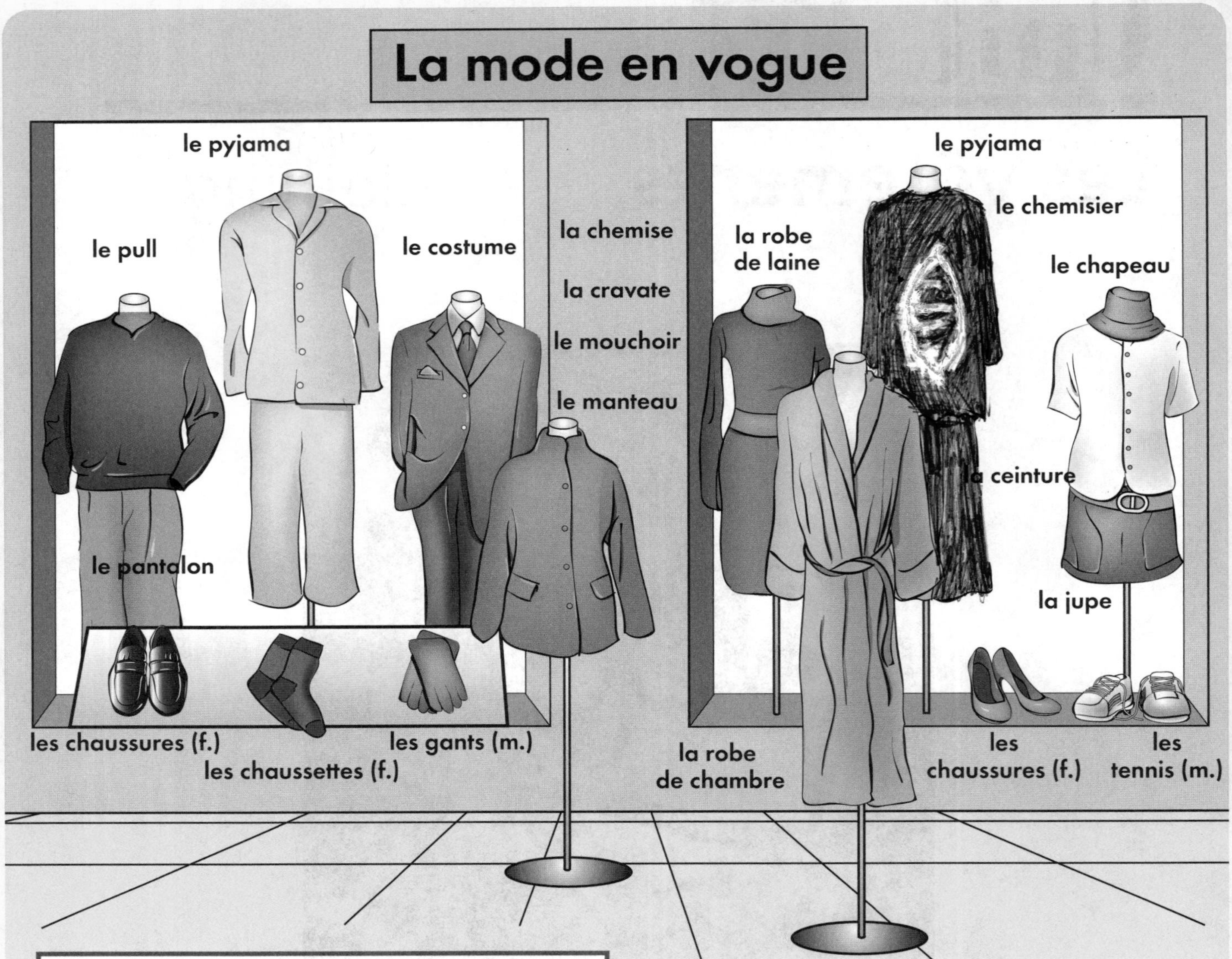
La mode en vogue
le pyjama
le pull
le costume
la chemise
la cravate
le mouchoir
le manteau
le pantalon
les chaussures (f.)
les chaussettes (f.)
les gants (m.)
la robe de laine
le pyjama
le chemisier
le chapeau
la ceinture
la jupe
la robe de chambre
les chaussures (f.)
les tennis (m.)

RENÉ: **Que portes-tu?**
What are you wearing?

PHILIPPE: **Je porte mon nouveau costume.**
I'm wearing my new suit.

RENÉ: **Pourquoi?**
Why?

PHILIPPE: **Parce que ce soir je vais à un concert.**
Because this evening I'm going to a concert.

ALEX: **Je vais dans le jardin.**
I'm going out to the yard.

MARIANNE: **Attends-moi. J'y vais avec toi. Mais d'abord je vais chercher mon blouson.**
Wait for me. I'm going with you. But first I'm going to get my jacket.

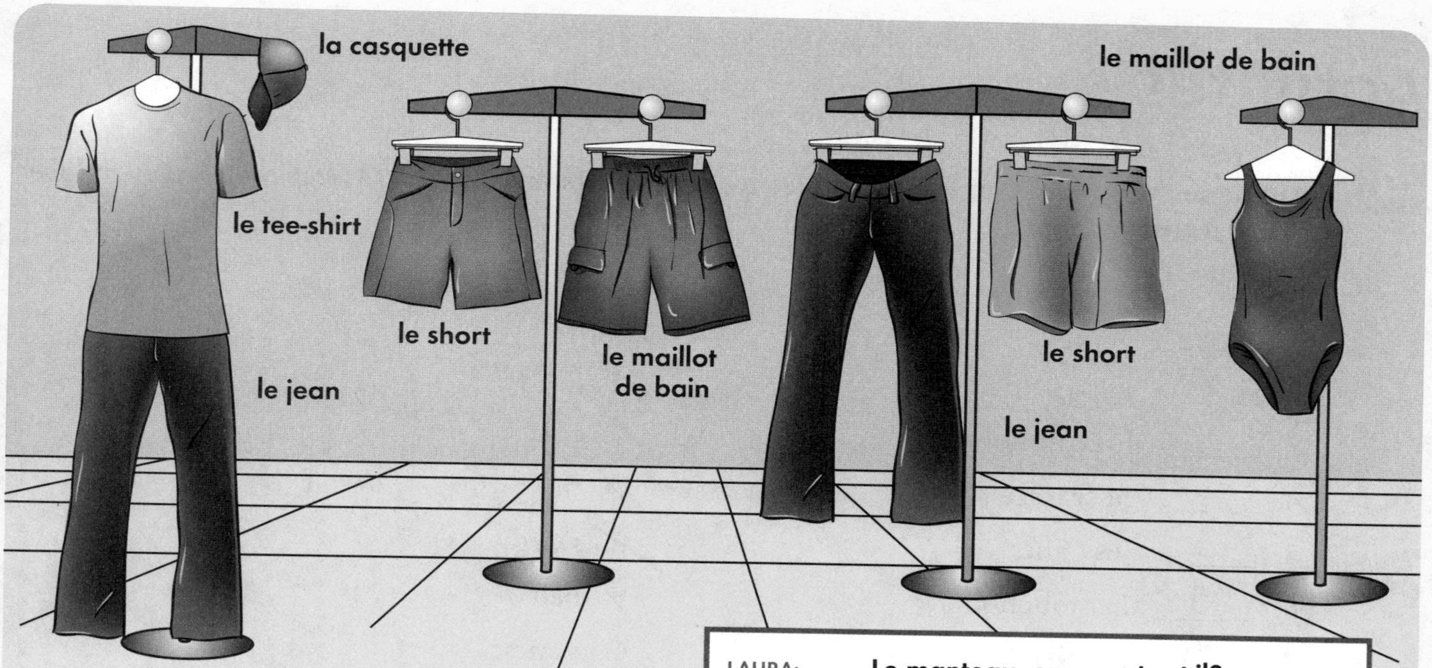
la casquette
le maillot de bain
le tee-shirt
le short
le maillot
de bain
le short
le jean
le jean

Monique

Vacances d'hiver
Winter vacation

la Suisse - janvier
Switzerland - January

2 robes de laine
3 chapeaux
1 pyjama
2 ceintures
1 blouson
1 pull
3 pantalons
3 chemisiers
1 jupe
manteau
chaussettes
chaussures
gants

LAURA: **Le manteau, comment est-il?**
How's the coat?

ANGÉLIQUE: **Il est beau!**
It's beautiful!

ANTOINE: **Qu'est-ce que tu fais, Monique?**
What are you doing, Monique?

MONIQUE: **Je fais ma valise.**
I'm packing my suitcase.

ANTOINE: **Pourquoi?**
Why?

MONIQUE: **Parce que je voyage bientôt en Suisse.**
Because I'm traveling to Switzerland soon.

ANTOINE: **N'oublie pas ta combinaison de ski!**
Don't forget your ski outfit!

Use **belle** to describe a word that begins with **la** or **une**.
La cravate est belle. *(The tie is beautiful.)*

Use **beau** to describe a word that begins with **le** or **un**.
Le manteau est beau. *(The coat is beautiful.)*

porter = to wear **Luc porte un beau manteau. Luc porte une belle cravate**.

Activités

A

Associe les vêtements en français avec les vêtements en anglais. ***(Match the French and the English words.)***

A		B
1. E	la jupe	A. handkerchief
2. F	la ceinture	B. jacket
3. G	le pantalon	C. coat
4. D	la cravate	D. tie
5. I	les gants	E. skirt
6. A	le mouchoir	F. belt
7. J	la robe de chambre	G. pants
8. C	le manteau	H. shoes
9. H	les chaussures	I. gloves
10. B	le blouson	J. bathrobe
11. L	le maillot de bain	K. baseball cap
12. K	la casquette	L. bathing suit

B

Que portes-tu? ***(What do you wear. . .)***

1. to school?

   le tee-shirt, la jupe et les tennis

2. to a symphony concert?

   la robe

3. to bed?

   le pyjama

4. in cool weather?

   ~~le jean~~ le short

5. in cold weather?

   le manteau, l'écharpe

C Complete the analogies.

1 gants: mains = tennis: pieds
2. tee-shirt: jupe = chemise: pantalon
3. robe de chambre: pyjama = manteau: ____________
4. cravate: chemise = cénture: pantalon

D Complète chaque phrase logiquement. *(Complete each sentence logically, based on the drawing.)*

1. Élodie porte la robe ____________.

2. Raphaël porte la costume ____________.

3. Je porte la robe de chambre ____________.

4. Chloé porte la jupe
et le chemise.

5. René porte le tee-shirt
et la cravate.

E **Écris les mots et les phrases en anglais.** ***(Write the words and phrases in English.)***

1. porter: to wear
2. il/elle porte: she/he wears
3. je porte: I wear
4. tu portes: you wear
5. mon nouveau chapeau: my new hat
6. J'y vais avec Jean.: I go there with Jean
7. Je vais chercher ma casquette.: I'm looking for a baseball hat
8. Le maillot de bain, comment est-il?: How's the bathing suit?
9. La robe est belle.: The dress is pretty
10. N'oublie pas ton chapeau!: Don't forget your hat

F Fill in the blanks with examples of the appropriate clothing according to the heading.

outdoor clothing

1. le chapeau
2. la robe
3. le short
4. le pantalon

accessories

5. les gants
6. le chapeau
7. les casquette

footwear

8. les chaussures th
9. les tennis
10. les chaussettes

sleepwear

11. le pyjama

G Choisis la réponse la plus logique pour compléter chaque phrase. *(Choose the most logical answer to complete each sentence.)*

1. Je fais __A__.
   A. ma valise
   B. "La Mode en vogue"
   C. mon jardín
   D. les vacances

2. Tu portes __D__.
   A. un mouchoir
   B. la santé
   C. la salle de classe
   D. une jupe et un chemisier

3. N'oublie pas __B__. *(Don't forget. . . .)*
   A. le jardin
   B. les gants
   C. la Suisse
   D. la soupe à l'oignon

4. Je vais chercher un blouson parce que __C__.
   A. j'ai faim
   B. je vais à la piscine
   C. je vais dans le jardin
   D. j'ouvre le livre

5. Je porte un nouveau costume parce que __C__.
   A. je voyage en Suisse
   B. j'ai un beau pyjama
   C. je vais ce soir à un concert
   D. je fais ma valise

6. Le manteau, comment est-il?
   A. Nouvelle.
   B. Bientôt.
   C. Ce soir.
   D. Beau.

H Lis le paragraphe, et choisis les bonnes réponses. *(Read the paragraph, and select the correct answers.)*

Monique *va en vacances* bientôt avec sa famille. Elle voyage à Berne, la capitale de la Suisse. Elle fait sa valise. Elle *emporte seulement* les vêtements *d'hiver*. Elle choisit deux pantalons, deux pulls, une robe, une jupe, un chemisier, et un blouson. Elle a déja *tous* les vêtements nécessaires pour *ses* vacances en Suisse. Monique est heureuse.

va en vacances	goes on vacation
emporte seulement	she takes only
d'hiver	of winter
tous	all
ses	her

1. Qui va en vacances?
   A. vacances
   B. Berne
   C. Suisse
   D. Monique

2. Qu'est ce qu'il y a dans la valise? *(What is there. . .?)*
   A. la Suisse
   B. la famille
   C. les vacances
   D. les vêtements d'hiver

3. Combien de pantalons emporte Monique?
   A. 4
   B. 3
   C. 2
   D. 1

4. Monique, emporte-elle une robe dans sa valise? *(Monique, does she take along. . .?)*
   A. Oui, elle emporte une robe.
   B. Non, elle emporte deux robes.
   C. Non, elle emporte trois robes.
   D. Non, elle emporte quatre robes.

I In your opinion, what other articles of clothing should Monique take along for the cold winter days of January in Switzerland? Answer in French.

____

____

____

____

____

____

J **Parlons!** Ask your speaking partner *Que portes-tu aujourd'hui?* He/she should begin a response with *Je porte. . .* and then name several articles of clothing. Then reverse roles.

K **C'est à toi!** Your partner will choose a category of clothing, such as indoor casual clothes, outdoor cold weather clothes, bedtime clothes, accessories, and clothes for special occasions. If you can correctly name all the items in that category in twenty seconds, give yourself a gold star. If you can't, or if the clock beats you, your partner takes over. This time, you select a category, and he/she will answer. Continue until all the categories are covered. The person with more gold stars wins.

Proverbe

"**L'habit ne fait pas le moine.**

Don't judge a book by its cover."

Langue vivante!

Mode et accessoires

Top Catégories

Vêtements d'extérieur pour enfants

Chemises - Hommes

Robes - Femmes

Sacs à main / Fourre-tout

Chaussures - Femmes

Kickers

Rentrée haute en couleurs chez **Kickers** qui vous dévoile sa nouvelle collection : une palette de 250 modèles de coloris. Des chaussures de qualité, doublées en chèvre et semelles cousues. Une finition irréprochable du 18 au 45.

Partez du bon pied...

Depuis quatre saisons, Martine Douvier expose ses collections au salon « The Train ». (DR.)

VÊTEMENTS-OCCASION

Référence A319.35

A vendre 1 paire de tennis PUMA femme de couleur bleu et noir, pointure 39. Valeur d'achat : 65 €. Prix : 35 €. Tennis de moins de 6 mois.

Localisation Île-de-France 75 France

Référence A352.69

Vends:
-combinaison de ski, Etirel, 16ans, bleu rouge jaune: 25 €
-coupe vent, 12 Nas rose vert violet: 5 €
-bottes après ski Bmenche, 35-37: 15 €
-bottes après ski, Patrick, rose, 38: 20 €
-pantalon de ski, Quiksilver, noir, S: 20 €
-Anorak de ski, Quiksilver, noir, L: 20 €
Prix négociables!

Localisation Doubs- Franche-Comté France

L **Review the clippings and answer the following questions.**

1. What is the name of the shoe brand advertised in the middle?

____

2. How many colored models of shoes does this brand make?

____

3. What sizes do the shoes come in?

____

4. Translate: *Ma pointure est quarante.*

____

5. For how many seasons has Mme Douvier been selling her clothing collection at the fashion show "The Train" in New York City? *(En français, s'il te plaît.)*

____

6. What article of clothing is Mme Douvier holding? *(En français, s'il te plaît.)*

____

7. Name the three available colors of the men's sports shirt. *(En français, s'il te plaît.)*

____

8. Can you find the French word for "fashion"?

____

9. Who can wear the sports jacket with the number 89 on it?

____

10. *Vêtements-occasion* means "second-hand clothing."

    a) Ad # A319.35: What size are the shoes?

    ____

    b) Ad # A352.69: What kinds of things are being sold?

    ____

Symtalk

M **Écris en français le mot ou l'expression qui correspond à chaque image.** ***(In the space, write the correct word or expression in French.)***

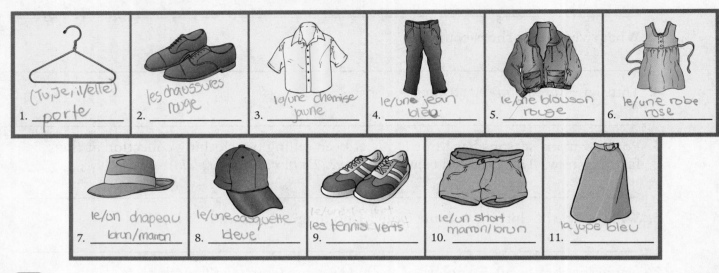

(Tu, Je, il/elle)
1. porte

2. les chaussures rouge

3. le/une chemise jaune

4. le/une jean bleu

5. le/une blouson rouge

6. le/une robe rose

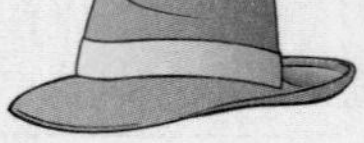
7. le/un chapeau brun/marron

8. le/une casquette bleue

9. les tennis verts

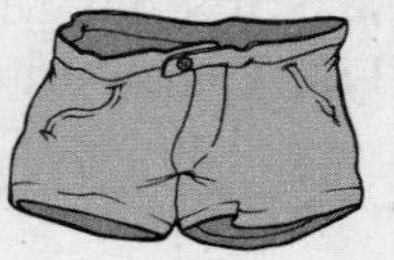
10. le/un short marron/brun

11. la jupe bleu

N **Dis les phrases, puis écris-les en français.** ***(Say the sentences, then write them in French.)***

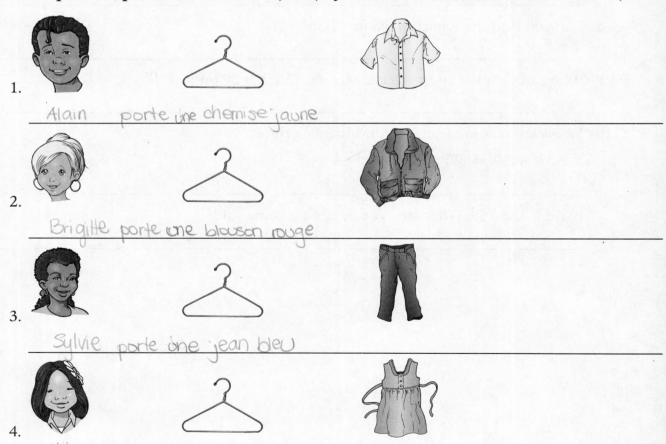

1.   

Alain porte une chemise jaune

2.   

Brigitte porte une blouson rouge

3.  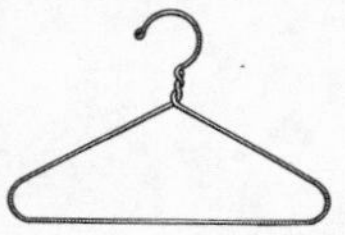 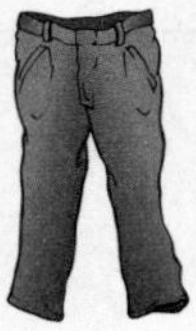

Sylvie porte une jean bleu

4.  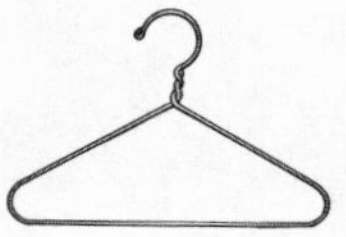 

Hiko porte une robe rose

5. Antoine porte les chassures rouge

O **Travaille avec un partenaire. Pose la question ou donne la réponse. Puis, écris le dialogue.** ***(Work with a partner. Ask the question or give the answer. Then, write the dialogue.)***

1. 
est-ce que
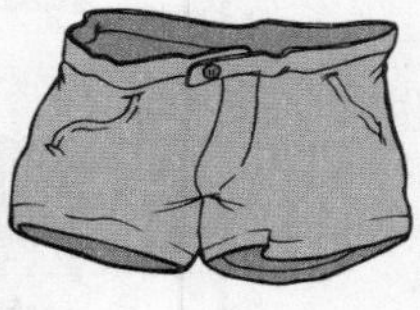

Est-ce que Alain porte une jean bleu? Non, il porte une short marron.

2. 
est-ce que
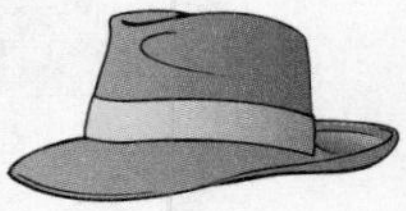

Est-ce que Antoine porte une casquette bleue? Non, il porte un chapeau brun.

3. 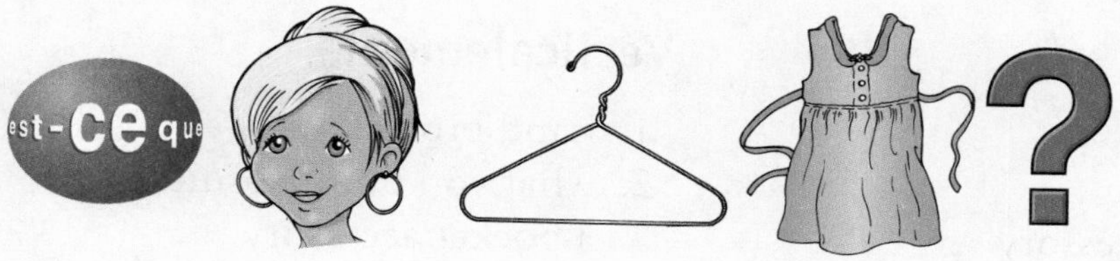
est-ce que

Est-ce que Brigitte porte une robe rose? Non, elle porte une jupe bleu.

4. 
est-ce que

Est-ce que Hiko porte les chassures rouge? Non, elle porte les tennis verts.

Mots croisés

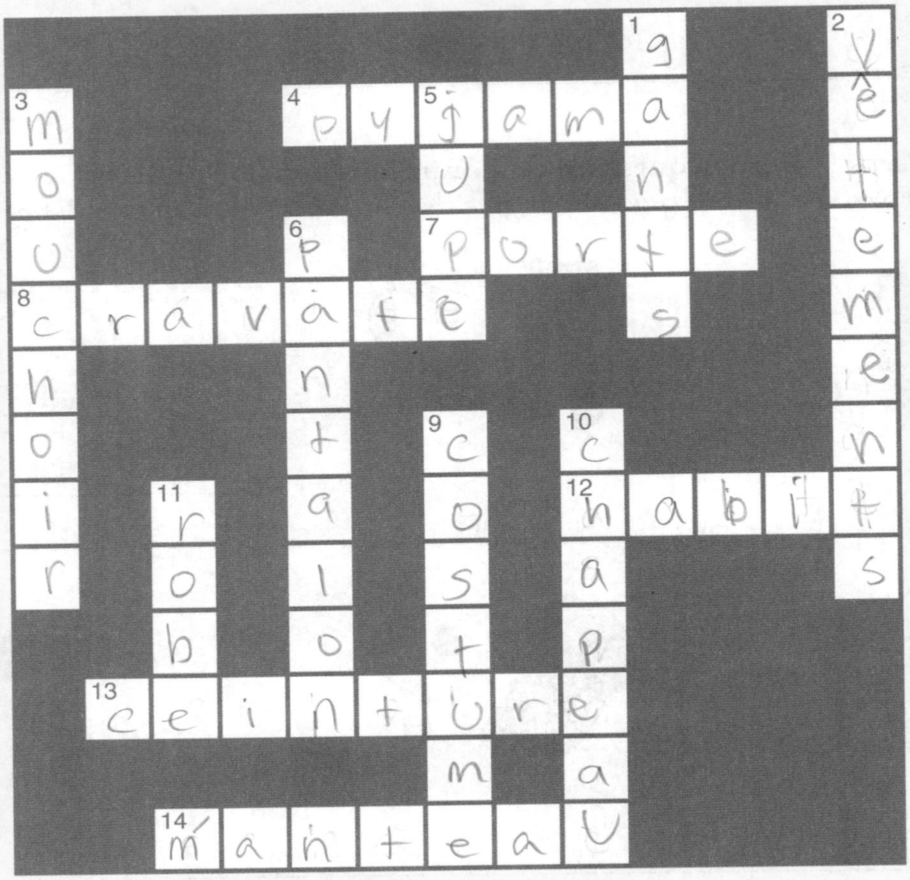
1 gants
2 vêtements
3 mouchoir
4 pyjama
5 jupe
6 pantalon
7 porte
8 cravate
9 costume
10 chapeau
11 robe
12 habits
13 ceinture
14 manteau

Horizontalement

4. clothes for sleeping
7. *Je _____ un chemisier.*
8. boy's formal shirt accessory
12. *L'_____ ne fait pas le moine.*
13. secures pants/trousers
14. outdoor garment for cold weather

Verticalement

1. hand protectors
2. what you put in a suitcase
3. a pocket accessory
5. usually worn with a blouse
6. pair of pants or trousers
9. man's matching pants, jacket, and vest
10. headgear
11. dressy garment for a girl

Unit 13

L'heure et les couleurs
Time and Colors

Vocabulaire

Quelle heure est-il?

What time is it?

Il est une heure et demie.

Il est trois heures.

Il est dix heures moins le quart.

Il est midi.

À quelle heure. . . ?

At what time. . . ?

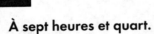

À deux heures cinq.

À sept heures et quart.

À midi moins cinq.

À minuit.

Transportation in Europe operates on the 24-hour clock. Official time is also used by school, radio and television stations, theaters, and cinemas. (Keep on counting after 12 noon: 13h00 = 1 P.M. etc., until 24h00 = 12 midnight.)

l'heure = literally, the hour; **les heures** = the hours

To differentiate between A.M. and P.M., use the phrase **du matin** (in the morning) for A.M. and de **l'après-midi** (in the afternoon) or **du soir** (in the evening) for P.M.
Il est dix heures du matin = 10 A.M. versus **Il est dix heures du soir** = 10 P.M.

De quelle couleur est. . . ?
What color is. . . ?

Il/Elle est. . .
It is. . . .

De quelle(s) couleur(s) sont. . . ?
What color(s) are. . . ?

Ils/Elles sont. . . .
They are. . . .

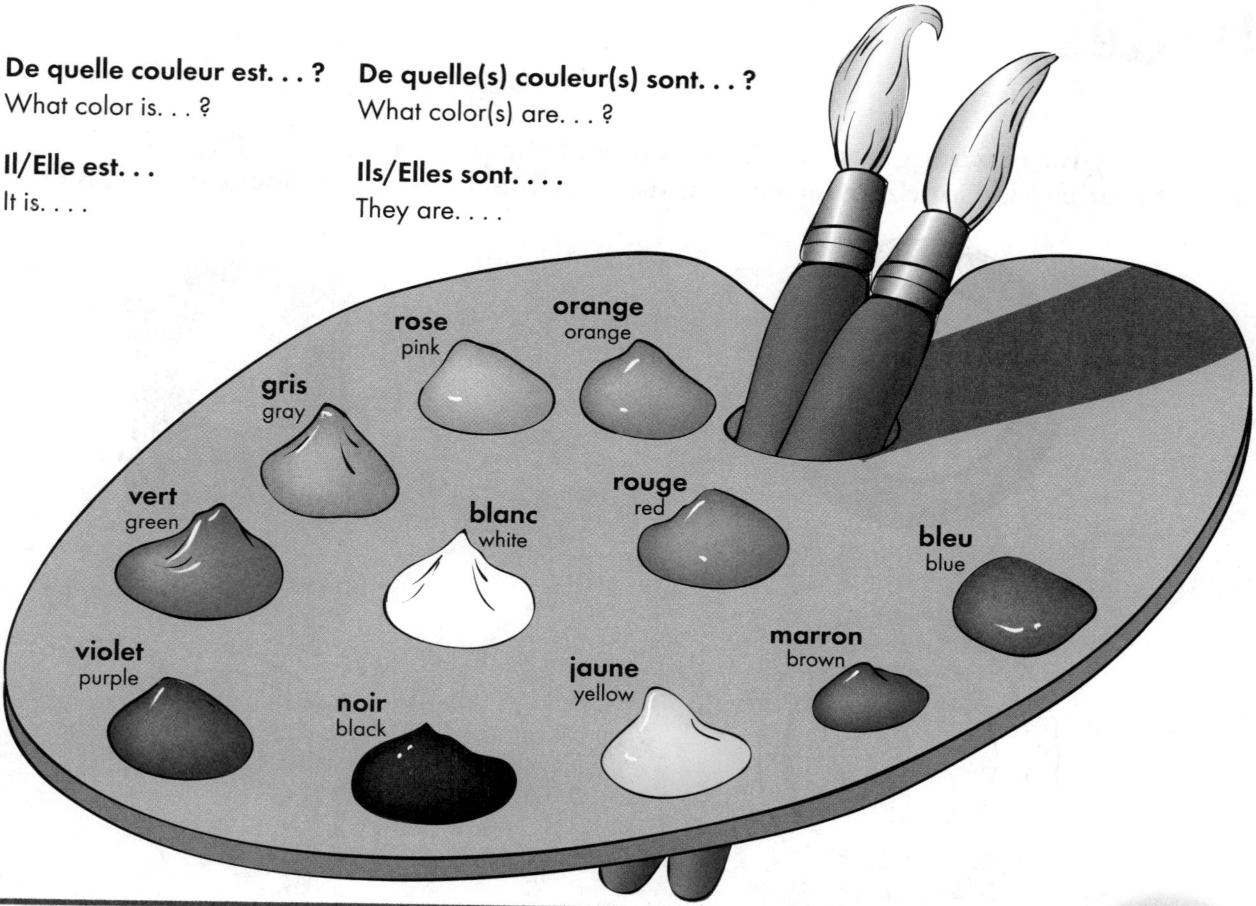

rose
pink
orange
orange
gris
gray
vert
green
blanc
white
rouge
red
bleu
blue
violet
purple
noir
black
jaune
yellow
marron
brown

Some of these adjectives require spelling changes when they are used to describe feminine nouns. Look at the different forms of each color:

Masculine	**Feminine**
Le manteau est **gris**.	La robe est **grise**.
Le chapeau est **vert**.	La cravate est **verte**.
Le chemisier est **violet**.	La chemise est **violette**.
Le blouson est **noir**.	La jupe est **noire**.
Le mouchoir est **blanc**.	La robe de chambre est **blanche**.
Le pantalon est **bleu**.	La chaussure est **bleue**.

An adjective ending in -**e** does not change when describing a masculine or a feminine noun.

Le manteau est **rouge**. La ceinture est **rouge**.

Add an -**s** to an adjective to make it describe a plural noun.

Les chapeaux sont **verts**. Les robes sont **vertes**.

An adjective ending in -**s**, (as in **gris**) does not change in the plural. The colors **orange** and **marron** do not change either.

Le costume est **gris**.
Les costumes sont **gris**.
Les robes sont **orange**.

CHRISTINE: **De quelle couleur est l'herbe (*grass*)?**
CLAUDE: **Il est vert.**

LAURENT: **De quelle couleur sont les tomates?**
GISÈLE: **Elles sont rouges.**

Activités

A **Listen as your teacher gives the time on one of the pictured clocks. Place an "A" to the left of that clock. Continue lettering until the time on all eight clocks has been given.**

1. ______

5. ______

2. ______

6. ______

3. ______

7. ______

4. ______

8. ______

B Complète les phrases en français. *(Complete the sentences in French.)*

1. Pink is called ______________________.
2. A bluebird or robin's egg is ______________________.
3. A piece of chocolate is ______________________.
4. A lemon is ______________________.
5. A leaf in the summer is ______________________.
6. A typical ant is ______________________.
7. A Florida fruit is ______________________.
8. The sky on a very cloudy or overcast day appears ______________________.
9. A marshmallow is ______________________.
10. The color of a strawberry is ______________________.

C Écris en français. *(Write in French.)*

1. at seven o'clock ______________________
2. It's half past one. ______________________
3. at 8:10 ______________________
4. It's 2:40. ______________________
5. at twenty after three ______________________

D Les objets, de quelle couleur sont-ils? *(What color are the objects? Match the items in column A with the colors in column B.)*

A | **B**

1. D

A. jaune

2. E

B. gris

3. A

C. bleu

4. B

D. rouge

5. C

E. vert

E **Réponds avec *oui* ou *non*. *(Answer with "yes" or "no.")***

1. Le gazon, est-il vert? ______________________
2. Les tomates, sont-elles bleues? ______________________
3. L'éléphant, est-il jaune? ______________________
4. Les bananes, sont-elles orange? ______________________
5. La pomme, est-elle rouge? ______________________

F **Lis le paragraphe, puis encercle les bonnes réponses. *(Read the paragraph, then circle the correct answers.)***

Christophe *va au cinéma avec son amie* Valérie. Le film *commence* à huit heures du soir. Christophe va porter son nouveau costume bleu, une chemise blanche, et une cravate rouge. Valérie va porter son chemisier jaune avec des chaussettes jaunes, et une nouvelle jupe verte. Les deux portent des chaussures noires. Il est *maintenant* sept heures et quart et Christophe va à la maison de Valérie.

va	is going
au cinéma	to the movies
avec son amie	with his friend
commence	starts
maintenant	now

1. Qui est l'amie de Christophe?
   A. sa mère
   B. Alain
   C. sa sœur
   D. Valérie

2. Christophe et Valérie, où vont-ils?
   (. . .where are they going?)
   A à la campagne
   B. au restaurant
   C. au cinéma
   D. au parc

3. De quelle couleur est la cravate de Christophe?
   A. verte
   B. rouge
   C. bleue
   D. blanche

4. De quelle couleur sont les chaussettes de Valérie?
   A. jaunes
   B. brunes
   C. noires
   D. grises

5. Christophe, à quelle heure va-t-il à la maison de Valérie?
   A. à 7h15 du soir
   B. à 6h45 du soir
   C. à 6h30 du soir
   D. à 8h00 du soir

6. À quelle heure commence le film?
   A. à sept heures
   B. à sept heures et quart
   C. à huit heures
   D. à huit heures et demie

G **Color the clock according to the directions.**

Il est 9h00.
12
1
2
3
4
5
6
7
8
9
10
11

1. le nez: jaune
2. les yeux: bleus
3. les cheveux: verts
4. la figure: orange
5. la bouche: marron
6. les pieds: gris
7. le chiffre *(numeral)* quatre: noir
8. le chiffre six: violet
9. le chiffre trois: rouge
10. la lettre "i": blanche
11. la lettre "h": rose
12. la lettre "e": noire

H **Parlons! Ask your speaking partner at what time certain events or activities take place by saying *"À quelle heure est. . .?"* Your partner will respond with a logical time during the day or at night. Here is a list of some events or activities you might include:**

le cours de maths | **le concert de rock**
le pique-nique | **le cours de français**

I **Les salutations. Your speaking partner will give you six times of day in French. In response to each, give an appropriate greeting: *Bonjour, Bonsoir,* or *Bonne nuit.* When you have finished, reverse roles.**

J **C'est à toi! Select a quizmaster from the students in your class. He or she will walk around the classroom and point to certain objects and ask, *"De quelle couleur est-il?" "De quelle couleur est-elle?"* The quizmaster calls on a classmate, who responds *"Il est. . . ." or "Elle est. . . ."***

Proverbe

"Mieux vaut tard que jamais.
Better late than never."

Langue vivante!

Les horaires du magasin
de 8h30 à 20h00
tous les jours sauf dimanche

30

Pochette
30 feutres.

COCOTTE EN FONTE
Ovale 33 cm.
Vert, marron ou bleu.

Liberté • Égalité • Fraternité
RÉPUBLIQUE FRANÇAISE

3 ROSIERS
3 COULEURS
OFFRE

LOT DE 3 ROSIERS BUISSON,
Catégorie II
3 couleurs.

NOE 2 FEMME
Livrée avec 2 bracelets, un jaune et et un noir.

UN DES PLUS GRANDS
DESIGNS DE CE SIÈCLE.
ET CERTAINEMENT DU PROCHAIN.

AP
AUDEMARS PIGUET
Le maître de l'horlogerie.

Audemars Piguet Noga Hilton, tél.: (022) 731 83 87
68, rue du Rhône, Genève, tél.: (022) 311 55 00

K **Look at the clippings and answer the following questions.**

1. The information shown with the small clock tells you when the store is open. What are the regular shopping hours? ______________________
2. *Il y a combien de feutres dans la pochette?* ______________________
3. *Une cocotte en fonte* is a cast-iron casserole, that is, a heavy duty cooking pot. Is it available (*disponible*) *en rouge*? ______________________
4. *Le drapeau français* consists of three colors.
   a. *De quelle couleur est l'égalité?* ______________
   b. *De quelle couleur est la fraternité?* ______________
   c. *De quelle couleur est la liberté?* ______________
5. What is a florist shop offering? ______________________
6. What three colors does the product have? *(En français, s'il te plaît.)* ______________________
7. The style of the woman's *montre* is called *Noe 2*. What is a *montre*? ______________________
8. Two *bracelets* are available with this *montre*. What are *bracelets*, as used in this context? ______________________
9. *AP Audemars Piquet* is a well-known *horlogerie*. What is that? ______________________
10. Where is it located? ______________________

Symtalk

L **Écris la couleur en français.** ***(On the blank, write the correct word in French.)***

1. rouge	2. rose	3. jaune	4. bleu	5. vert

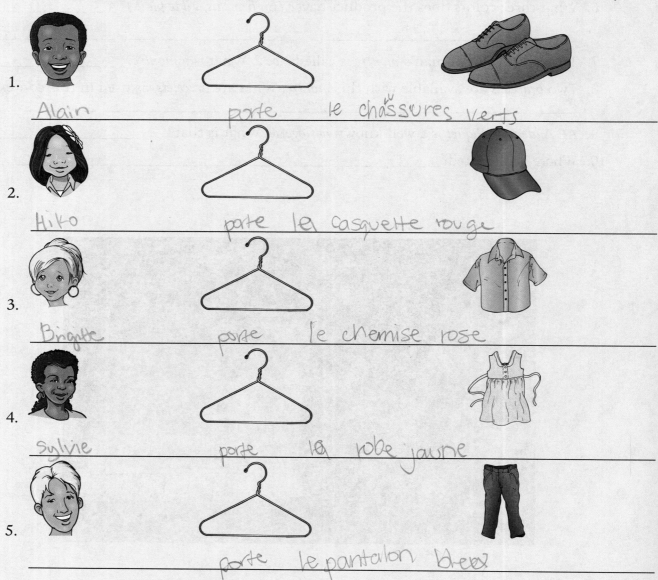

M **Dis les phrases, puis écris-les en français.** ***(Say the sentences, then write them in French.)***

1. 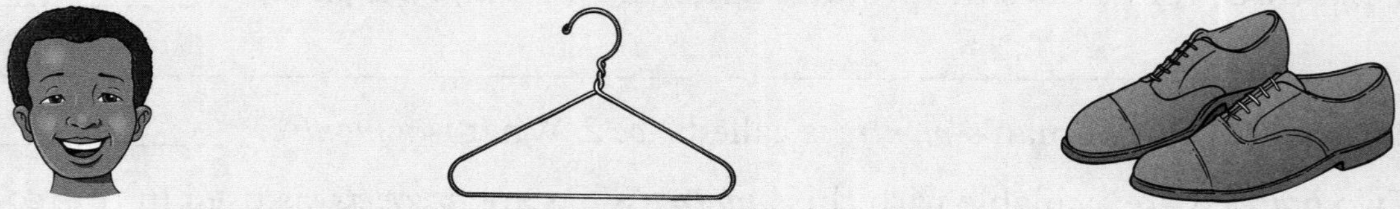

Alain porte le chaussures verts

2. 

Hiko porte la casquette rouge

3. 

Brigitte porte le chemise rose

4. 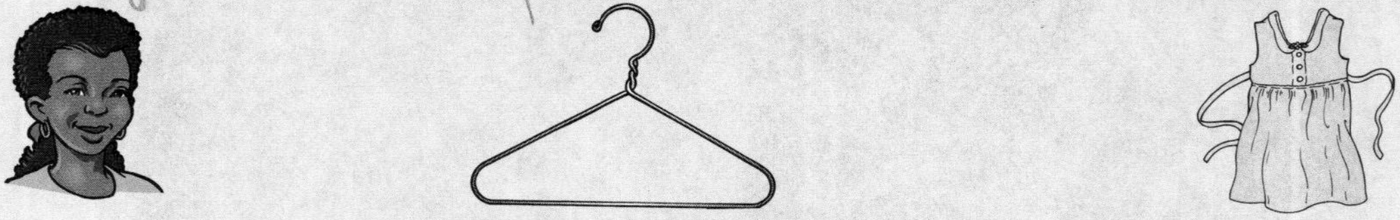

Sylvie porte la robe jaune

5. 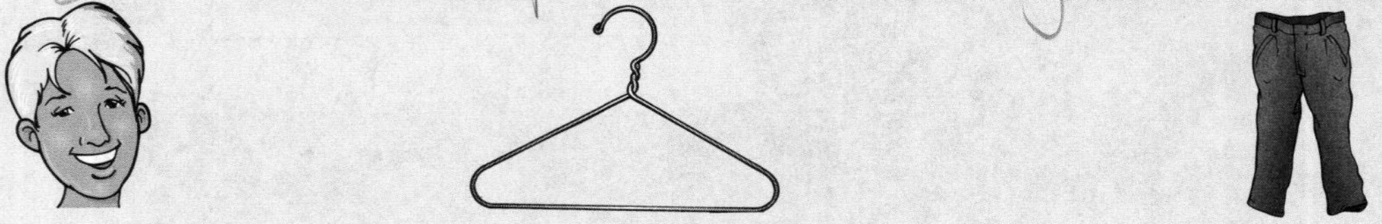

porte le pantalon bleu

N **Travaille avec un partenaire. Pose la question ou donne la response. Puis, écris le dialogue.** ***(Work with a partner. Ask the question or give the answer. Then, write the dialogue.)***

1. 
est-ce que

est-ceque Alain porte le chaussures rouges? Non, Alain porte le chaussures vert.

2. 
est-ce que

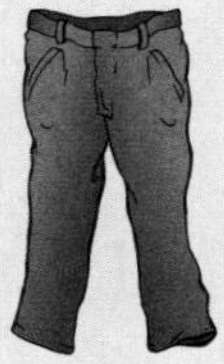

______________________ Non, ______________________.

3. 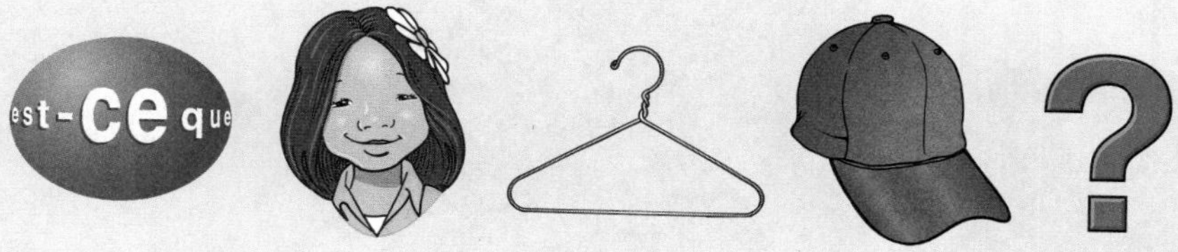
est-ce que

Hiko ______________________ Non, ______________________.

4. 
est-ce que

Brigitte ______________________ Non, ______________________.

5. 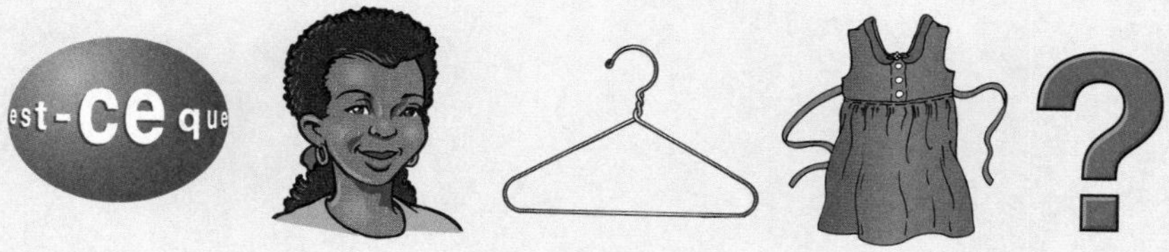
est-ce que

______________________ Non, ______________________.

Mots croisés

Horizontalement

4. couleur du lait
5. couleur du chocolat
7. Quelle ____ est-il?
9. couleur des épinards
11. À deux heures et ____. (2:15)
12. Il est trois heures et ____. (3:30)
13. Il ____ midi.

Verticalement

1. couleur d'une orange
2. couleur du beurre
3. Il est dix heures ____ cinq. (9:55)
6. Il est ____ heure. (1:00)
8. couleur d'une fraise
10. "Mieux vaut ____ que jamais."
11. À ____ heure est le pique-nique?

Unit 14

La musique

Music

Des musiciens merveilleux (Great musicians)

RAMEAU

Jean Philippe Rameau

1683-1764

Jean Philippe Rameau (1683-1764) was born in Dijon. A superb musician, he played the organ and the harpsichord. He also wrote a book, *Le Traité d'harmonie*, about the rules of musical harmony. Rameau is considered today *the* outstanding French composer of the **Baroque** period. He wrote 21 operas and ballets, church music, and special music for the harpsichord. Some of his works are *Castor and Pollux*, an opera based on the mythological story of Greek and Roman twins, and *Pieces for the Harpsichord (Pièces pour le clavecin)*. This French composer's style has been compared to that of Johann Sebastian Bach of Germany and Antonio Vivaldi of Italy.

Georges Bizet (1838-75) was born in Paris. He began his musical studies at age six and at nine he entered the Paris Conservatory of Music. At 17 he composed a delightful piece of music called *Symphony in C.* At 19 he won the *Prix de Rome*, an award for achievements in music and art.

Bizet's musical style is considered **Romantic,** that is, based on the movement called **Romanticism.** Some of his works are musical adaptations of famous stories. He wrote the music for *The Woman from Arles (L'Arlésienne),* which was based on a play by compatriot Alphonse Daudet, and an opera called *Carmen*, which was based on a story by another Frenchman, Prosper Mérimée. *Carmen* is about gypsies, smugglers, toreadors, and soldiers. Today this opera is considered the best ever written by a French composer because it is colorful, exciting, and dramatic. The music critics of the time, however, were extremely harsh in their reviews. Bizet became very depressed by their rejection, and his health got worse. He died at the age of 37.

Maurice Ravel

1875-1937

Maurice Ravel (1875-1937) was born in Ciboure, a Basque village near Bordeaux. Like many of the composers of his time, such as Aaron Copland and Manuel de Falla, he worked folk music into his compositions. He created music for his favorite instrument, the piano, and for a large orchestra. He used wind and percussive instruments to create dramatic sound effects, hoping that the different sounds would create different impressions on the listener. (This style of music is called **Impressionistic**, that is, based on a movement called **Impressionism**.) Unlike the Baroque composer Rameau, Ravel did not use the standard rules of harmony. He was freer and more inventive in terms of creating sounds. Much of Ravel's music reflects his Basque heritage.

Ravel's works include *Daphne and Chloe (Daphnis et Chloé),* a ballet; *Mother Goose Suite (Ma mère l'oye),* a piece for the piano; *The Spanish Hour (L'heure espagnole),* a comic opera; *The Waltz (La Valse),* a ballet to represent the Viennese spirit; *Bolero*, a very popular ballet; and finally, *The Spanish Rhapsody (Rapsodie espagnole),* a work for the full orchestra.

Popular Music

Contemporary rock music in Europe has been greatly influenced by the English speaking world. The blues, jazz, rock and roll, country western, and rap from the United States and rock from England have all had an effect on the new sounds in other countries. Many French bands lean heavily on these models, while others create their own unique styles. Some groups, including *Manau,* sing and rap in French.

The Gipsy Kings are members of two related families from Arles and Montpellier.

Traditional music is largely folk music, that is, music that reflects the cultural heritage of a certain region. It could be a folk song, dance music, or another kind of instrumental music. You can hear this music at regional dances and annual folk festivals. Some French groups play songs in the Breton and Basque languages or perform on traditional instruments. The *Gipsy Kings*, a very popular band, creates music based on their Basque heritage. The rock/rap band *Manau* has recently brought out a Celtic album, which highlights the Breton heritage of its members. A type of music imported from North Africa is called *le raï***,** which combines Arabic folk music with electronic sounds.

Manau chose its name from the old Gaelic name for the Isle of Man.

Céline Dion sings in both French and English.

The musical influences of Angélique Kidjo include Afropop, Jazz, Gospel, Congolese rumba, and Caribbean zouk.

The **entertainment world** is always eager for singers and song writers. Back in the 1930's and 1940's there was the world-famous Parisian singer Édith Piaf, called the *la Môme*, or "Little Sparrow." Recognized by her very distinctive and powerful voice, Édith was a cabaret singer who sang about the troubles and problems of ordinary people. Currently popular is Céline Dion, a singer from Québec, Canada. She has made soundtracks for motion pictures such as *Beauty and the Beast (La Belle et la Bête)* and *Titanic*. She became a hit in France as well, winning at the Music Awards Festival at Cannes and receiving an honor from the French government.

There are other popular celebrities. Patricia Kaas, a singer from Alsace in northeastern France, sings in French, German, and English. Angélique Kidjo, a singer from the African country of Bénin, sings in both French and her native language Fon. (As a Goodwill Ambassador for UNICEF, she uses her music to call attention to the problems facing the world's children.) Like Céline Dion, she has also recorded soundtracks for many movies. Jean-Jacques Goldman has a huge following in Europe. His songs are a combination of folk and rock, somewhat similar to the style of Bob Dylan. Finally, there is Patrick Bruel, a singer and actor originally from Algeria, a former French colony.

Activités

A Give the full name of the composer who. . .

1. . . . used folk songs in his music. ______________________
2. . . . wrote a book about harmony. ______________________
3. . . . wrote music for a play and a story. ______________________

B Match the work in column A with its description in column B.

A		B
1. _____	*Carmen*	A. a play set to music
2. _____	*Castor and Pollux*	B. opera that at first displeased the public
3. _____	*The Waltz*	C. full orchestral work
4. _____	*The Woman from Arles*	D. ballet inspired by the city of Vienna
5. _____	*The Spanish Rhapsody*	E. opera inspired by mythological twins

C Identifie. . . (*Identify*. . .)

1. . . . the name of the city referenced in *L'Arlésienne.*

____

2. . . . the ethnic heritage of Maurice Ravel.

____

3. . . . the nationality of Céline Dion.

____

4. . . . the name of the singer from Bénin.

____

5. . . . the region of France that Patricia Kaas calls home.

____

D **Complete the analogies.**

1. *Daphnis and Chloé*: Ravel = *Castor and Pollux*: ______________________
2. Maurice Ravel: composer = Jean-Jacques Goldman: ______________________
3. Ravel: ______________________ = Rameau: harpsichord
4. ______________________: Kidjo = Édith: Piaf
5. Georges: Bizet = Céline: ______________________

E **Match the composer with his style of music.**

A		B
1. _____	Ravel	A. Romantic
2. _____	Rameau	B. Impressionistic
3. _____	Bizet	C. Baroque

F **Write the correct name of the musician associated with the idea represented by the image.**

1. ______________________

Harpsichord

2. ______________________

3. ______________________

G Contemporary Music

Can you name a female singer. . .

from Africa? ______________________

from Europe? ______________________

from North America? ______________________

H

C'est à toi! Choose one of the following composers, musicians, or singers. Find out as much as you can about the person's life and musical works. Report to the class about your findings. A musical excerpt on an audio CD or a printout of a song's lyrics would add a nice touch to your presentation.

Aznavour, Charles

Berlioz, Héctor

Brassens, Georges

Brel, Jacques

Debussy, Claude

Gainsbourg, Serge

Goldman, Jean-Jacques

Gounod, Charles

Hallyday, Johnny

Khaled

Massenet, Jules

Saint-Saëns, Camille

Proverbe

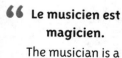

"**Le musicien est magicien.**
The musician is a magician."

Langue vivante!

Depuis l'été 1998, le rap celtique est sur toutes les ondes !

Manau, composé de Martial, Cédric et R.V. (Hervé), 3 garçons de banlieue parisienne qui revendiquent leurs racines bretonnes. Après l'immense succès de *La tribu de Dana*, et plus de 1 700 000 singles vendus, Manau enchaîne avec *Panique Celtique*.

Cela fait plusieurs années que tous les 3 ils utilisent les platines et qu'ils évoluent dans l'univers de la musique, entre rap, groove et techno.

Le Monde DE MOZART
UNE COLLECTION UNIQUE
NOUVELLE SÉRIE
30 CD AVEC LEURS LIVRETS
Le Monde 2
Le Monde

PARIS CULTUREL
Fête de la MUSIQUE
21 JUIN
Ne ratez pas votre soirée !
Tous les concerts, tous les lieux, tous les horaires, dans le programme officiel de la Fête de la Musique publié le 21 juin dans
le Parisien
En vente 4,80 F chez votre marchand de journaux

I

Look at the screen-shot from the Web site of the musical group Manau; then answer the questions.

1. What kind of music does it play?

   ____

2. How many musicians make up the group?

   ____

3. The group's members all have Breton roots, that is, they come from the province of Brittany. Can you find the phrase "Breton roots"?

   ____

4. Breton roots mean the members share a Celtic heritage. Can you find a phrase that includes the word *"celtique"*?

   ____

5. What is the title of one of their albums?

   ____

J

The newspaper *Le Monde* has a musical offer for the reader.

1. What is the name of the composer featured in this offer?

   ____

2. *Il y combien de CD?*

   ____

3. What accompanies each CD?

   ____

K

***Le Parisien* is another newspaper featuring a musical event. Answer the following questions about it.**

1. What event is being advertised in the picture?

   ____

2. In what month does it take place?

   ____

3. What information about this event can you find in the paper?

   ____

   ____

   ____

Symtalk

L

Écris en français le mot ou l'expression qui correspond à chaque image. ***(In the spaces, write the correct words in French.)***

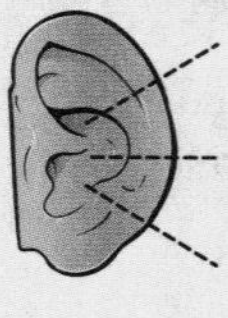 1. ____________ ____________	 2. ____________	 3. ____________	 4. ____________

M

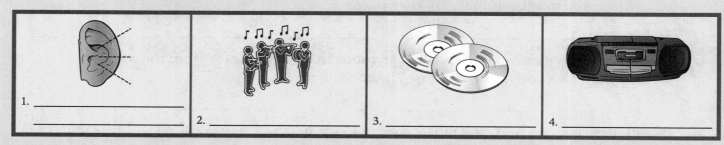

Dis les phrases, puis écris-les en français. ***(Say the sentences, then write them in French.)***

1.  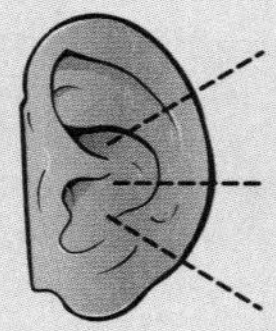 

____

2.  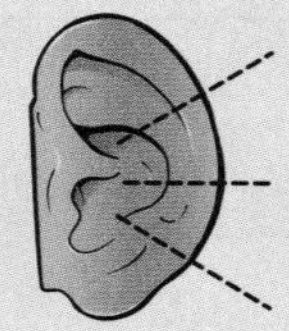 

____

3.  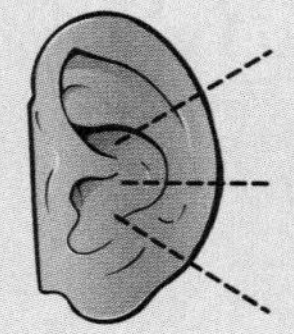 

____

4.  et  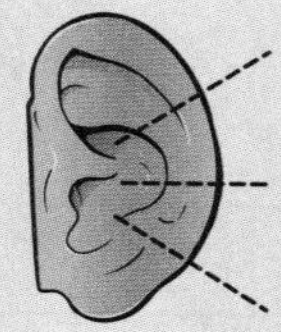 

____

5. 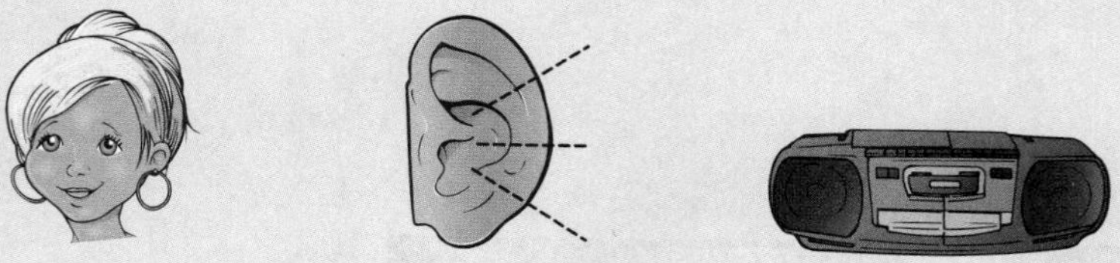

____

N **Travaille avec un partenaire. Pose la question ou donne la response. Puis, écris le dialogue.** ***(Work with a partner. Ask the question or give the answer. Then, write the dialogue.)***

1. 
est-ce que

____ ______________

2. 
est-ce que

____ ______________

3. 
est-ce que
et

____ ______________

4. 
est-ce que

____ ______________

Mots croisés

1
2
3
4
5
6
7
8
9
10
11
12
13
14
15

Horizontalement

4. birthplace of Georges Bizet
6. used entirely by Ravel
10. first name of Impressionist composer
12. Jean-Jacques ____
14. birthplace of Ravel
15. Angélique Kidjo's first language

Verticalement

1. singer from Africa
2. *Mother ____ Suite*
3. composer of *Carmen*
4. one of the mythological brothers
5. sings in French, German, and English
7. Rameau believed in the rules of ____.
8. Céline's last name
9. Baroque composer
11. most famous French opera
13. world famous singer of the 1930's and 1940's

Unit 15

Le temps et les saisons
Weather and Seasons

Vocabulaire

Quel temps fait-il? How's the weather?

Il fait beau.
It's nice out.

Il fait du soleil.
It's sunny.

Il fait (très) chaud.
It's (very) warm (hot).

Comme ci, comme ça.
So-so.

Il fait frais.
It's cool.

Il fait du vent.
It's windy.

Il fait humide.
It's humid.

Il est nuageux.
It's cloudy.

Il fait mauvais.

Il tonne.
It's thundering.

Il pleut.
It's raining.

Il y a des éclairs.
There's lightning.

Il fait froid.
It's cold.

Il neige.
It's snowing.

Quelle est la saison? What's the season?

C'est. . . It's. . .

Les quatre saisons

l'été (m.)

le printemps

l'hiver (m.)

l'automne (m.)

au printemps	=	in (the) spring
en été	=	in (the) summer
en automne	=	in (the) fall / in autumn
en hiver	=	in (the) winter

Notice the nouns related to some of the verbs:

le tonnere	=	thunder	→	**Il tonne.**	=	It's thundering.
l'éclair (m.)	=	lightning	→	**Il y a des éclairs.**	=	There's lightning.
la pluie	=	rain	→	**Il pleut.**	=	It's raining.
la neige	=	snow	→	**Il neige.**	=	It's snowing.

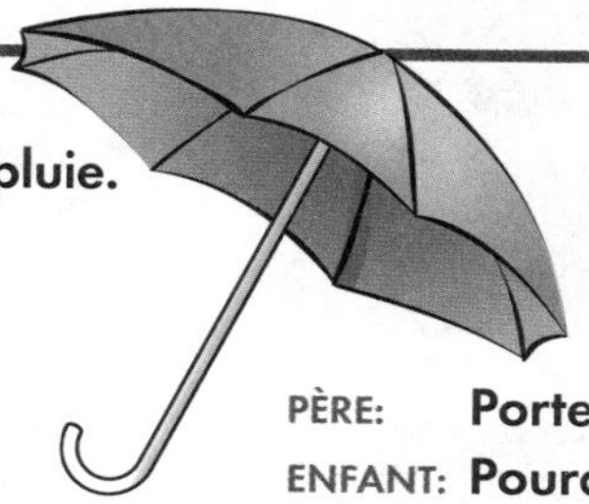

MÈRE: **Prends ton parapluie.**
ENFANT: **Pourquoi?**
MÈRE: **Il pleut.**

MÈRE: **Porte tes lunettes de soleil.**
ENFANT: **Pourquoi?**
MÈRE: **Il fait beaucoup de soleil.**

PÈRE: **Porte ton chapeau.**
ENFANT: **Pourquoi?**
PÈRE: **Il fait très froid.**

prends	=	take
porte	=	wear

Activités

A **Quelle image correspond à chaque phrase?** ***(Match each picture with a sentence.)***

A. Il fait du soleil.
B. Il y a des éclairs.
C. Il pleut.
D. Il fait du vent.
E. Il fait froid.

1. ________

2. ________

3. ________

4. ________

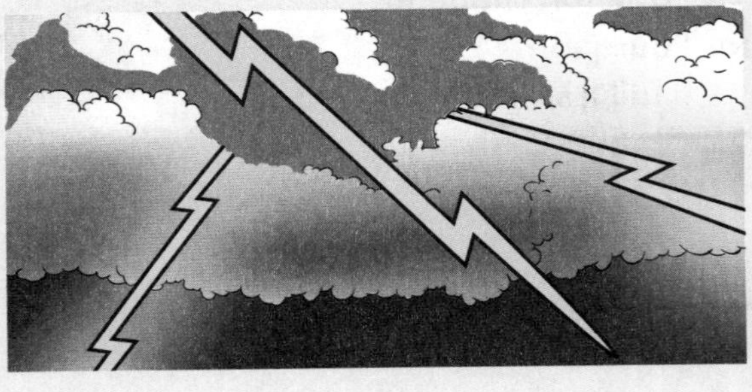

5. ________

B **Quel temps fait-il? Réponds à cette question en français selon chaque image.** ***(How's the weather? Answer this question in French according to each picture.)***

1.  ____________________

2.  ____________________

3.  ____________________

4.  ____________________

5.  ____________________

C **Associe l'image à la saison.** ***(Match the picture with the season.)***

A	B
	A. l'été
	B. l'hiver
	C. le printemps
	D. l'automne

1. ________

2. ________

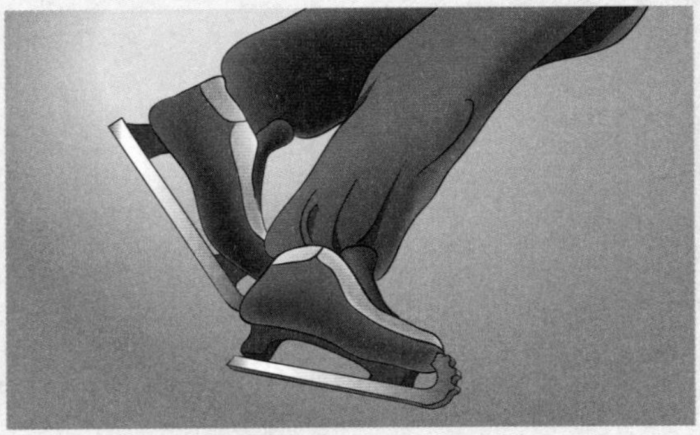

3. ________

4. ________

D **Write in *Column 1* the English meaning of each French word. When you have finished the entire column, cover the column of French words at the left. Then in *Column 2*, change the English words into French.**

	Column 1 (English)	**Column 2** (French)
1. le soleil	______	______
2. les éclairs	______	______
3. le printemps	______	______
4. l'été	______	______
5. le temps	______	______
6. l'automne	______	______
7. la saison	______	______
8. frais	______	______
9. très chaud	______	______
10. Il pleut.	______	______
11. l'hiver	______	______
12. mauvais	______	______
13. Il tonne.	______	______
14. froid	______	______

E **Match the noun in column *A* with the related verb in column *B*.**

A	**B**
1. ______ la pluie	A. faire du soleil
2. ______ la neige	B. tonner
3. ______ le tonnerre	C. faire du vent
4. ______ le vent	D. neiger
5. ______ le soleil	E. pleuvoir

F ***Quel temps fait-il?* Use each cue to write a statement in French about the weather.**

1. mittens and parka

____

2. sunglasses

____

3. lightning rod

____

4. light sweater

____

5. outdoor tennis court

____

6. umbrella

____

7. snowflakes

____

8. air conditioner

____

9. sailboat

____

10. rain, wind, and hail

____

G

Lis le paragraphe; puis, encercle la lettre correcte. ***(Read the passage; then, circle the correct letter.)***

Les quatres saisons

En hiver il fait très froid. Il neige beaucoup. La neige est blanche. Au printemps il fait frais et il pleut beaucoup. Il fait chaud et il fait du soleil en été. En automne il fait *encore* du vent et il fait frais aussi. Les quatre saisons sont *très* intéressantes.

encore	again
très	very

1. En hiver ____.
   A. il est humide
   B. il tonne
   C. il fait froid
   D. il fait chaud

2. Il pleut beaucoup ____.
   A. au printemps
   B. en été
   C. en hiver
   D. en automne

3. Il fait très chaud ____.
   A. en hiver
   B. en automne
   C. au printemps
   D. en été

4. Il y a ____ saisons.
   A. cinq
   B. quatre
   C. six
   D. trois

H

Parlons! Think of three clothing items or accessories. For each one you select, ask your speaking partner to say how the weather is. Then reverse the roles. He/she will suggest to you three new cues that you can respond to.

> **Modèle:** A: lunettes de soleil
> Quel temps fait-il?
> B: Il fait du soleil.

I

C'est à toi! Select five cities in various parts of the world and five different months. Use cities in different continents and hemispheres. Ask your partner about the weather in the first city. Your partner should then respond appropriately according to the city and month. (Don't forget that when it's summer in the northern hemisphere, it is winter in the southern hemisphere!) Write your answers on a piece of paper.

> **Modèle:** A: Quel temps fait-il à Tokyo en janvier?
> B: Il fait froid.

Proverbe

“Une hirondelle ne fait pas le printemps.

One swallow doesn't make a spring.”

Langue vivante!

En France

Jeudi, la dépression pluvio-neigeuse de la veille se sera évacuée totalement vers l'Italie et l'Europe centrale, pendant qu'un anticyclone aura repris position sur notre territoire. Le ciel sera généralement bien dégagé et la très large partie du pays profitera d'un bon ensoleillement. Quelques nappes de nuages bas ou de brumes matinales se formeront toutefois ici et là le matin, notamment sur Rhône-Alpes, au nord de la Seine et au pied des Pyrénées. Il fera froid le matin avec de nombreuses gelées matinales. Même type de temps vendredi avant une dégradation progressive ce week-end.

Jours suivants

Région	Samedi	Dimanche	Lundi
Nord-Ouest	1° / 14°	6° / 11°	6° / 11°
Ile-de-France	1° / 15°	6° / 10°	5° / 7°
Nord-Est	0° / 15°	7° / 9°	5° / 6°
Sud-Ouest	7° / 16°	10° / 19°	12° / 19°
Sud-Est	6° / 18°	12° / 19°	14° / 24°

Beau mais froid le matin
30 km/h
10 km/h
50 km/h
60 km/h
11° / 22° Températures à l'aube et l'après-midi
Lille 0° 11°
Cherbourg -2° 12°
Amiens -3° 12°
Rouen -3° 12°
Caen -2° 12°
PARIS -3° 12°
-4° 11°
Metz -5° 10°
Châlons-en-Champagne
Strasbourg -3° 9°
Brest -1° 12°
Rennes -2° 12°
Orléans -3° 11°
Dijon -3° 10°
Besançon -2° 7°
Nantes -2° 12°
Poitiers -2° 11°
Chamonix -3° 8°
Clermont-Ferrand -1° 10°
Lyon 2° 11°
Limoges -1° 11°
Grenoble 2° 11°
Bordeaux 0° 14°
Nice 7° 20°
Toulouse 2° 15°
Montpellier 5° 15°
Marseille 5° 17°
Biarritz 4° 14°
Perpignan 6° 16°
Ajaccio 8° 20°
-5 à 0° | 0 à 5° | 5 à 10° | 10 à 15° | 15 à 20° | 20 à 25° | 25 à 30° | 30 à 35°
ST-MARCELLIN
COEFF. DE MARÉE:28
LEVER: 07.17 COUCHER: 20.27 PARIS
LEVER: 12.39 COUCHER: 04.54 PARIS

Les Quatre saisons de Vivaldi

Eté
GUIDE D'INFORMATIONS PRATIQUES

Printemps HAUSSMANN
64, bd Haussmann - 75009 - Paris - France - **Tél. :** 01 42 82 50 00

Printemps Haussmann
- Mode Femme
- Luxe
- Accessoires
- Lingerie
- Enfant
- Homme
- Beauté
- Maison

à cet hiver...
haute savoie
mont blanc
Lausanne
Thonon - Lac Léman
Genève - TGV
Vallée d'aulps
Avoriaz
Morzine
Les Gets
SUISSE
Bellegarde - TGV
LYON
Cluses
Chamonix
Annecy
GRENOBLE
ITALIE

Retrouvez- nous sur Internet : www.valleedaulps.com
Communauté de Communes de la Vallée d'Aulps 74430 LE BIOT
Tél 04 50 72 15 15 - Fax : 04 50 72 14 59

J *Regarde la météo.* Look at the weather map and answer the questions.

1. The large weather map for Thursday shows city temperatures at dawn and in the afternoon. Look for the following combinations and write their corresponding cities.
   A. 0°/11° ______________________
   B. 4°/14° ______________________
   C. 7°/20° ______________________
   D. –5°/10° ______________________
   E. 8°/20° ______________________
   F. –1°/10° ______________________
2. How would you describe the weather in France on this day (Thursday)? *(En français, s'il te plaît.)*
   ____
3. What is the general weather forecast from Saturday to Tuesday for the five main regions of France?
   ____

K Now answer questions about the remaining clippings.

1. In what region is Mont Blanc, the highest mountain in France?
   ____
2. During what season would most tourists visit this area?
   ____
3. This season is also the name of a large store located in Boulevard Haussmann in Paris.
   A. Write the name of the season in French. ______________________
   B. What kind of a store do you think it is? ______________________
4. Antonio Vivaldi (1678-1741) was an Italian composer. Can you find the French name of his most famous concerto?
   ____
5. What is the weather like on the beach? *(En français, s'il te plaît.)*
   ____
6. What is the weather like on the ski slope? *(En français, s'il te plaît.)*
   ____
7. What is the weather like at tulip time? *(En français, s'il te plaît.)*
   ____

Symtalk

L **Écris en français l'expression qui correspond à chaque image.** ***(In the space, write the correct expression in French.)***

 1. ______	 2. ______	 3. ______	 4. ______	 5. ______

M **Dis les phrases, puis écris-les en français.** ***(Say the sentences, then write them in French.)***

1. 

____

2. 

____

3. 

____

4. 

____

5. 

____

N

Travaille avec un partenaire. Pose la question ou donne la response. Puis, écris le dialogue. ***(Work with a partner. Ask the question or give the answer. Then, write the dialogue.)***

1. 
est-ce que

_______________________________ Non, _______________________.

2. 
est-ce que

_______________________________ Non, _______________________.

3. 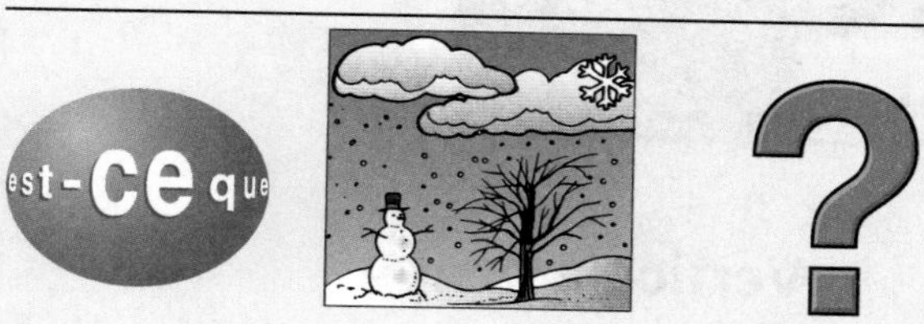
est-ce que

_______________________________ Oui, _______________________.

4. 
est-ce que

_______________________________ Non, _______________________.

5 
est-ce que

_______________________________ Non, _______________________.

Mots croisés

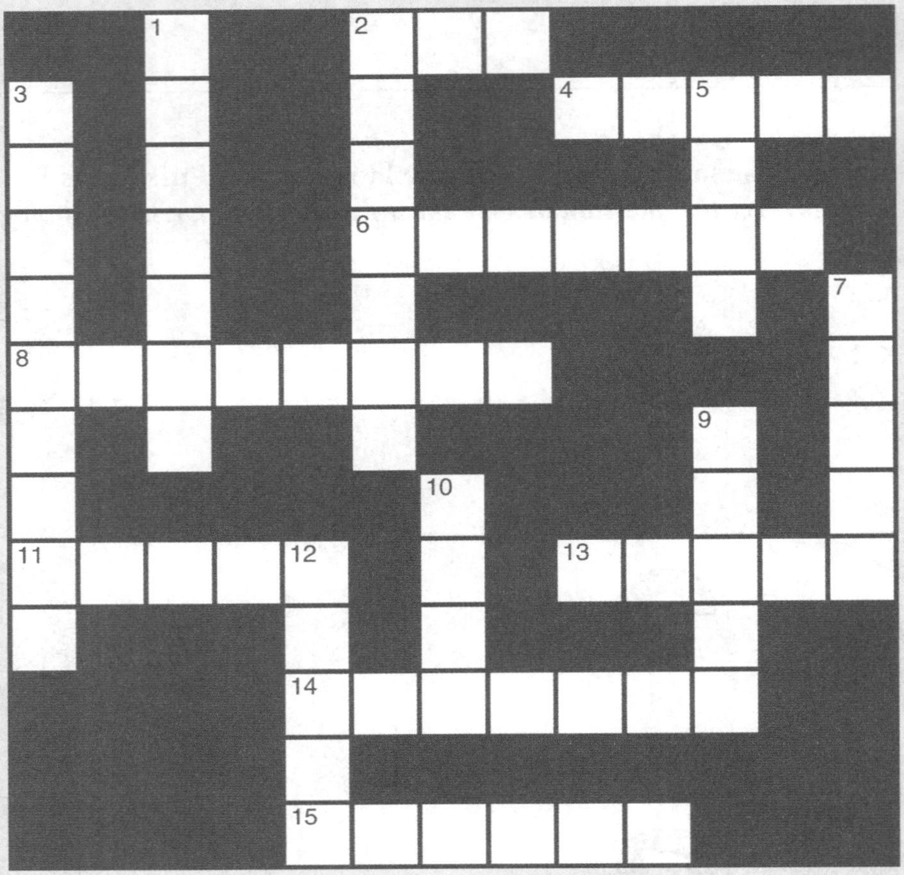

Horizontalement

2. season after *printemps*
4. time for some animals to hibernate
6. season after *été*
8. big noise during a storm
11. time for a *parapluie: Il* ____.
13. weather in the summer
14. opposite of *beau*
15. gives us warmth and light

Verticalement

1. A temperate climate has four ____.
2. white bolts that light up the sky
3. season of new flowers
5. needed to fly kites
7. weather in the winter
9. between *chaud* and *froid*
10. nice, pleasant weather: *Il fait* ____.
12. *Quel* ____ *fait-il*?

Unit 16

Les jours et les mois
Days and Months

Vocabulaire

Quel jour est-ce?
What day is today?

Nous sommes. . .
Today is. . .

Monday **lundi**	Tuesday **mardi**	Wednesday **mercredi**	Thursday **jeudi**	Friday **vendredi**	Saturday **samedi**	Sunday **dimanche**
	1	2	3	4	5	6
7	8	9	10	11	12	13
14	15	16	17	18	19	20
21	22	23	24	25	26	27
28	29	30	31			

C'est quand, le jour de fête?	When is the holiday?
C'est demain.	It's tomorrow.
Quelle est la date aujourd'hui?	What is the date today?
C'est le premier mai.	It's May first.
Le quatorze juillet.	July 14
Le vingt-cinq novembre.	November 25
29.4 (le 29 avril)	4 - 29 (April 29)

mars
avril
mai
septembre
octobre
novembre
juin
juillet
août
décembre
janvier
février

When you say the first day of any month, use the word **premier**: **C'est le premier juin**.

When you write the date, be sure to put the day before the month: **le 15 mai**.

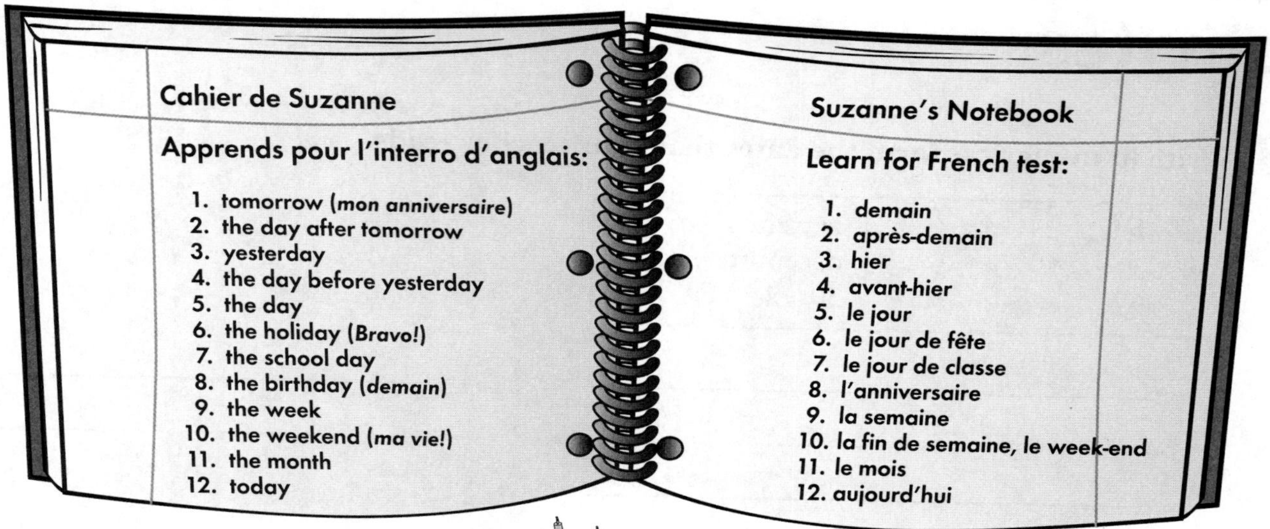
Cahier de Suzanne
Apprends pour l'interro d'anglais:
1. tomorrow (*mon anniversaire*)
2. the day after tomorrow
3. yesterday
4. the day before yesterday
5. the day
6. the holiday (*Bravo!*)
7. the school day
8. the birthday (*demain*)
9. the week
10. the weekend (*ma vie!*)
11. the month
12. today
Suzanne's Notebook
Learn for French test:
1. demain
2. après-demain
3. hier
4. avant-hier
5. le jour
6. le jour de fête
7. le jour de classe
8. l'anniversaire
9. la semaine
10. la fin de semaine, le week-end
11. le mois
12. aujourd'hui

HENRI: **C'est quand, ton anniversaire, Loïc?**
When's your birthday, Loïc?

LOÏC: **C'est après-demain, le 8 juin.**
It's the day after tomorrow, on June 8th.

MIDORI: **C'est quel jour, l'interro d'anglais?**
On what day is the English test?

MICHEL: **C'est mardi.**
It's on Tuesday.

mardi
1
2
7
8
9
15

SANDRINE: **Qu'est ce que tu as mercredi?**
What do you have on Wednesday?

MAGALI: **J'ai ma leçon de piano.**
I have my piano lesson.

NICOLE: **Qu'est-ce que tu as aujourd'hui, André?**
What do you have today, André?

ANDRÉ: **Je n'ai rien! Aujourd'hui je suis libre.**
Nothing! Today I'm free.

Weekdays and Mythology

Derivations and Comparisons

French Day	Roman Mythology
lundi	Day honoring the moon god (*luna* = Latin name for moon)
mardi	Day honoring Mars, god of war
mercredi	Day honoring Mercury, messenger of the gods
jeudi	Day honoring Jupiter, or Jove, "father of all the gods"
vendredi	Day honoring Venus, goddess of love
samedi	Day honoring Saturn, god of the harvest and agriculture
dimanche	Day honoring the Lord (*Dominus* = Latin name for the Lord; Christian conversion of *solis dies* = day of the sun, or Sunday, or day honoring the god of the sun)

Activités

A **Write in numerical form the dates that your teacher reads.**

> **Modèle:** **Teacher says:** le trente décembre
> **You write:** 30/12

1. ______________________
2. ______________________
3. ______________________
4. ______________________
5. ______________________

B **Make a calendar of the current month. Include the names of the days and all the numbers.**

C Écris les dates. *(Write the dates.)*

Modèle: *Tuesday, February 11th*
mardi, le 11 février

1. Wednesday, October 22

   ____

2. Sunday, August 13th

   ____

3. Thursday, May 1st

   ____

4. Friday, April 26th

   ____

5. Saturday, February 9th

   ____

D Answer the following questions in English.

1. If the French date is 16.3, what is the month and what is the day?

   ____

2. Which part of the solar system is associated with the name *solis dies*?

   ____

3. Which Roman god, do you suppose, was a fast runner?

   ____

E Encercle les réponses correctes. *(Circle the correct answers.)*

1. C'est quel jour demain?
   A. semaine
   B. lundi
   C. juillet
   D. mois

2. Quelle est la date aujourd'hui?
   A. Aujourd'hui c'est un jour de fête.
   B. Aujourd'hui je suis libre.
   C. C'est aujourd'hui le 10 janvier.
   D. C'est aujourd'hui dimanche.

The following questions are based on the dialogues presented on page 205. Review them before you choose your answers.

3. Loïc, qu'est-ce qu'il a le 8 juin? *(What does he have. . .?)*
   A. une fin de semaine
   B. mars
   C. un anniveraire
   D. mardi

4. Michel, qu'est-ce que tu as mardi?
   A. J'ai un chien et deux chats.
   B. J'ai une interro d'anglais.
   C. J'ai une maison à Nantes.
   D. Je suis libre.

5. C'est quel jour, la leçon de piano de Magali?
   A. mercredi
   B. mardi
   C. vendredi
   D. lundi

6. Qui est libre aujourd'hui?
   A. Henri
   B Midori
   C. Nicole
   D. André

F Associe les termes français avec les termes anglais. *(Match the French expressions with the English.)*

1. _____ aujourd'hui
2. _____ après-demain
3. _____ avant-hier
4. _____ demain
5. _____ hier

A. yesterday
B. day after tomorrow
C. today
D. tomorrow
E. day before yesterday

G Écris en français. *(Write in French.)*

1. the third month of the year ______________________________
2. the day that honors the Roman "father of all the gods" ______________________________
3. the day that honors the Roman goddess, Venus ______________________________
4. the month that brings May flowers ______________________________
5. the first day of the French week ______________________________
6. the month of the national holiday in France ______________________________
7. the month in which Halloween is celebrated in the U.S. ______________________________
8. the month of your *anniversaire* ______________________________

On July 14 the French celebrate their national holiday, known as Bastille Day.

H **Écris le nom du jour selon l'image.** ***(Identify the French weekday according to the illustration.)***

1.  ______________________

2.  ______________________

3.  ______________________

4.  ______________________

5.  ____________________

6.  ____________________

7.  ____________________

I **Lis le paragraphe, puis encercle les réponses correctes.** ***(Read the paragraph and then circle the correct answers.)***

C'est aujourd'hui un jour spécial pour Jean-Claude, un garçon français. Jean-Claude habite à *l'Île* de la Réunion dans l'Océan Indien. *Cet été* il *rend visite* à son ami, Didier. Didier habite à Paris. C'est samedi, le 9 juillet. C'est aussi le *dernier* jour du *championnat de football* le plus important dans le monde. L'Argentine *joue contre* la France pour la *Coupe du monde*. Les deux *équipes* jouent à Paris. Normalement il est difficile d'obtenir les *billets d'entrée* mais Jean-Claude et Didier ont *de la chance*. Jean-Claude est très heureux aujourd'hui.

l'île	island	**joue contre**	plays against
Cet été	This summer	**Coupe du monde**	World Cup
rend visite	visits	**équipes**	teams
dernier	last	**billets d'entrée**	entrance tickets
championnat de football	soccer championship	**ont de la chance**	are lucky

1. Quel jour est-ce aujourd'hui?
   A. lundi
   B. vendredi
   C. mardi
   D. samedi

2. Quelle est la date?
   A. le dix juillet
   B. le neuf juillet
   C. le douze juillet
   D. le vingt juillet

3. C'est un jour spécial pour Jean-Claude?
   A. Oui.
   B. Non.
   C. Comme ci, comme ça.
   D. C'est Noël *(Christmas)*.

4. Qui est Didier?
   A. un frère de Jean-Claude
   B. un oncle de Jean-Claude
   C. un professeur de Didier
   D. un ami de Jean-Claude

5. Où est le championnat de football?
   A. à la Réunion
   B. en Italie
   C. à Paris
   D en Allemagne

6. Jean-Claude, comment est-il?
   A. heureux
   B. triste
   C. malade
   D. intéressant

J **Parlons!** Find out from your speaking partner on what day three things occur: his/her birthday *(son anniversaire)* his/her music lesson or sports practice *(la leçon de musique, la répétition de sport)*, and his/her next test *(son interro prochaine)*. Start with *C'est quel jour?* He/she answers by saying a specific day of the week. Then your partner will ask you when three other things are: *le jour de fête, l'anniversaire de ta mère* and *le pique-nique.* He/she should start with *C'est quand. . .?* You should answer with a day or a date.

K **C'est à toi!** Find out whether you and your classmate know your days. You start by saying *"C'est aujourd'hui lundi."* Your classmate says, *"C'est demain mardi."* You finish by saying *"C'est après-demain mercredi."* Then your partner goes back to: *"C'est aujourd'hui. . ."* Continue until you have both identified all the weekdays.

Proverbe

"Ne remettez pas au lendemain ce que vous pouvez faire aujourd'hui.

Don't put off until tomorrow what you can do today."

CHORES for DEMAIN
· Clean Room
CHORES for AUJOURD'HUI
· Clean Room
· Dishes
· Mow Lawn

Langue vivante!

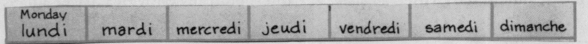

Monday lundi	mardi	mercredi	jeudi	vendredi	samedi	dimanche

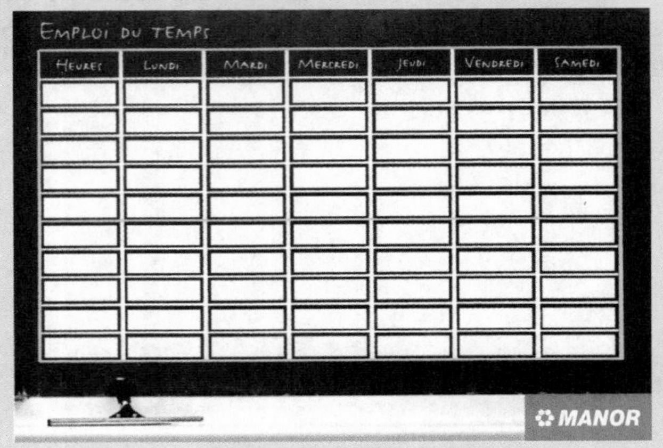

Emploi du temps
Heures
Lundi
Mardi
Mercredi
Jeudi
Vendredi
Samedi
MANOR

RENNES, les curiosités

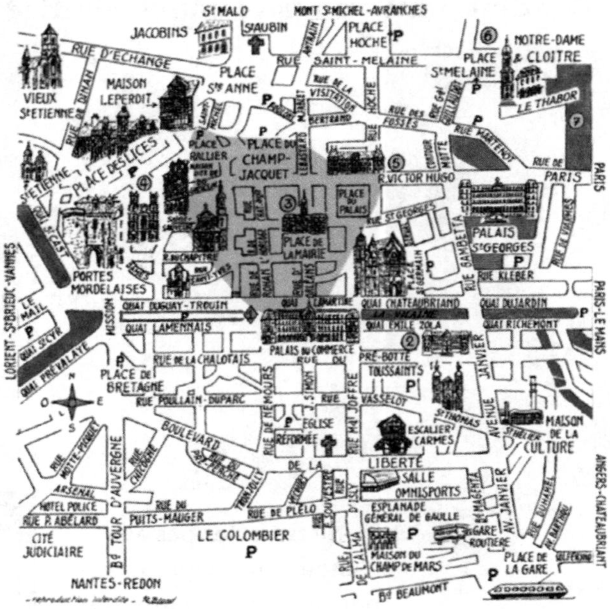

St MALO
MONT St MICHEL-AVRANCHES
JACOBINS
St AUBIN
PLACE HOCHE
NOTRE-DAME & CLOITRE
RUE D'ECHANGE
PLACE Ste ANNE
RUE SAINT-MELAINE
PLACE St MELAINE
MAISON LEPERDIT
VIEUX St ETIENNE
LE THABOR
PLACE DES LICES
PLACE RALLIER
PLACE DU CHAMP-JACQUET
R. VICTOR HUGO
RUE DE PARIS
PLACE DU PALAIS
PALAIS St GEORGES
PLACE DE LA MAIRIE
RUE KLEBER
PORTES MORDELAISES
LE MAIL
QUAI DUGUAY-TROUIN
QUAI LAMENNAIS
QUAI CHATEAUBRIAND
QUAI DUJARDIN
QUAI EMILE ZOLA
QUAI RICHEMONT
PALAIS DU COMMERCE
PRÉ-BOTTE
TOUSSAINTS
PLACE DE BRETAGNE
RUE POULLAIN-DUPARC
RUE VASSELOT
ÉGLISE RÉFORMÉE
ESCALIER CARMES
MAISON DE LA CULTURE
LIBERTÉ
SALLE OMNISPORTS
ESPLANADE GÉNÉRAL DE GAULLE
ARSENAL
HOTEL POLICE
RUE P. ABÉLARD
CITÉ JUDICIAIRE
LE COLOMBIER
MAISON DU CHAMP DE MARS
GARE ROUTIÈRE
PLACE DE LA GARE
Bd BEAUMONT
NANTES-REDON
LORIENT-St BRIEUC-VANNES
PARIS-LE MANS
ANGERS-CHATEAUBRIANT
PARIS

1 SYNDICAT D'INITIATIVE
OFFICE DU TOURISME
hiver : 9h-12h30 - 14h-18h30
sauf dimanche et lundi matin
été : 9h-19h30 sauf dimanche
Juillet - Août : idem + dimanche :
10h-12h - 14h17h

2 MUSÉES
10h-12h - 14-18h sauf mardi et fériés

3 HOTEL DE VILLE 9h - 17h

4 CATHÉDRALE St PIERRE
8h30-12h - 14h-17h

5 ANCIEN PARLEMENT
DE BRETAGNE
10h-12h - 14h-18h sauf mardi

6 ÉGLISE NOTRE DAME
ET CLOITRE St MELAINE
9h-19h

7 JARDIN DU THABOR
Horaires variables selon la saison

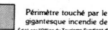

Périmètre touché par le gigantesque incendie de 1720.

RENNES

A 3 heures de Paris par fer (10 liaisons quotidiennes) et autoroute.
A 2 heures de Paris par le T.G.V. en 1989.
A 2h30 de Quimper. A 3 heures de Brest. A 1h15 de St-Malo (car ferry).
Lignes aériennes régulières avec Paris, Lyon, Caen et Londres.

Édité par l'Office du Tourisme Syndicat d'Initiative avec le concours de la Ville de Rennes - Imprimerie des Lices 99.30.38.30

Welcome to Invalides - the Musée de L'Armée

Renseignements pratiques

Ouvert tous les jours
(sauf le 1/1 - 1/5 - 1/11 - 25/12)

Horaires:
de 10h à17h du 1/10 au 31/3
de 10h à 18h du1/04 au 30/09
Le tombeau de Napoléon 1er est accessible
jusqu'à 19 h du 1er juin au 31 août

L **Look at the clippings and answer the following questions.**

1. *Le Musée de l'Armée* in Paris is open every day except on certain days of the year. Can you figure out what four days these are? *(En français, s'il te plaît.)*

2. During what months is the museum open from *10h* to *17h*?

3. During what months is the museum open until *18h*?

4. When may a visitor see Napoléon's Tomb until *19h* each day? *(En français, s'il te plaît.)*

5. Using the schedule, or *emploi du temps*, as a model, create your own weekly schedule on a separate piece of paper. Include your school subjects and after-school activities.

6. The French calendar begins with Monday. What are the fourth and sixth days of the week?

7. Rennes, a city in the province of *Bretagne* (Brittany), has many interesting things to see. What is the French name of these sights of special interest?

8. What are the winter hours of the *Office du Tourisme*? (# 1 on the legend)

9. During which hours is the cathedral closed for lunch?

10. Name a month when it would be pleasant to have a *pique-nique* in the *Jardin du Thabor*.

Symtalk

M **Écris en français le mot qui correspond à chaque image.** ***(On the blank, write the correct word in French.)***

 1. ______	 2. ______	 3. ______	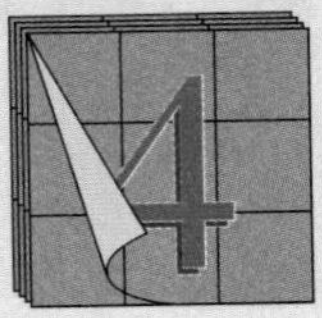 4. ______
 5. ______	 6. ______	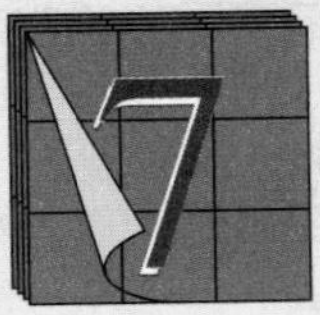 7. ______	 Monday JUNE 8. ______

N **Dis les phrases, puis écris-les en français.** ***(Say the sentences, then write them in French.)***

1.  

______

2.  

______

3.  

______

4.  

______

O **Travaille avec un partenaire. Pose la question ou donne la response. Puis, écris le dialogue.** ***(Work with a partner. Ask the question or give the answer. Then, write the dialogue.)***

1. 
Monday
JUNE
est-ce que
1

2. 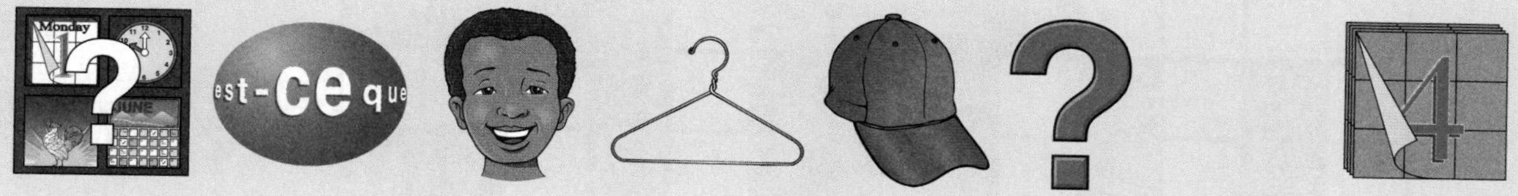
Monday
JUNE
est-ce que
4

3. 
Monday
JUNE
est-ce que
5

4. 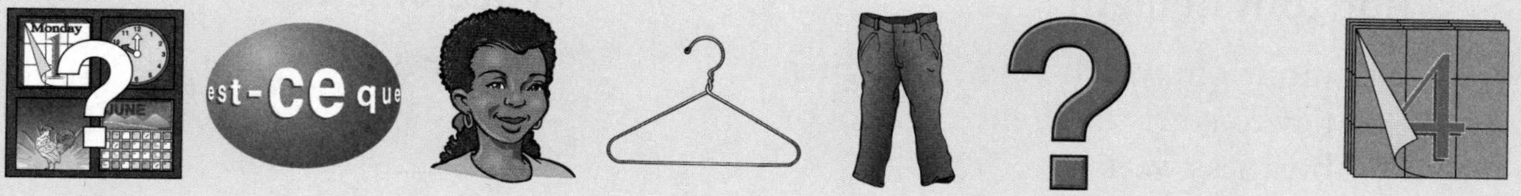
Monday
JUNE
est-ce que
4

5. 
Monday
JUNE
est-ce que
2

Mots croisés

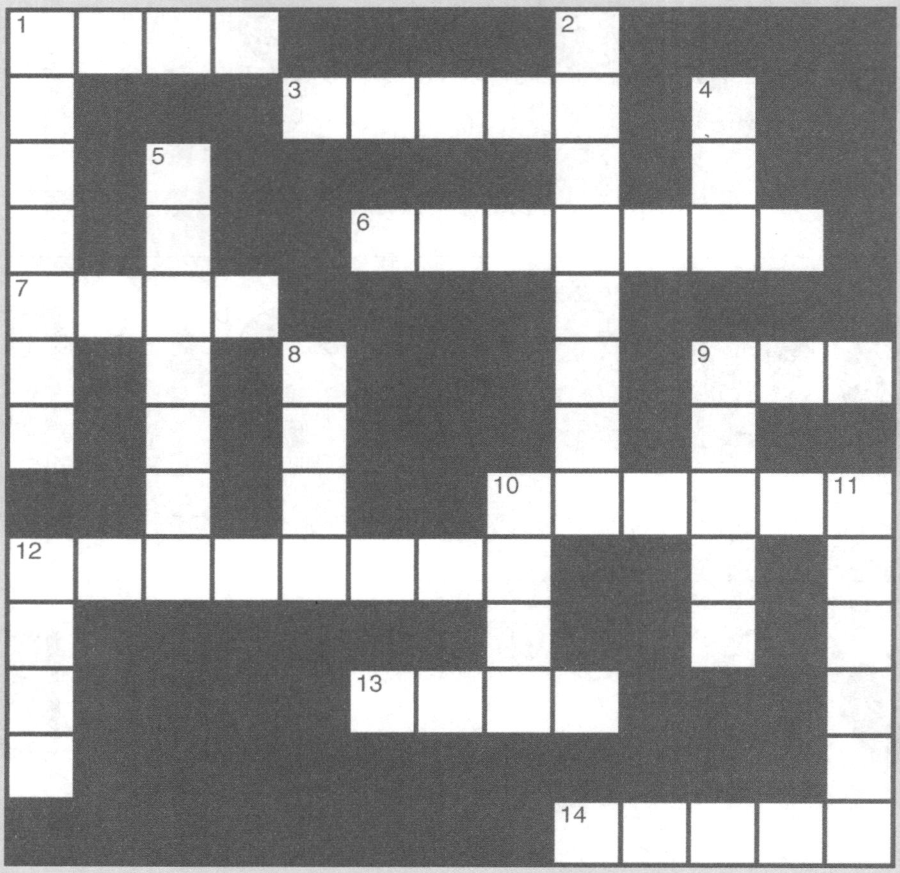
1
2
3
4
5
6
7
8
9
10
11
12
13
14

Horizontalement

1. month in which summer begins
3. day to start the French school or business week
6. *sept jours,* all together
7. Latin source of *lundi*
9. month of flowers
10. A day has 24 of these.
12. day in honor of Mercury
13. the Roman god honored by a day and a month
14. day to honor the Romans' chief god of the universe

Verticalement

1. warmest summer month
2. last day of the French week
4. *la ____ de semaine*
5. month of new resolutions
8. one seventh of a week
9. the second school day of the week
10. the day just past
11. day to give thanks to Saturn
12. year is divided into twelve of these

Unit 17

La littérature Literature

Les Misérables
Math 76

Des écrivains merveilleux (Great Authors)

Pierre Corneille

1606-1684

Pierre Corneille (1606-84) was born in Rouen. Educated according to the classical tradition, he studied Latin and Greek and became a lawyer. Encouraged, however, by the popularity of his first play, *Mélite*, Corneille soon gave up law, moved to Paris and began to write plays for Cardinal Richelieu at the French royal court.

Corneille's plays are **Classical** in style, that is, they conform to the Greek rules of drama. Many of his plays are based on the adventures of Greek and Roman heroes and deal with the themes of honor and duty. The author wrote many tragedies, such as *Polyeucte*, and many comedies, such as *The Liar (Le Menteur)*. Eventually the dramatist became too creative and independent for Cardinal Richelieu's taste. The play *Le Cid*, which uses a national hero of Spain as its principal character, became an instant success with the public but it displeased Richelieu. Today Corneille is considered the greatest example of a French Classical dramatist.

Victor Hugo (1802-85) was born in Besançon and educated in Paris. With an appreciation for detail as well as feeling, Hugo wrote about topics such as love, liberty, and nature. As a follower of the **Romantic** style of literature, he ignored all the rules of Classical style and created his own. He had an extraordinary talent for using words to express feelings. *The Autumn Leaves (Les feuilles d'automne)* is a collection of poems and *Hernani* is a play about love and honor in 16th century Spain.

As a Romantic novelist, Hugo wrote about the lives of the less fortunate, the poor, and the handicapped. These were the people who were generally the innocent victims of unjust laws. As a politician he voted for fair laws and improvements in the quality of life. In doing so, however, he angered many politicians. Hugo was exiled twice for his political views. Two of his historical novels are *Notre-Dame de Paris,* the story of the deformed bell-ringer, Quasimodo; and *Les Misérables,* the story of a poor man who steals a loaf of bread and is sentenced to years in prison.

Victor Hugo

1802-1885

Charles Baudelaire

1821-1867

Charles Baudelaire (1821-67) was born in Paris and educated in Lyon and Paris. His mother and stepfather wanted him to have a traditional career, but Charles was attracted to languages and literature. He enjoyed learning German and English. Of all the German poets, he liked E.T.A. Hoffmann best, and of all the American poets, he preferred Edgar Allen Poe. Baudelaire translated the entire prose works of Poe into French. In order to make a living, he wrote essays on the new art of the period, including reviews of the artists Eugène Delacroix and Édouard Manet (See Unit 10) and on French writers, including Victor Hugo.

Baudelaire, a Symbolist poet, interpreted life as a struggle between good and evil. In his most famous collection of poems, titled *The Flowers of Evil (Les Fleurs du mal)* the poet explains life with word pictures, or symbols. A pretty flower could be a sign of joy or good, while a wilting flower could be a sign of sorrow or evil. This is called **Symbolism**. Baudelaire had tremendous influence on the symbolist poets who followed him. The young poet suffered tremendously from poverty and ill-health, dying at the age of 46.

Marguerite Duras

1914-1996

Marguerite Duras (1914-96) was born in Southeast Asia in the former colony of French Indochina. She spent her childhood in Saigon, where her parents taught school. Her father died when she was four. The hardships of rural life in Vietnam provided the young girl with much material for future novels. Later in France she wrote more than 50 novels and several film scripts. Duras frequently wrote about life and love in Vietnam and India, and human relationships in general. She objected strongly to the French colonial policy of the time, and was concerned about the lives of ordinary people.

Duras' writing style is simple and direct. Her stories have to do with the isolation some people feel and how they try to communicate with others. With little background or description, her novels concentrate on dialogues and confrontations between people. One of her best known novels is *The Square (Le Square)*. Written entirely in dialogue form, it is about two strangers who meet on a park bench. *Moderato Cantabile is* about a woman who is bored with her own life and then finds excitement when she becomes involved in a murder mystery. This story has been made into a motion picture. The author also wrote the screenplay for *Hiroshima Mon Amour,* which in 1984 won the *Prix Goncourt*, the highest literary honor in France.

Nathalie Sarraute (1900-99) was born in Russia but lived most of her life in France. Like Corneille, she began her career as a lawyer and soon became a writer. But unlike him, she did not care for the traditional ways of story-telling. She thought that writing should show confusion and conflict just as modern life does. She and her friends helped establish a new style of writing called The New Novel *(le nouveau roman)*. Two of her novels are *Portrait of an Unknown Person (Portrait d'un inconnu)* and *The Planetarium (Le Planétarium)*. In this last novel there is no narrator at all, and the reader has no help in figuring out the strange lives and problems of the characters.

French students specializing in literature read novels and plays by great authors at the lycée *(high school).*

Activités

A Qui suis-je? *(Who am I?)*

1. I abandoned law to write plays.

   Pierre Corneielle

2. I spoke German and English.

   charles Baudelaire

3. I wrote about people in southeast Asia.

   Marguerite Duras

4. I was exiled by my government.

   Victor Hugo

5. I rejected the traditional style of writing novels.

   Nathalie sarraute

B Associe les noms avec les descriptions. *(Match the names with the descriptions.)*

	A	B
1. D	Marguerite Duras	A. This writer discards many rules, like using a narrator.
2. E	Victor Hugo	B. This writer expresses thoughts through symbols.
3. C	Pierre Corneille	C. This writer uses many rules.
4. A	Nathalie Sarraute	D. This writer uses many dialogues.
5. B	Charles Baudelaire	E. This writer strives to create many feelings.

novelist, playwright, and poet Victor Hugo

C Write the full name of the author of each work listed below.

1. *Le Cid* Pierre Corneille
2. *Le Planétarium* Nathalie Sarraute
3. *Le Square* Marguerite Duras
4. *Les Misérables* Victor Hugo
5. *Les Fleurs du mal* Charles Baudelaire

D Complete the analogies.

1. Roman heroes: Classicism = the less fortunate: Angered politicians
2. Symbols: Baudelaire = drama: Corneille
3. feelings: Romanticism = poetry: Symbolism
4. marguerite: Duras = Charles: Baudelaire
5. plays: Corneille = The New Novel: Sarraute

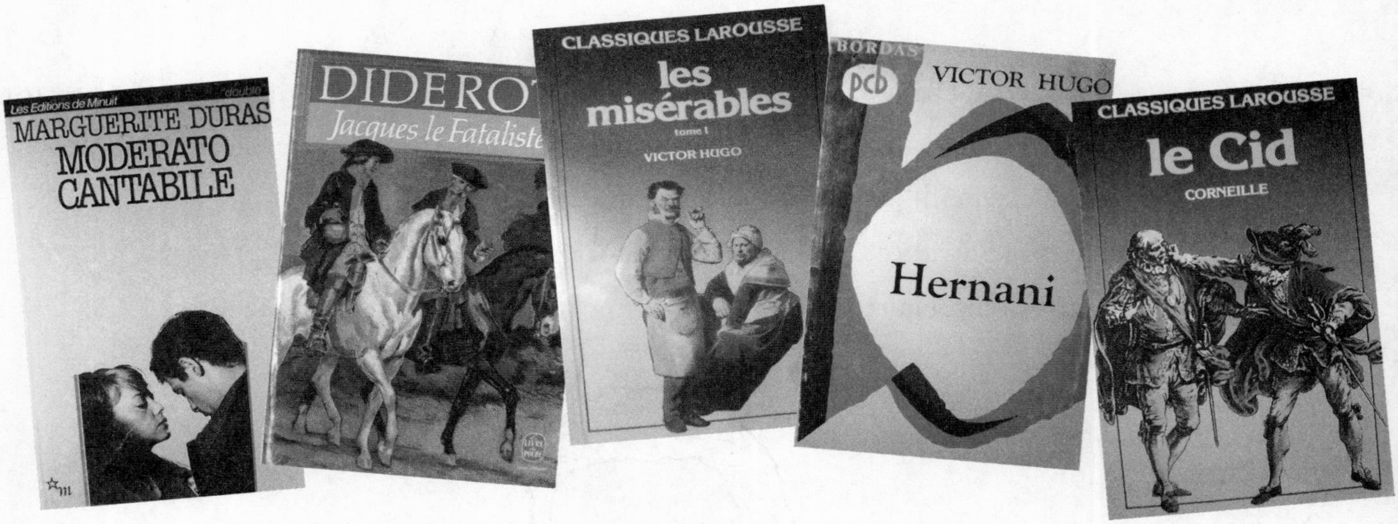
Les Editions de Minuit
MARGUERITE DURAS
MODERATO CANTABILE
DIDEROT
Jacques le Fataliste
CLASSIQUES LAROUSSE
les misérables
tome I
VICTOR HUGO
BORDAS
pcb
VICTOR HUGO
Hernani
CLASSIQUES LAROUSSE
le Cid
CORNEILLE

E Write the correct name of the writer associated with the idea represented by the image.

1. 

Pierre Corneille

2. 
Les Fleurs
du mal

Charles Baudelaire

3. 

Victor Hugo

F Which author would most likely. . .

1. enjoy looking at ancient Egyptian hieroglyphics (word pictures)?

   Charles Baudelaire

2. enjoy describing the budding of trees and flowers in the spring?

   Victor Hugo

3. give a talk describing living conditions in Southeast Asia?

   Marguerite Duras

4. be eager to talk about new trends in literature?

   Nathalie Sarraute

5. enjoy visiting the amphitheaters of the ancient Greek and Roman empires?

   Pierre Corneille

G Label each plot described below as Modern, Romantic, or Classical.

1. Professor Horatio Allgood has the opportunity to be appointed Commissioner of Education for the Republic of Scholarium. To receive this honor he must agree to be silent about a national committee that has unjustly fired a fellow professor. The professor does his duty and speaks out. His courageous action clears his colleague's name, but Professor Allgood loses the appointment.

   Classical

2. Jean-Pierre L'Amour is devastated over the loss of his girlfriend, Gigi. He joins the French Foreign Legion and dies heroically. In his hand is found a picture of Gigi.

   Romantic

3. In the poem, "Singing Salamander," the square tomato is about to take a trip on the jet stream to see the orange-colored odor about conducting business with the silver soundwaves.

   Modern

H

Complète les phrases avec les noms des auteurs. ***(Complete the sentences with the names of the authors.)***

1. Marguerite Duras spent her childhood in Saigon, Vietnam.
2. Victor Hugo was educated in Paris.
3. Pierre Corneille followed his parents' advice to become a lawyer.
4. Charles Baudelaire did not follow his parents' career advice.
5. Nathalie Sarraute was born in Russia.
6. Pierre Corneille wrote plays called comedies and tragedies.
7. Marguerite Duras wrote novels with characters who have trouble talking to each other.
8. Victor Hugo wrote a novel about Quasimodo, a cathedral bell-ringer.
9. Charles Baudelaire wrote poetry with word pictures and hidden meanings.
10. Nathalie Sarraute experimented with writing styles.

I

C'est à toi! Choose one of the novels or plays mentioned in this chapter. Ask the librarian for help in finding information about the work's plot and themes. Look over carefully what you have found, and then, in your own words, retell the story to your classmates. You may wish to use visuals to relate the story and the names of the main characters.

Proverbe

"**La table est bien couverte quand elle est bien tapissée de livres.**
A well-set table is covered with books."

Langue vivante!

BAUDELAIRE
Les fleurs du Mal
HUGO
Les Misérables
BALZAC
La Duchesse de Langeais
Une ténébreuse affaire
PROUST
A l'ombre des jeunes filles en fleurs
MAUPASSANT
Mont-Oriol
DICTIONNAIRE DE LA LANGUE FRANÇAISE
DICTIONNAIRE

ABONNEZ-VOUS
À VOS MAGAZINES PRÉFÉRÉS !
PASSE-TEMPS ET APPRENTISSAGES
Télé 7 Jeux
39,00 $ / 12 numéros
Une synthèse des jeux de lettres les plus connus sur le marché : mots fléchés, énigmes, jeux de logique et de réflexion.
Bien Dire
94,00 $ / 6 numéros
Spécialement conçu pour les adultes qui apprennent le français. Un CD accompagne chaque numéro pour aider à parfaire sa prononciation !
L'ami des jardins et de la maison
100,00 $ / 12 numéros
Pour tout savoir sur le jardinage, l'art de vivre, l'aménagement de la maison, la gastronomie et les saveurs venues du jardin. Avec un carnet pratique central détachable.
Sandra - Le magazine du tricot
61,00 $ / 11 numéros
Sandra vous offre des modèles pour réinventer les mailles. Tous les styles, du rustique au romantique en passant par le raffiné.
30 millions d'amis
94,00 $ / 12 numéros
Ce magazine vous apporte des histoires, interviews et dossiers traitant de la vie des animaux dans la société comme dans la nature.
Détachez ici, humectez, scellez et postez dès aujourd'hui.

www.salondulivreparis.com
L'Italie à l'honneur
22e Salon du Livre
livres
revues
multimédia
presse
22-27 mars
Paris Expo, Porte de Versailles

La Société des Écrivains
édite chaque mois 10 nouveaux auteurs
Catalogue sur simple demande
Aux Éditions des Écrivains
147-149, rue Saint-Honoré
75001 PARIS
(adresse postale pour toute correspondance ou envoi de manuscrit)
tél : 01 39 08 05 38
fax : 01 39 75 60 11
Indicatif éditeur 2-7480 – Contrat participatif.

J **Look at the clippings of books and answer the following questions.**

1. Write the name of each book's author.
   - A. *Les fleurs du mal* Charles Baudelaire
   - B. *La Duchesse de Langeais; Une ténébreuse affaire* Balzac
   - C. *Mont-Oriel* Maupassant
   - D. *Les Misérables* Victor Hugo
   - E. *À l'ombre des jeunes filles en fleurs* Proust
2. How are the two dictionaries different? The first one is the French dictionary and the second is a French-to-English dictionary

K **A magazine company is looking for subscribers. Five magazines are shown. Write the title that corresponds to each description. This magazine is about . . .**

1. caring for pets. 30 millions d'amis
2. learning French. Bien dire
3. knitting clothes. Sandra - Le magazine du tricot
4. decorating the house. L'ami des jardins et de la maison
5. playing puzzles and games. Télé 7 jeux

L **Look at the remaining clippings and answer the following questions.**

1. What is the *22e Salon du Livre*?

   website / honors club
2. What is the theme of the *22e Salon du Livre*?

   online news and literature
3. What kind of people might like to join the *Société des Écrivains*?

   authors
4. What are *nouveaux auteurs*?

   new authors
5. What can you probably find out by looking at the catalog each month?

   simple demands

Symtalk

M **Écris en français le mot ou l'expression qui correspond à chaque image.** ***(In the space, write the correct word or expression in French.)***

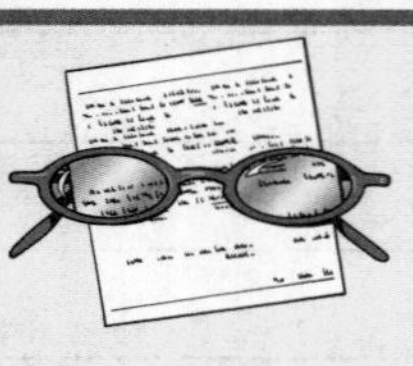

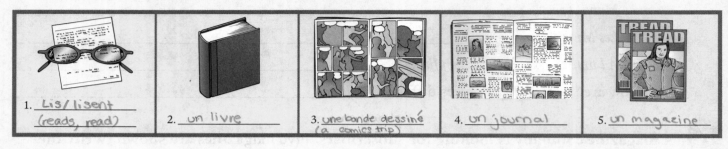

1. Lis/lisent (reads, read)

2. un livre

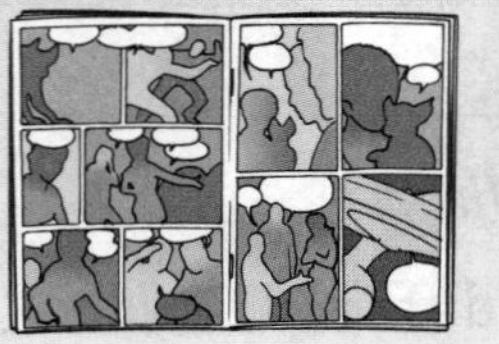

3. une bande dessiné (a comics trip)

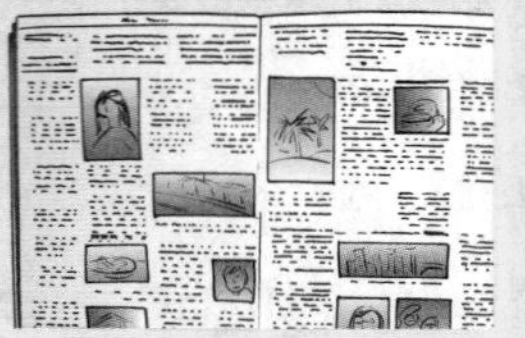

4. un journal

TREAD

5. un magazine

N **Dis les phrases, puis écris-les en français.** ***(Say the sentences, then write them in French.)***

1. 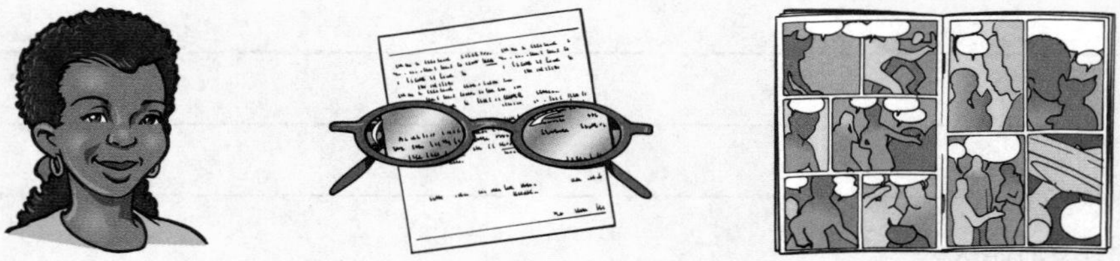

Sylvie lit une bande dessiné (Sylvie reads a comictrip)

2. 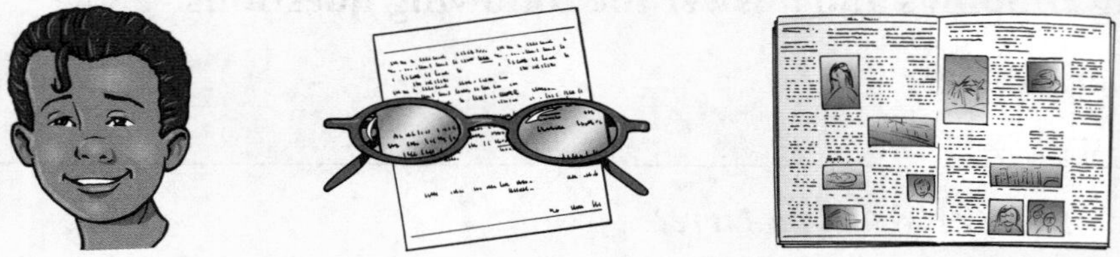

Alain lit un journal (Alain reads a journal

3. 

et
TREAD

Antoine et Brigitte lisent un magazine (Antoine and Brigitte read a magazine)

4. 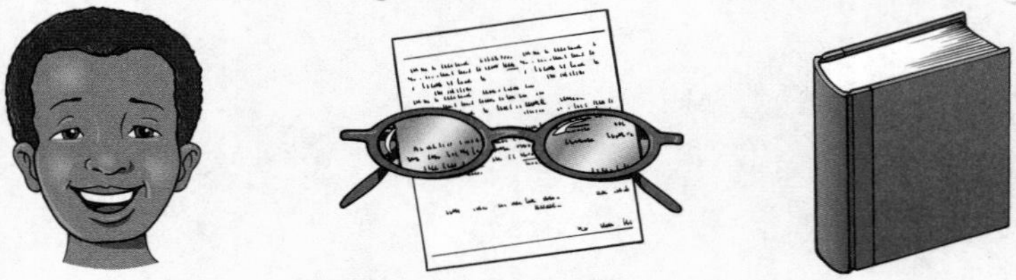

Gérard lit un livre (Gérard reads a book)

O

Décris oralement et par écrit chaque scène en français. *(Say and write a description of each scene in French. Mention different types of reading material.)*

1.

2.

3.

4.

RAIDERS

Mots croisés

1
2
3
4
5
6
7
8
9
10
11

Horizontalement

2. what a well-set table has on it (proverb)
3. ____ *Leaves* by Hugo
6. lived in Southeast Asia
8. writing style with rules
9. concerned about the lives of the poor and handicapped
10. Corneille's first name
11. Baudelaire's first name

Verticalement

1. *The* ____, novel by Sarraute
2. was excellent in languages, art, and poetry
4. what Sarraute and her friends liked to write
5. Sarraute's first name
7. Hugo's first name
10. *Le Menteur* is an example of this genre of literature.

Unit 18

Les loisirs et les divertissements
Leisure and Recreation

Vocabulaire

Où vas-tu?
Where are you going?

Je vais au match.
I'm going to the game.

Je vais au musée.
I'm going to the museum.

Je vais à la boum.
I'm going to the party.

Je vais à la plage.
I'm going to the beach.

SOPHIE:	**Où vas-tu ce soir?**	Where are you going tonight?
MICHEL:	**Je vais au match.**	I'm going to the game.
SOPHIE:	**Moi aussi!**	Me, too!

❀✿❀✿❀

JEAN:	**Où vas-tu aujourd'hui?**	Where are you going today?
CATHERINE:	**Je vais au musée... au Louvre.***	I'm going to the museum... to the Louvre.
JEAN:	**Pourquoi?**	Why?
CATHERINE:	**Pour voir le Festival Delacroix.**	To see the Delacroix Festival.

*The Louvre, France's best known art museum, is located in Paris.

Je fais du volleyball.
I play volleyball.

Je fais du football.
I play soccer.

Quels sports fais-tu?
What sports do you play?

Je fais du tennis.
I play tennis.

Je fais du basketball.
I play basketball.

Je fais du baseball.
I play baseball.

Je fais du football américain. I play football.

le football (soccer) is often called **le foot**
le volleyball is called **le volley**
le basketball is called **le basket**

Qu'est-ce que tu aimes faire?
What do you like to do?

J'aime faire du ski.
I like skiing.

J'aime danser.
I like dancing.

J'aime lire.
I like reading.

J'aime faire du cheval.
I like horseback riding.

J'aime nager.
I like swimming.

J'aime faire du vélo.
I like biking.

J'aime le football américain.	I like football.
J'aime faire du football américain.	I like playing football.

MARC:	**Il y a demain un pique-nique.**	Tomorrow there's a picnic.
SUZANNE:	**Où ça?**	Where is it?
MARC:	**À la plage. Tu veux m'accompagner?**	At the beach. Do you want to go with me?
SUZANNE:	**Oui, je veux bien. J'aime nager.**	Yes, very much. I like to swim.

❀✿❀✿❀

MARGUERITE:	**Tu vas à la boum ce soir?**	Are you going to the party tonight?
FABIEN:	**Bien sûr. Il y a de la musique, n'est-ce pas?**	Of course. There'll be music, right?
MARGUERITE:	**Oui. J'adore danser!**	Yes. I love to dance!

Activités

A **Où vas-tu? Complète chaque phrase en français, en employant les mots entre parenthèses.** ***(Where are you going? Complete each sentence in French, using the cues in parentheses.)***

1. Je vais au ______________________. *(game)*
2. Je vais au ______________________. *(picnic)*
3. Je vais au ______________________. *(museum)*
4. Je vais à la ______________________. *(beach)*
5. Je vais à la ______________________. *(party)*

B **The following questions are based on all the dialogues presented in this unit. Refer to them if you don't know the correct answer. Circle the right answer.**

1. C'est quand, le match?
   A. demain
   B. vendredi
   C. ce soir
   D. à huit heures
2. Le Louvre, qu'est-ce que c'est?
   A. un cheval
   B. un match
   C. un festival
   D. un musée
3. Delacroix, qui est-ce?
   A. un professeur d'art
   B. le directeur d'un musée
   C. un artiste français
   D. un acteur français
4. C'est quand, le pique-nique?
   A. demain
   B. aujourd'hui
   C. après-demain
   D. hier
5. Où est le pique-nique?
   A. à la boum
   B. au Louvre
   C. du baseball
   D. à la plage

C **Quels sports fais-tu? Complète chaque phrase en français.** ***(What sports do you play? Complete each sentence in French.)***

1. Je fais ______________________________.

2. Je fais ______________________________.

3. Je fais ______________________________.

4. Je fais ______________________________.

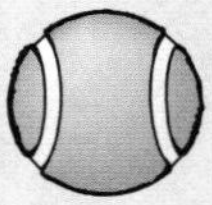

5. Je fais ______________________________.

D **Écris les mots correctement.** ***(Unscramble the words.)***

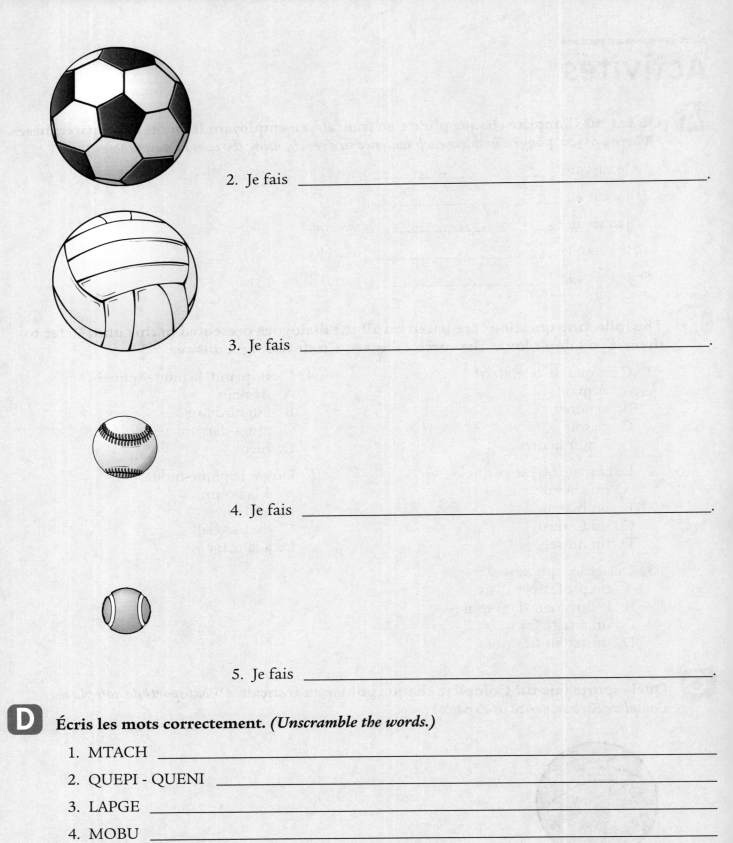

1. MTACH ______________________________
2. QUEPI - QUENI ______________________________
3. LAPGE ______________________________
4. MOBU ______________________________
5. SÉEUM ______________________________

E

Qu'est-ce que tu aimes faire? Complète chaque phrase en français. ***(What do you like to do? Complete each sentence in French.)***

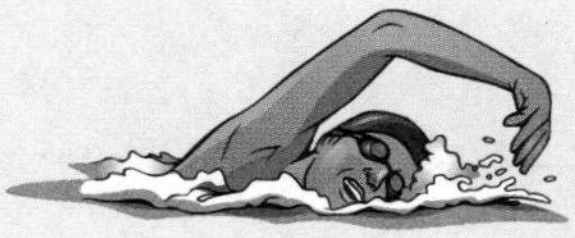

1. J'aime ______________________________.

2. J'aime ______________________________.

3. J'aime ______________________________.

4. J'aime ______________________________.

5. J'aime ______________________________.

6. J'aime ______________________________.

7. J'aime ______________________________.

F **Complète le dialogue en français.** ***(Complete the dialogue in French.)***

THIERRY: Où (1) ________________ -tu aujourd'hui?

PATRICE: Je vais (2) ________________ plage. Tu (3) ________________ m'accompagner?

THIERRY: Bien (4) ________________. J'adore la plage.

PATRICE: Moi (5) ________________! Qu'est-ce que tu aimes faire à la plage?

THIERRY: J'aime (6) ________________ du volley-ball.

PATRICE: Et moi, j'adore (7) ________________ dans l'océan.

G **Lis le paragraphe, puis encercle les meilleures réponses.** ***(Read the passage, then circle the best answers.)***

Claude organise une petite fête à la plage pour son anniversaire. Aujourd'hui il *a* douze *ans*. Il invite *ses* amis Hélène, Abdul, Marylène, Sabine, et Jean-Paul à la fête. La fête commence à trois heures. Il fait chaud et la plage est très belle. Les amis aiment nager dans l'océan et faire du volley-ball. Après les *divertissements*, *tout le monde* a faim. Il y a un bon pique-nique avec des sandwichs, des boissons, de la glace, et naturellement, un gâteau d'anniversaire. Une fête d'anniversaire à la plage est magnifique! Claude est très heureux aujourd'hui.

a ____ ans	is ____ years old
ses	his
divertissements	recreation, fun and games
tout le monde	everyone

1. Quel âge a Claude aujourd'hui?
   A. 13 ans
   B. 14 ans
   C. 12 ans
   D. 11 ans
2. Qui sont les invités *(guests)*?
   A. ses parents
   B. ses amis
   C. ses sœurs
   D. ses cousins
3. Quel temps fait-il?
   A. Il fait beau.
   B. Il neige.
   C. Il pleut.
   D. Il fait mauvais.
4. Quel sport aime faire tout le monde?
   A. Tout le monde aime faire du ski.
   B. Tout le monde aime faire du baseball.
   C. Tout le monde aime faire du volleyball.
   D. Tout le monde aime faire du vélo.
5. Qu'est-ce qu'il y à manger?
   A. un gâteau
   B. une plage
   C. un restaurant
   D. une fête

H **Parlons! Think of three places where you could go this weekend, *i.e.*, a museum, a beach, a picnic. Your speaking partner will ask you where you are going and you should answer appropriately. Then reverse the roles, using new places.**

Modèle: A: Où vas-tu?
B: Je vais à la plage.

I **C'est à toi! Try a word association game with a partner. Each of you will prepare a list of five nouns from this unit and exchange them. Within a time frame decided by the teacher, your partner will say a word that in some way is related to each noun on the list, for example: *un livre, lire; un musée, le Louvre*. If your partner successfully offers a related word within the time frame, he or she earns a gold star or a prize from the grab bag. If not, or when the time is up, it is your turn.**

Proverbe

"**Diversité réjouit.**

Variety is the spice of life."

Langue vivante!

AQUALAND
DECOUVREZ LES 7 PARCS AQUALAND DU SUD DE LA FRANCE
Les bons plans
LE SAVIEZ-VOUS ?
1 Pas besoin de pique-nique ! Dans tous les parcs, une offre restauration à petits prix !
2 Le samedi est le jour où il y a le moins d'affluence.
3 Pour bien profiter des glisses, mieux vaut arriver tôt !
LE MONDIAL SAQ
Montréal
En automobile / By car: pont Jacques-Cartier Bridge
Sortie «Parc Jean-Drapeau» Exit
Renseignements / Information: (514) 397-2000
www.laronde.com
LaRonde
7 nouveaux manèges!
7 new rides!
LA DESCENTE DÉMENTE DE L'ÉTÉ!
INFO : 1 888 215-4418
WWW.TREMBLANT.CA
Dévalez la montagne en conduisant votre « Kart » à la vitesse que vous désirez sur une piste de 1.4 km.
Vivez les vacances à leur meilleur à Mont-Tremblant !
690, rue Sherbrooke Ouest
Montréal
(514) 398-7100
www.musee-mccord.qc.ca
metro McGill / bus 24
MUSÉE
McCORD
MUSEUM
Musée d'histoire canadienne
Les Sports
Canoë Kayak, canoë raft et kayak / Canoes kayak
Au lac de Montriond et sur rivière avec le club de kayak de Montriond et des Hauts de Dranse
Tél. : 04 50 75 98 92
Canyoning
Dans le lit d'une rivière, avec cordes et baudriers, pour descendre les toboggans naturels des cascades.
- Franck Aubry. Tél. : 04 50 79 64 13
- 7 Aventure à Bioge.
Tél. : 04 50 72 15 12
Rafting, Hydrospeedd, Kayak Raft / Wild watersports activities
Découverte et perfectionnement
7 Aventure à Bioge.
Tél. : 04 50 72 15 12
Centre équestre / Horse riding
- Avec "Le Ranch de l'Avenir" à Montriond.
Pierre Premat et Françoise Saint-Marc.
Tél. : 04 50 75 79 12.
- Avec le centre équestre de l'Abbaye à Saint Jean d'Aulps.
Patrick Muffat. Tél. : 04 50 74 82 15
(portable 06 86 82 02 57)
FÉDÉRATION FRANÇAISE DE TENNIS
Stade Roland-Garros
CHAMPIONNATS INTERNATIONAUX DE FRANCE 2005
Lundi 23 mai 2005
Ouverture des portes : 10H00
COURTS ANNEXES
Tribune Escalier Rang Place
Prix : 19,00€
ROLAND GARROS
IBM
BNP PARIBAS
WTA
TENNISEUM

J **Look at the clippings about attractions in France and Canada and answer the following questions.**

1. *Aqualand* is a popular water park franchise in southern France. *Il y a combien de parcs? (En français, s'il te plaît.)*

____

2. On what day is *Aqualand* the least crowded?

____

3. In what city is the *La Ronde* amusement park located?

____

4. *La Ronde* has seven new rides or attractions. What is the French word for "rides" or "attractions"?

____

5. *Mont Tremblant*, a ski resort in the Laurentian Mountains of Québec province, provides off-season recreational activities. What is the distance in kilometers of the downhill "kart" ride?

____

6. During what season is the downhill "kart" ride popular? *(En français, s'il te plaît.)*

____

7. What is the address of the *Musée McCord*?

____

8. What kind of exhibits do you think the *Musée McCord* displays?

____

K **Look at the clippings about sports and answer the following questions.**

1. Name some water sports that are offered.

____

2. Where can one go horseback riding?

____

3. What is the name of the organization sponsoring the tennis championship?

____

4. What is the name of the stadium where the tennis championship will take place?

____

5. How much does a ticket for the tennis championship cost?

____

Symtalk

L **Écris en français le mot ou l'expression qui correspond à chaque image.** *(In the space, write the correct word or expression in French.)*

1. ______________ ______________

2. ______________ ______________

3. ______________

4. ______________

5. ______________

6. ______________

M **Dis les phrases, puis écris-les en français.** *(Say the sentences, then write them in French.)*

1. 

____

2. 

____

3. 
et

____

4. 

____

5. 
et

____

N **Travaille avec un partenaire. Pose la question ou donne la response. Puis, écris le dialogue.** *(Work with a partner. Ask the question or give the answer. Then, write the dialogue.)*

1. 
est-ce que

______________________________ Non, ______________________________

______________________________ ______________________________.

2. 
est-ce que
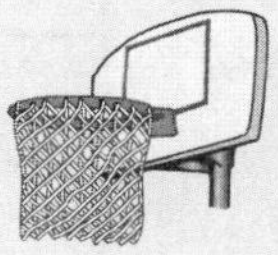

______________________________ Non, ______________________________

______________________________ ______________________________.

3. 
est-ce que

______________________________ Non, ______________________________

______________________________ ______________________________.

4. 
est-ce que
et

______________________________ Non, ______________________________

______________________________ ______________________________.

Mots croisés

1
2
3
4
5
6
7
8
9
10
11
12
13
14

Horizontalement

1. place where friends, music, games, and food converge
4. *Je ____ au musée du Louvre.*
6. what you do on a ranch: *faire du ____*
7. *Qu'est-ce que tu aimes ____?*
11. *____ vas-tu?*
12. game with a net and a ball
14. game with a racquet and a ball

Verticalement

1. game with a hoop and a ball
2. athletic event
3. what you do in the water
5. game with a bat and a ball
7. *Je ____ du tennis.*
8. game with a black and white ball
9. famous museum in Paris
10. *____ sports fais-tu?*
13. what you do with a book

Unit 19

Les achats

Shopping

FOIES GR

Vocabulaire

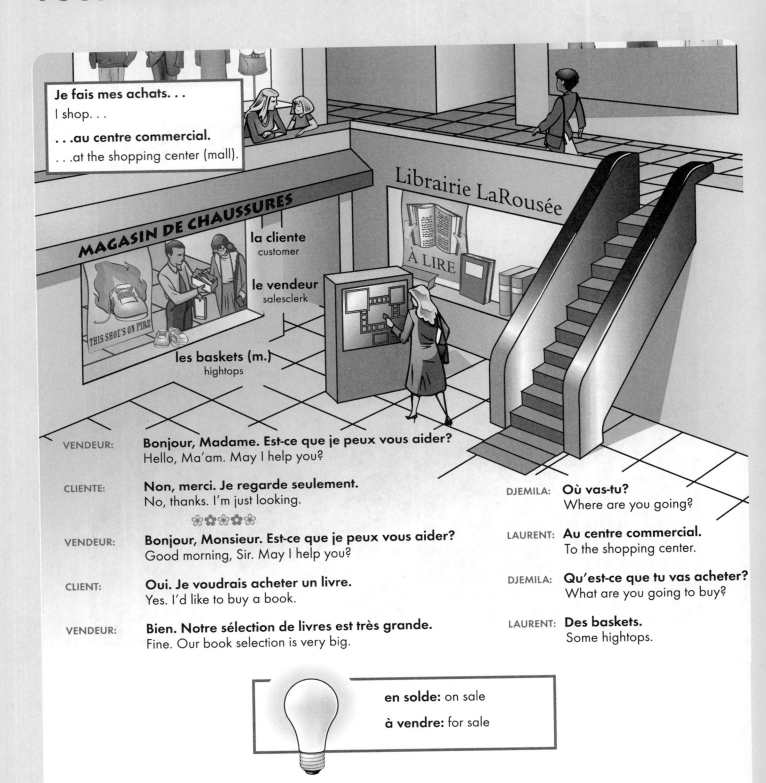

Je fais mes achats. . .
I shop. . .
. . .au centre commercial.
. . .at the shopping center (mall).
MAGASIN DE CHAUSSURES
THIS SHOE'S ON FIRE
Librairie LaRousée
À LIRE
la cliente
customer
le vendeur
salesclerk
les baskets (m.)
hightops

VENDEUR: **Bonjour, Madame. Est-ce que je peux vous aider?**
Hello, Ma'am. May I help you?

CLIENTE: **Non, merci. Je regarde seulement.**
No, thanks. I'm just looking.

❀✿❀✿❀

VENDEUR: **Bonjour, Monsieur. Est-ce que je peux vous aider?**
Good morning, Sir. May I help you?

CLIENT: **Oui. Je voudrais acheter un livre.**
Yes. I'd like to buy a book.

VENDEUR: **Bien. Notre sélection de livres est très grande.**
Fine. Our book selection is very big.

DJEMILA: **Où vas-tu?**
Where are you going?

LAURENT: **Au centre commercial.**
To the shopping center.

DJEMILA: **Qu'est-ce que tu vas acheter?**
What are you going to buy?

LAURENT: **Des baskets.**
Some hightops.

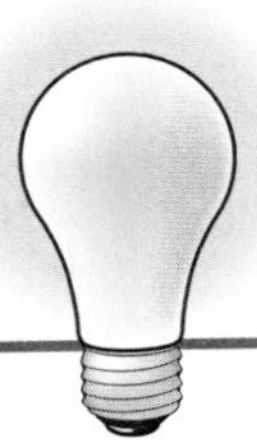

en solde: on sale

à vendre: for sale

. . . au magasin.
. . . at the store.
Soldes
Sale
la caissière
cashier
le client
customer
l'argent (m.)
money
la caisse
cash register
la monnaie
change (coins)
le disque compact;
le CD
compact disc, CD

CLIENT:	**Ce disc compact, c'est combien?**	How much is this compact disc?
CAISSIÈRE:	**Ça coûte 12 euros.**	It costs 12 euros.
CLIENT:	**C'est un peu cher!**	That's a little expensive!
CAISSIÈRE:	**Mais non, c'est bon marché.**	No, it's cheap.
CLIENT:	**Bon, je l'achète. Voilà l'argent, Mademoiselle.**	OK, I'll buy it. There you are, Miss.
CAISSIÈRE:	**Merci, beaucoup. Voilà votre monnaie.**	Thank you very much. Here's your change.

. . . au marché.
. . . at the market.
la vendeuse
vendor
la cliente
customer
les pêches
peaches
les haricots verts (m.)
green or string beans

VENDEUSE:	**Quelque chose d'autre?**	Anything else?
CLIENTE:	**Euh. . . trois tomates, cinq pêches, et des haricots verts. Oui, c'est tout.**	Uhm. . . three tomatoes, five peaches, and some green beans. Yes, that's all.

Vocabulaire Extra!

acheter
to buy

j'achète
I'm buying or I buy

faire des achats
to shop (make purchases)

coûter
to cost

ne. . . pas
not

Activités

A Match the items for sale with the stores in which they can be found.

A		B
1. B	les baskets	A. market
2. A	les haricots verts	B. shoe store
3. E	les CDs	C. furniture store
4. C	les chaises et les tables	D. stationery store
5. D	les stylos et les cahiers	E. music store

B Complète chaque phrase selon l'illustration. *(Complete each sentence according to the illustration.)*

1. J'adore les pêches.

2. Madame Thibault choisit de beaux fruits au le marché.

Librairie LaRousée
MAGASIN DE CHAUSSURES

3. Je fais mes achats au ___centre commercial___.

4. Voilà la ___monnaie___, Monsieur.

PATRICK
BRUEL

5. Le CD est bon marché. Il ___coûte___ 12 euros.

C

Choose the word or expression from the following list that completes each sentence correctly.

bon marché   acheter   euros   magasin   caisse

Thierry va au ___magasin___ de musique. Il va ___acheter___ un CD de musique classique. Voilà un bon CD à 10 ___euros___. Ce n'est pas cher. C'est ___bon marché___. Il va à la ___caisse___ avec son CD.

100
50 EURO
20 EURO

D Encercle la réponse correcte. *(Circle the correct answers.)*

1. If you see the sign *soldes*, what would you expect the price of the object to be?
   A. bon marché
   B. l'argent
   C. cher
   D. la monnaie

2. What do you reply if the cashier says "*Ça coûte 20 euros*"?
   A. Voilà l'argent.
   B. C'est combien?
   C. Où est le magasin?
   D. Merci, c'est tout.

3. What do you get back if you give the cashier too much money?
   A. la caisse
   B. le centre commercial
   C. le magasin
   D. la monnaie

4. Who helps you find what you need?
   A. les pêches
   B. le vendeur
   C. la caissière
   D. la cliente

5. What do you say if you don't need the salesclerk's help right now?
   A. Est-ce que je peux vous aider?
   B. C'est un peu cher!
   C. Je regarde seulement.
   D. Quelque chose d'autre?

E Write the following sentences in English.

1. J'achète des baskets.

   I buy the shoes

2. Tu achètes sept pêches.

   You buy 7 peaches

3. Elle achète un CD. (**Hint:** *Elle* refers to *La cliente.*)

   She buys a CD

F Encercle la réponse correcte pour chaque question. *(Circle the correct answer for each question.)*

1. C'est tout?
   A. Non, je ne peux pas vous aider.
   B. Non. . . euh. . . des pêches, s'il vous plaît.
   C. Mais non, c'est bon marché.
   D. Non, je regarde seulement.

2. Pourquoi vas-tu au magasin?
   A. Je n'ai pas soif.
   B. Je porte une robe.
   C. Je vais faire mes achats.
   D. Il y a un pique-nique.

3. Les baskets, elles sont bon marché?
   A. Oui, voilà la monnaie.
   B. Non, c'est le vendeur.
   C. Oui, c'est tout.
   D. Non, elles sont cher.

4. Le CD, c'est combien?
   A. C'est 19,00 euros.
   B. Euh. . . je regarde seulement.
   C. C'est tout.
   D. Au centre commercial.

5. Qu'est-ce que tu vas acheter?
   A. soldes
   B. un vendeur
   C. des tomates et des haricots verts
   D. la monnaie

G

Khadim is shopping in a clothing store. Complete his conversation with the salesclerk.

VENDEUR: Bonjour, Monsieur. Est-ce que je peux vous (1) ___aider___?

KHADIM: Non, merci. Je (2) ___regarde___ seulement.

VENDEUR: C'est la saison des soldes. Tout est (3) ___à vendre___: les chemises, les pantalons, les manteaux, et les chaussures.

KHADIM: Merci, Monsieur. Euh. . . ce pantalon noir, c'est (4) ___tout___?

VENDEUR: Ça coûte 59 euros.

KHADIM: C'est un peu (5) ___cher!___. Je ne peux pas acheter le pantalon. Je n'ai pas les cinquante-neuf euros.

H

Parlons! Think of three things you would like to buy, for example, a notebook, a shirt, a sandwich. Ask your speaking partner how much each item costs, for example, *La chemise, c'est combien?* After he/she gives you an exact price in euros, then react to the price by using an expression such as *C'est cher* or *C'est bon marché* or *C'est bon.*

I

C'est à toi! You and your partner are going to role-play a situation in a store. The salesclerk will greet the customer and ask to help. The customer will say that he/she would like to buy a certain item. (You may want to use props.) The salesclerk will mention the large selection of those items. The customer will ask how much the item costs. The clerk will proceed with the purchase, thank the customer, and say good-bye. (You may want to use play money in your cash register.) Hang the store owner's sign above the store, *e.g., Le magasin de Jean-Luc, Le coin de Djemila* or *Le marché de Louis.* After the dialogue, switch roles.

Langue vivante!

Sony KV 28 CS70

28 - 71 - 100 Hertz - Son: Stéréo

★★★★★ Lire 1 avis | Rédigez un avis

Salut à tous, Je viens d'aquérir un nouveau téléviseur 16/9ème. si vous voulez savoir pourquoi lire mon avis sur le Sharp Attack.... Mon choix s'est finalement orienté pour ce modèle dont voici un peu les caractéristiques: - Taille de l'écran (diagonale) 82 cm - Taille de l'image 76

Téléviseur 16/9 100hz - 71cm - tube FD Trinitron WEGA Sony KV-28CS70 **669,90 €**

LA TERRE EST NOTRE SOLEIL

Carrefour bio

bio
AGIR
Muesli
croustillant
quinoa-chocolat

Muesli croustillant au quinoa-chocolat Issu de l' agriculture biologique

Ancienne marque : Carrefour Bio

bio **3€** 500g

"J'AI TOUJOURS ENVIE D'ALLER AUX GALERIES"

GALERIES Lafayette

L'EXPRESS vous propose
ce superbe sac reporter.

Toujours prêt pour une nouvelle journée trépidante !

Une ligne sobre et élégante et une foule de détails parfaitement pensés en font l'accessoire indispensable de tous vos déplacements professionnels ou personnels.

...OU
ce mini radio-réveil.

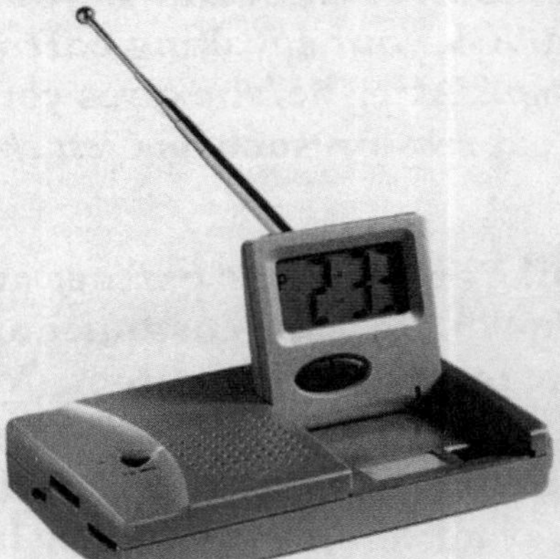

Pratique et compact, il adore les voyages...

Pour ne rater ni l'avion, ni un rendez-vous important... Ce radio-réveil se plie, s'emporte partout et vous réveille en douceur, au son de votre station préférée.

J **Look at the clippings and answer the following questions.**

1. Look at the television ad from the Internet. How much is the TV set being sold for?

   ____

2. Carrefour Bio sells *muesli,* a cereal of grains, nuts, and fruit originally from Switzerland. How much does a 500 gram bag of muesli cost?

   ____

3. What is the name of a famous department store found all over France?

   ____

4. The magazine *L'Express* offers free gifts with a subscription.

   a) Find the French word in the ad which means "organizer bag."

   ____

   b) Find the seven words that say: "Always ready for another busy day!"

   ____

   c) What are some French adjectives that describe how wonderful this bag is?

   ____

   d) What color is the bag?

   ____

5. *L'Express* also offers a *mini radio-réveil* as a free gift.

   a) What two French adjectives indicate the usefulness of this gift for travelers?

   ____

   b) What do you think the *réveil* does that an ordinary clock does not do?

   ____

Proverbe

"**Premier arrivé, premier servi.**
First come, first served."

Librairie de
René
caisse

Symtalk

K **Écris en français le mot ou l'expression qui correspond à chaque image.** *(In the space, write the correct word or expression in French.)*

1. ____________________
____

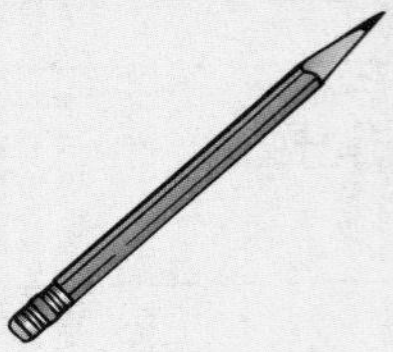

2. ____________________

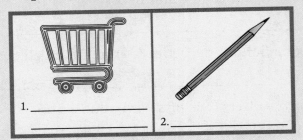

L **Dis les phrases, puis écris-les en français.** *(Say the sentences, then write them in French.)*

1.   

____

2.   

____

3.   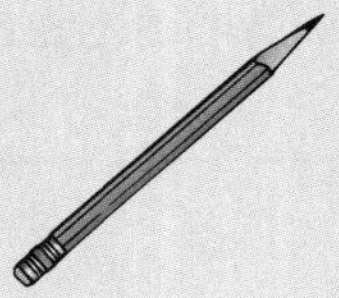

____

4.  et   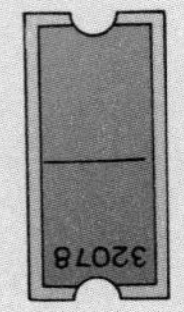

____

5.  et   

____

M **Travaille avec un partenaire. Pose la question ou donne la réponse. Puis, écris le dialogue.** ***(Work with a partner. Ask the question or give the answer. Then, write the dialogue.)***

1.  

_______________________________ _______________________________

2.  

_______________________________ _______________________________

3.  

_______________________________ _______________________________

4.  

_______________________________ _______________________________

5.  

_______________________________ _______________________________

Mots croisés

Horizontalement

1. *Premier ____, premier servi.* (proverb)
6. female customer
7. *____ vas-tu? À la plage?*
8. chaussures pour les sports
12. *Non, merci. Je regarde ____.*
13. opposite of *bon marché*
14. cash register

Verticalement

1. what you pay your bill with
2. female salesclerk
3. where you buy fresh produce
4. *les ____ verts* (vegetable)
5. fruit with a fuzzy exterior (plural)
9. *Est-ce que je peux vous ____?*
10. *C'est ____, Madame.*
11. *Quelque chose d'____?*
13. *le disque compact* (abbreviation)

Unit 20

Les voyages et les moyens de transport

Travel and Transportation

Vocabulaire

Comment voyages-tu?
How do you travel?

voler	to fly
Je vole.	I fly.
à velo	by bike
à pied	on foot

Je voyage en avion.
I travel by plane.

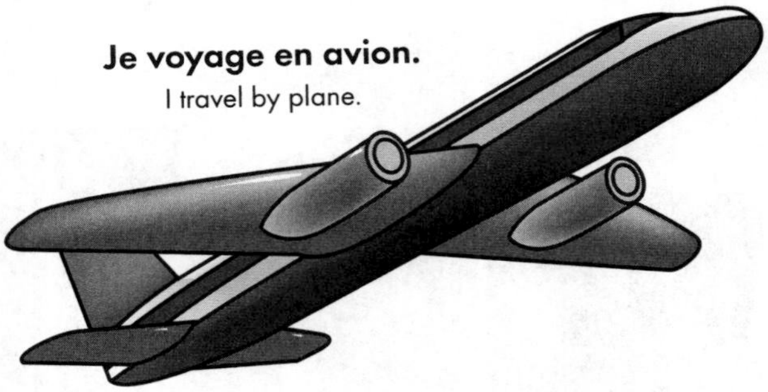

Je voyage en autobus.
I travel by bus.

Je voyage en voiture.
I travel by car.

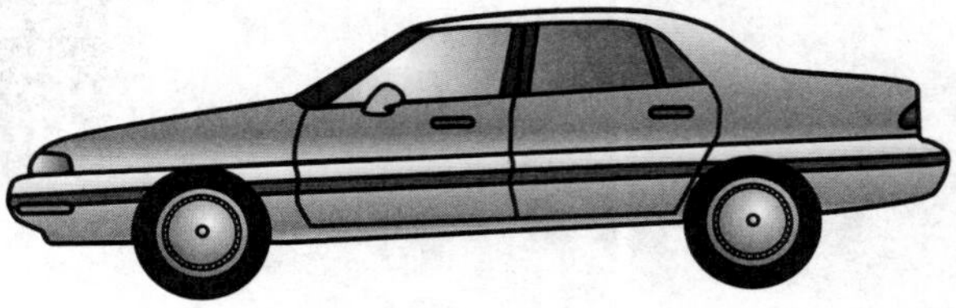

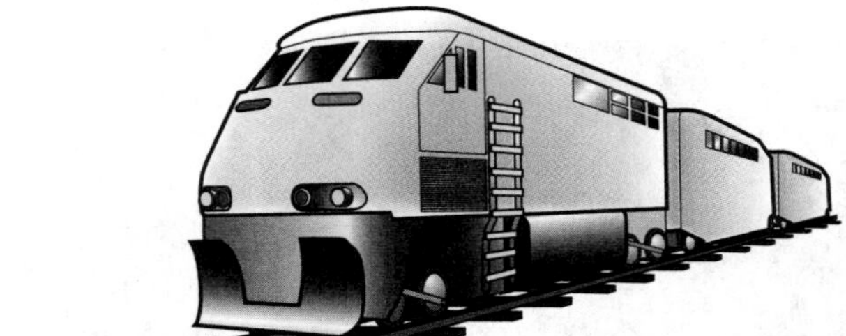

Je voyage en train.
I travel by train.

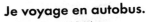

Je voyage en navire.
I travel by ship.

À l'aéroport
At the airport

l'employée (f.)
clerk, agent
le voyageur
traveler
le passeport
passport
le guichet
ticket counter
la valise
suitcase

EMPLOYÉE:	**Votre passeport, Monsieur?**	Your passport, Sir?
VOYAGEUR:	**C'est dans ma valise, Mademoiselle.**	It's in my suitcase, Miss.
EMPLOYÉE:	**Mais il faut l'avoir sur vous. . . et surtout au contrôle des passeports en arrivant.**	But you must have it on you. . . and especially at passport control upon arrival.
VOYAGEUR:	**D'accord. Attendez, s'il vous plaît. Le voilà! Et on monte où?**	O.K. Wait, please. There it is! And where do we board?
EMPLOYÉE:	**À la porte 20, à droite. Bon voyage!**	At gate 20, on your right. Have a good trip!

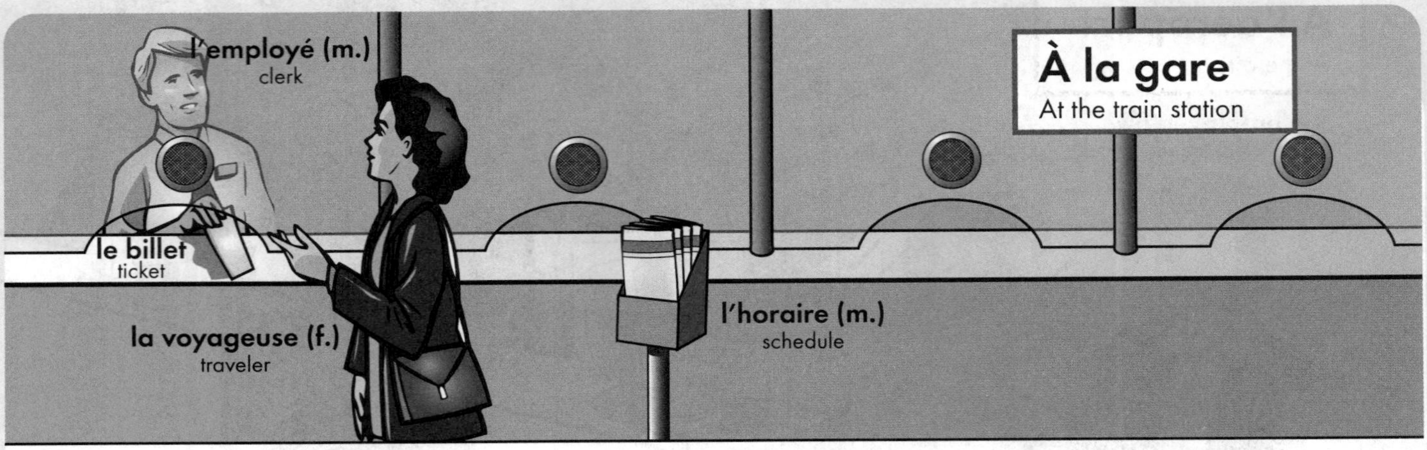
À la gare
At the train station
l'employé (m.)
clerk
le billet
ticket
la voyageuse (f.)
traveler
l'horaire (m.)
schedule

VOYAGEUSE:	**Monsieur, le prochain train pour Paris part à quelle heure?**	Sir, at what time does the next train for Paris leave?
EMPLOYÉ:	**À midi, Madame. Voilà l'horaire.**	At noon, Ma'am. Here's the schedule.
VOYAGEUSE:	**Bon, alors je voudrais acheter un aller-retour en seconde.**	Good, then I'd like to buy a round-trip (ticket) in second class.
EMPLOYÉ:	**Voilà le billet. Ça fait 200 euros.**	There's the ticket. It's 200 euros.

Dans la rue
On the street
l'autobus (m.)
bus

M. BREL:	**Pardon, Madame. . . pour aller à l'Hôtel Couronne?**	Excuse me, Ma'am. How do I get to the Couronne Hotel?
MME PIAF:	**Prenez l'autobus numéro 2 et descendez à la poste. L'hôtel est à gauche.**	Take bus number 2 and get off at the post office. The hotel is on the left.
M. BREL:	**Merci, Madame.**	Thank you, Ma'am.
MME PIAF:	**De rien.**	You're welcome.

Use **prendre** to express taking the bus, the train, etc.

Je prends le train. Elle prend l'autobus.

Activités

A Match the French with the English.

A		B
1. _____	Attendez.	A. a round-trip ticket
2. _____	Je voudrais. . .	B. on the right
3. _____	à gauche	C. Where do we board?
4. _____	Descendez à la poste.	D. There's the schedule.
5. _____	On monte où?	E. Get off at the post office.
6. _____	Prenez l'autobus.	F. You must have it on you.
7. _____	un aller-retour	G. Wait.
8. _____	Il faut l'avoir.	H. I would like. . .
9. _____	Voilà l'horaire.	I. Take the bus.
10. _____	à droite	J. on the left

B Comment voyages-tu? Complète chaque phrase en français. *(How do you travel? Complete each sentence in French.)*

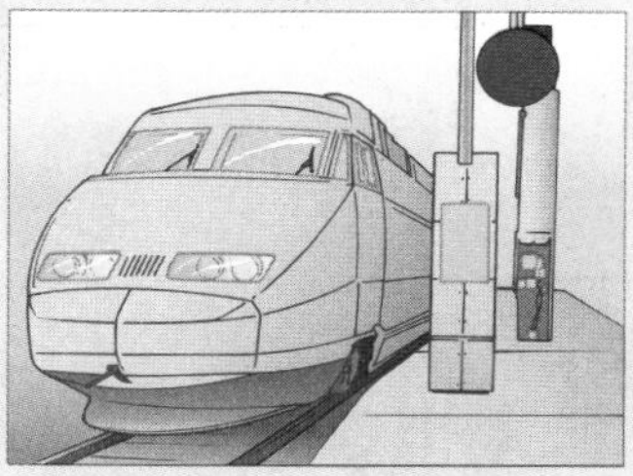

1. Je voyage ____.

2. Je voyage ____.

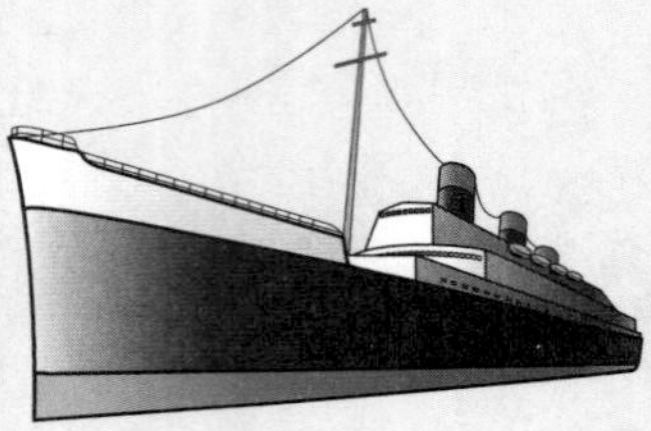

3. Je voyage ____.

4. Je voyage ____.

5. Je voyage ____.

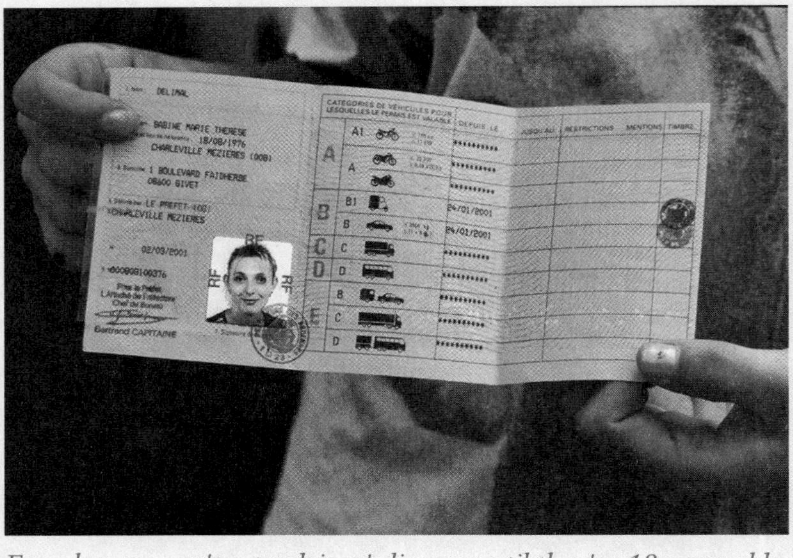

French teens can't get a driver's license until they're 18 years old.

C Encercle la réponse correcte. *(Circle the correct answer.)*

1. Where do you go to take a train?
   A. à l'aéroport
   B. au contrôle des passeports
   C. à la gare
   D. dans la rue
2. What do you ask if you want directions to the train station?
   A. Et on monte où?
   B. Pour aller à la gare?
   C. Le train part à quelle heure?
   D. Est-ce que je peux vous aider?
3. What do you look at to find the times when trains, buses, and planes arrive and leave?
   A. l'horaire
   B. le guichet
   C. le passeport
   D. la valise
4. What do you say when you want to buy a ticket?
   A. Voilà mon passeport.
   B. Je voudrais acheter un billet.
   C. Où vas-tu?
   D. Pour aller à la poste?
5. If you want a roundtrip ticket, what do you say?
   A. un aller-retour
   B. un billet
   C. l'autobus numéro deux
   D. en seconde

D Écris les mots correctement. *(Unscramble the words and write them correctly.)*

1. CUTIGEH ______________________
2. ROHIEAR ______________________
3. LEVISA ______________________
4. YOGRUEVA ______________________
5. SOPERAPTS ______________________

POUR
TOUS

In France, passengers must stamp their ticket in le composteur *before boarding a train.*

E Lis le paragraphe, puis encercle la réponse correcte. *(Read the passage, then circle the correct answer.)*

Il fait beau aujourd'hui. Karine et Jasmin *vont* voyager en train. Elles sont au guichet de la gare où Karine achète deux billets pour Bordeaux. Les grands-parents de Karine habitent à Bordeaux. Les deux amies *compostent* les billets. Elles *attendent* le train sur *le quai* numéro quatre. Le train arrive dans la gare à quatorze heures. Les jeunes filles *montent dans* le train. Jasmin choisit une place à la fenêtre. Les amies parlent de la visite à Bordeaux où il y a *beaucoup à faire*. Elles sont heureuses. À Bordeaux elles *prennent* l'autobus à la maison des grands-parents de Karine.

vont	are going
compostent	stamp (cancel the ticket by inserting it into an orange machine)
attendent	wait for
le quai	platform
montent dans	climb into
beaucoup à faire	lots to do
prennent	take

1. Où sont Karine et Jasmin?
   A. à l'aéroport
   B. dans l'autobus
   C. dans un taxi
   D. à la gare

2. Où est-ce que Karine et Jasmin vont voyager?
   A. à Lille
   B. à Bordeaux
   C. à Reims
   D. à Lyon

3. Combien de billets achète Karine?
   A. deux
   B. un
   C. quatorze
   D. quatre

4. Où est le train?
   A. à la fenêtre
   B. au guichet
   C. sur le quai numéro 4
   D. dans les valises

5. Comment est-ce que les jeunes filles voyagent de *(from)* la gare à *(to)* la maison des grand-parents?
   A. en train
   B. en autobus
   C. en voiture
   D. en navire

F **Complete the analogies.**

1. employé: ____________________ = voyageur: voyageuse
2. avion: aéroport = train: ____________________
3. navire: océan = autobus: ____________________
4. employé: ____________________ = professeur: bureau
5. une: deux = première: ____________________

G **Parlons! Look at the pictures of a bus, an airplane, a car, a ship, and a train. Ask your speaking partner what each one is: *"Qu'est-ce que c'est?"* He/she will answer. Then you get to ask him/her *"Comment voyages-tu?"* as you point to a specific picture. He/she will answer again. Then switch roles.**

H **C'est à toi! With a partner, act out a dialogue that takes place *dans la rue.* One of you will be Monsieur Debussy and the other Madame Berlioz. This time, however, M. Debussy wants to go to another destination within the city. He will substitute *à l'Hôtel Couronne (i.e., à l'Hôtel Ritz, au Musée du Louvre, au Parc zoologique).* Mme Berlioz will recommend a different bus number. She will finish giving directions by saying that the place is on the right. Don't forget to say "thank you" and "you're welcome!"**

Proverbe

"**On s'instruit en voyageant.**

Traveling is an education in itself."

Langue vivante!

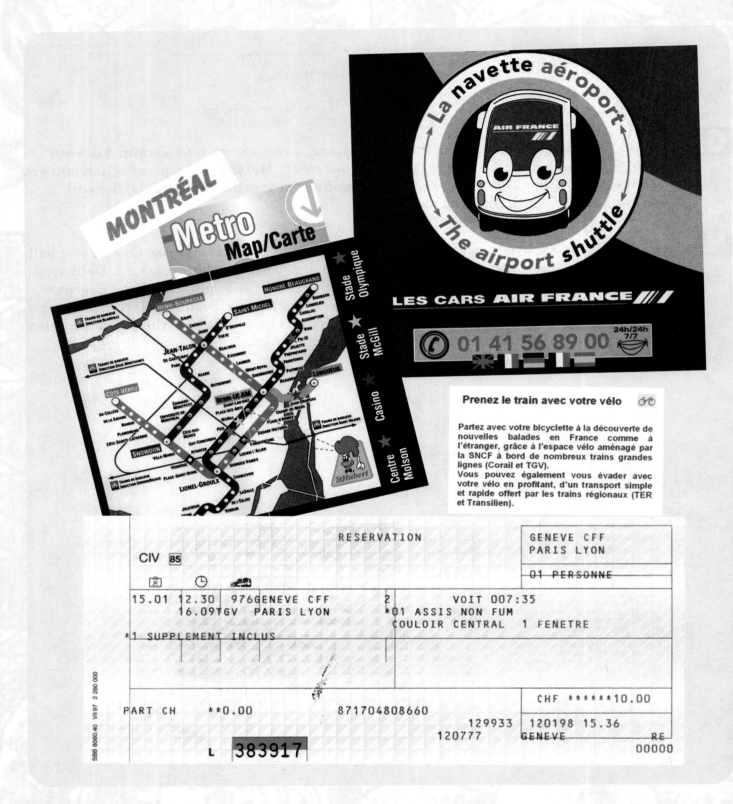

MONTRÉAL
Metro
Map/Carte
Stade Olympique
Stade McGill
Casino
Centre Molson
HONORÉ-BEAUGRAND
HENRI-BOURASSA
SAINT-MICHEL
JEAN-TALON
CÔTE-VERTU
BERRI-UQAM
LONGUEUIL
SNOWDON
LIONEL-GROULX
StHubert

La navette aéroport
AIR FRANCE
The airport shuttle
LES CARS AIR FRANCE
01 41 56 89 00
24h/24h
7/7

Prenez le train avec votre vélo

Partez avec votre bicyclette à la découverte de nouvelles balades en France comme à l'étranger, grâce à l'espace vélo aménagé par la SNCF à bord de nombreux trains grandes lignes (Corail et TGV).
Vous pouvez également vous évader avec votre vélo en profitant, d'un transport simple et rapide offert par les trains régionaux (TER et Transilien).

```
                         RESERVATION              GENEVE CFF
                                                  PARIS LYON
 CIV 85
                                                  01 PERSONNE
15.01 12.30  976GENEVE CFF        2       VOIT 007:35
      16.09TGV  PARIS LYON        *01 ASSIS NON FUM
                                   COULOIR CENTRAL   1 FENETRE
*1 SUPPLEMENT INCLUS

                                                  CHF ******10.00
PART CH      **0.00         871704808660
                                         129933   120198 15.36
                                   120777         GENEVE       RE
       L  383917                                               00000
SBB 8060.40  VII 97  2 280 000
```

I **Look at the map of the Montréal metro and answer the following questions.**

1. The city of Montréal has a *métro.* What is this?

____

2. How many *lignes* (lines) are there?

____

3. What are the names of the two end-point stations of *la ligne bleue*?

____

4. How many transfers *(correspondances)* are needed to ride from *Côte-des-Neiges (la ligne bleue)* to *Place des Arts (la ligne verte)?*

____

5. Is it possible to transfer *métro* lines at Rosemont?

____

J **Look at the remaining clippings and answer the following questions.**

1. What does the reservation ticket reserve?

____

2. For how many passengers is this reservation intended?

____

3. What does *"la fenêtre"* mean in this context?

____

4. What is the city of departure?

____

5. How long will it take to reach Paris at the Lyon Terminal?

____

6. What does the *Société Nationale de Chemins de Fer* (French National Railroad) suggest to bike riders?

____

7. What is the abbreviation of the French National Railroad?

____

8. How does one say "airport shuttle" in French?

____

9. What is the purpose of this vehicle?

____

Symtalk

K **Écris en français le mot ou l'expression qui correspond à chaque image.** ***(In the space, write the correct word or expression in French.)***

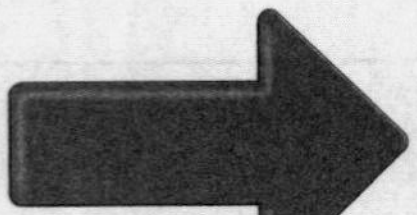
1. ______________

2. ______________

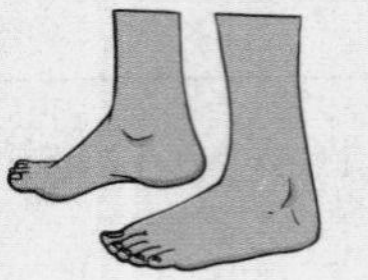
3. ______________

4. ______________

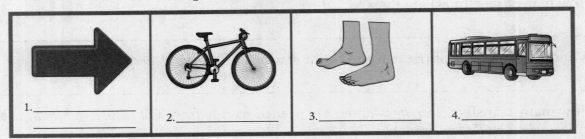

L **Lis les phrases, puis écris-les en français.** ***(Read the sentences, then write them in French.)***

1. 
et

____

2. 

____

3. 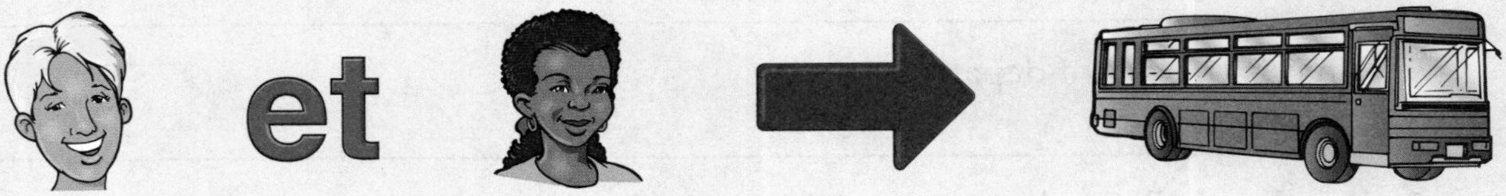
et

____

4. 

____

5. 

____

M **Décris chaque scène en français oralement et par écrit.** ***(Say and write a description of each scene in French.)***

1. 

____

____

____

____

____

2. 

____

____

____

____

____

3. 
Aux Bonnes Affaires

____

____

____

____

____

4. 

____

____

____

____

____

Mots croisés

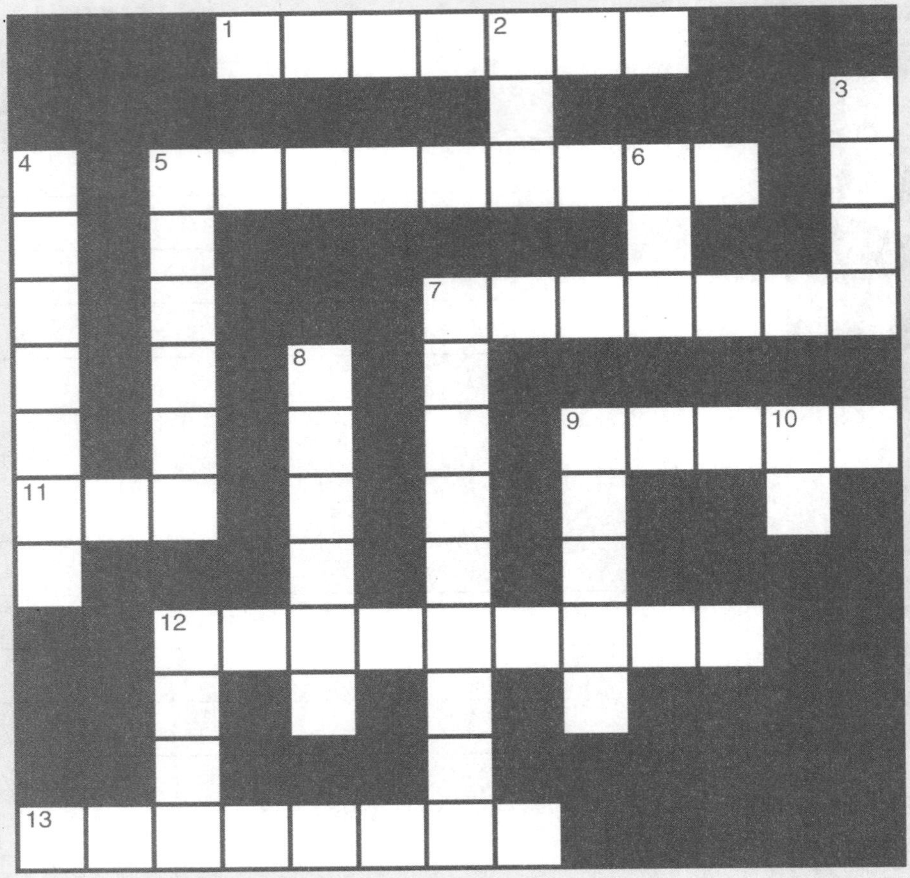

Horizontalement

1. public city transportation
5. ____ *à la poste.* (Get off. . .)
7. personal vehicle
9. one-way ticket: *un ____-retour*
11. street
12. document showing identification and citizenship
13. Wait.

Verticalement

2. good
3. place where you can find trains
4. shows at what time a bus or plane departs and arrives
5. opposite of *gauche*
6. *Mon passeport ____ dans ma valise.*
7. female traveler
8. where a *voyageur* would put his clothes
9. airplane
10. *Je voyage ____ train.*
12. *Le train ____ à 17h00.*